THE HEART OF ARYAVARTA

THE HEART OF ARYAVARTA

A STUDY OF THE PSYCHOLOGY OF INDIAN UNREST

EARL OF RONALDSHAY

GYAN

Published by

Gyan Publishing House
5, Ansari Road
Daryaganj, New Delhi-110002
Phone: 011-47034999, 9811692060
E-mail: books@gyanbooks.com

Distribution Network
gyanbooks.com
India, USA, Canada, UK, Australia

ISBN: 978-93-7447-658-1 (PB)

First Published, 1925

2nd Impression 2026

Printed at: Gyan Press, Delhi.

THE HEART OF ARYAVARTA
Author: EARL OF RONALDSHAY

THE HEART OF ÂRYÂVARTA

THE HEART OF ARYÂVARTA

A STUDY OF THE PSYCHOLOGY OF INDIAN UNREST

BY THE

EARL OF RONALDSHAY

P.C., G.C.S.I., G.C.I.E.

HON. D.LITT. CALCUTTA; HON. D.L. DACCA; HON. D.LITT. LEEDS
PRESIDENT OF THE ROYAL GEOGRAPHICAL SOCIETY
AUTHOR OF
'INDIA: A BIRD'S-EYE VIEW' 'LANDS OF THE THUNDERBOLT', ETC.

CONSTABLE AND COMPANY LIMITED
LONDON BOMBAY SYDNEY
1925

PREFACE

THE pages which follow form the last of three volumes designed to acquaint the reader with the nature of the problem which has arisen out of one of the most engrossing and fateful episodes in the recent history of mankind—the creation under the ægis of Great Britain of a vast Asiatic empire, Eastern by birth and tradition, to a large extent Western by training and upbringing. For such is modern India. The first volume,[1] which, as I explained in the Preface, was concerned for the most part with external things, was designed to picture the stage upon which the drama of British-Indian history is being enacted. The second, read in conjunction with the concluding chapters of the first, was intended to give to the Western reader some idea of the orientation of the Indian mind, with a view to familiarising him with the mental atmosphere in which he will now find himself. For it is certainly the case, as Dr. Macnicol has recently stated, that a veil that it requires an intellectual effort to penetrate hangs between the minds of the two peoples, through which the voice of India comes muffled and

[1] "India: A Bird's-eye View." Although for reasons into which I need not enter this volume was not actually issued until after its companion entitled "Lands of the Thunderbolt", it is organically the first of the sequence.

dim.[1] If the problem with which Great Britain is faced had remained what it originally was, a mere question of administration, it would have been a comparatively simple one, and one with which British genius is particularly well adapted to cope. It has, however, lost its original simplicity, and has acquired a much more subtle character, for it is now dominated by the psychology of the two peoples whose contact and interaction during the past one hundred and fifty years have been instrumental in fashioning the India of to-day. A factor of fundamental importance in the present problem is, consequently, the spirit of modern India, and it is this subtle and illusive element in a complex whole that I here seek to interpret. Hence the title which I have given to this volume.

* * * * * *

It is laid down in the Institutes of Manu that the country which lies between the Himavat and the Vindhya mountains, which extends as far as the Eastern and Western oceans, the wise call Āryâvarta. "That land where the black antelope naturally roams one must know to be fit for the performance of sacrifices. . . . Let twice-born men seek to dwell there." Later the Aryans spilled over the Vindhya hills and spread their civilisation over large tracts of Southern India; but Āryâvarta was the cradle of the civilisation and culture of the twice-born peoples, the call of which rings so insistently in the ears of their descendants at the present day. When, therefore, I speak of the Heart of Āryâvarta I am thinking not so much of the geographical centre of a

[1] In an article in the *British Weekly* of July 31, 1924.

tract of country, as of the feelings of pride and affection for all that Hinduism stands for in the eyes of the twentieth century heirs of those early Aryan tribes, which were exhorted to dwell in the sacred land lying between the Himâlaya and Vindhya mountains. And the spirit of modern India is in large measure a manifestation of the pride of race of the intellectual Hindu—a thing born of a rapidly awakened consciousness of past greatness, giving birth in its turn to an extreme sensitiveness to any suggestion of inferiority where East and West come into contact.

* * * * * *

My own experience has led me to the conclusion that there are few among those who are styled compendiously the Hindu intelligentsia who are not imbued to a greater or less extent with the spirit which I have described above, and who do not look back with feelings of something approaching repugnance to the time, not long past, when their own class permitted itself to be dominated by the mental outlook and the mode of life of Europe. An observant Indian writer, Mr. St. Nihal Singh, who after an absence of eleven years returned to India in 1921 and spent two years in travelling over the country, has declared that what struck him most was the revolution in the spiritual and intellectual outlook upon life of those with whom he came in contact. "The people in general", he asserts, "are becoming more and more dissatisfied with being turned into *mock Englishmen.* An ever-deepening national impulse is compelling India to go back to the fount of her own traditions and her own culture, to insist upon developing along her own lines so that she may be

This phase had now passed; the gaze of India was turned back once more to her own inheritance; she was lighting once again the fires upon her own altars. Yet the shadow of the West still lay heavy upon her. "Without being consciously aware of it, our thought is dominated by the West. Hating it with all our heart we may not yet get away from it." The dominant feature in Indian life to-day was the idea of political nationalism, a thing which had come out of the West. "This works itself out in its external aspect in a suspicion, distrust, and even dislike of foreigners. . . . There is an under-current of violent suspicion against all foreigners in Asia." And this was not to be explained by "a mere fear of financial and industrial exploitation".[1]

It is this consuming hatred of the West that is gripping the spirit of modern India, with a tenacity comparable with that displayed by the amazing vegetable growth known as the water hyacinth, which has laid hold of and is rapidly choking the great waterways of Bengal. What is required to avert the tragedy in which British-Indian relations are becoming enveloped is a *will* to thrust under foot this malignant growth. But it is precisely the *will* to do so that is lacking, and that no one seems able to bring into being. Indeed, far from a desire to improve relations there is evidence of the existence in some quarters of a determination to foster hatred and widen the gulf that has opened between India and Great Britain. For it is difficult to see what else can have been the motive by which Mr. C. R. Das and

[1] Mr. K. M. Panikkar, M.A. (Oxon.), Editor of the *Swarajya* of Madras, writing in the *Modern Review* for October 1923.

his followers were actuated when carrying a resolution at a political gathering in Eastern Bengal in June 1924, extolling the patriotism of a young Bengali, Gopi Nath Saha, who six months before had been guilty of the cold-blooded murder of an Englishman in Calcutta. In face of this gratuitous and sinister gesture and of the subsequent attitude of the left wing of the Nationalist party, it would be futile to close one's eyes to the spread of a spirit which if not checked, must end by bringing crashing to the ground the hopes so fondly cherished by many men of both races, of a future India the product of the constructive genius of the two peoples working in willing and fruitful co-operation.

* * * * * *

If in trying to make clear the mental outlook of modern India I have drawn more largely upon the speeches and writings of men of extreme views than upon those of moderate opinions, it is because the former are the more vocal and give more uncompromising expression to their feelings. But as I have already pointed out, the reaction against undue Westernisation is not confined to men of extreme views; if not universal amongst the educated Hindu middle classes it is at least very widespread. And in this particular matter the extremist often says what the moderate thinks. The difference between them is one of degree rather than of kind. And herein is to be found the explanation of the failure of the so-called moderate political party to carry the day in the controversies of the past few years. When the reformed constitution provided for by the Government of India Act of 1919 came into operation, the moderates had an unique opportunity of working the new constitution with success and establishing themselves as the dominant political party in the country, for the extremists by boycotting the elections left them a free field. After a promising start they failed, largely because their heart was not in the work. While they condemned the extravagances of the extremists and dissented from their methods, there was nevertheless a bond of sentiment between them. There were Ministers who strove gallantly to make of the new constitution the success which in a more friendly atmosphere it almost certainly might have become; but they received only lukewarm support from the legislative councils, and an impartial onlooker would often have been hard put to it to distinguish between the views expressed by the nominal moderates in the legislative bodies and the full-blown extremists outside.

The speeches and writings of the extremists provide a key, consequently, to the mentality of the Hindu educated classes generally, and it is in the light of that mentality that the spirit of modern India must be studied. It is this spirit which in the following pages I seek to explain. If I have succeeded in my attempt, I shall have made it clear that there is much in the aspirations of the modern educated Indian that calls for sympathy. For the political extremist with his bitter racial animosity, his acrid polemics against Great Britain, his extravagant unreason and his threats of criminal violence, the Englishman will find it difficult to entertain sympathy. But to the cultured Indian who does not fall into the error of mistaking hatred of other people for love of his own, with his innate courtesy, his responsive nature, his intellectual attainments and his high ideals, he will assuredly be attracted. And out of a growing understanding by each of the point of view of the other, will be born a greater capacity for fruitful co-operation, in which alone lies the hope of a future for India and Great Britain worthy of the high purpose with which their association has been consecrated in the past.

* * * * * *

I have concentrated upon this one aspect of the Indian problem—the revivalist tendencies of the Hindus—because while it is, in my opinion, one which is of fundamental importance, it is at the same time the one which is least generally understood. I do not underestimate the importance of the many other factors which add to the complexity of the situation—of the Akali movement among the Sikhs in the Punjab, which, if local in its operation, is nevertheless a source of no little anxiety; of the antagonism between the Brahmans and non-Brahmans in southern India; or of the presence in India of seventy million Moslems. Of this latter factor I have written in the first of these three volumes;[1] and I have made no further reference to it here, for to have dealt with this or any other of the factors of which the statesman and administrator have to take account would have diverted attention from the very matter to which it is my object to direct it, namely, the revolt of the rising generation of

[1] "India: A Bird's-eye View"; in particular, chapters xviii. and xix.

Western-educated Hindus against what it regards as the subordination of the soul of India to the cultural and political outlook of the West.

* * * * * *

A word is necessary in explanation of the spelling of Sanskrit terms. When writing of the *thought* of India the employment of a certain number of technical Sanskrit words is unavoidable, and with their use the question of transliteration at once presents itself. Generally speaking, I have employed the system laid down by Max Müller for use in the Sacred Books of the East. But since I am writing for the general reader rather than for the orientalist I have restricted my use of any system of scientific transliteration, and in the case of names and words that seem to me to have acquired a certain degree of currency in English I have discarded accents and diacritical marks altogether. Thus I have written Krishna rather than Kr̲ishn̲a, Shiva rather than S̲iva, and Rajendra rather than Râg̲endra. On the other hand, I have written g̲ñ̲âna, s̲ûnyavâda and Yâg̲ñ̲avalkya. It will probably be objected that my decision in each case is purely arbitrary. I admit it.

* * * * * *

My acknowledgements are due to the editor of the "Nineteenth Century and After" for permission to make use of certain passages from an article written for the July number in 1924; and I gladly avail myself of this opportunity of thanking him for the courtesy which he has thus shown me.

RONALDSHAY.

January 1925.

CONTENTS

PAGE

Prologue 1

CHAPTER I

An Unique Experiment 8

CHAPTER II

Origin and Growth of the System . . . 16

CHAPTER III

The Flowering of an Indian Language . . 28

CHAPTER IV

Navadvîpa and its Associations . . . 35

CHAPTER V

The New Wine of the West 44

CHAPTER VI

At the Cross-roads 55

CHAPTER VII

A Re-orientation of Aim ? 66

CHAPTER VIII

PAGE

Perverted Patriotism 80

CHAPTER IX

Panegyrics of the Past 88

CHAPTER X

"Ananda Math" 103

CHAPTER XI

The Song of the Lord 117

CHAPTER XII

Characteristics of Indian Art . . . 132

CHAPTER XIII

Sex Symbolism 143

CHAPTER XIV

An Indian Renaissance 151

CHAPTER XV

Indian Monism 161

CHAPTER XVI

A Problem for the Pundits 172

CHAPTER XVII

The Letter of the Vedanta 181

CHAPTER XVIII

PAGE

The Spirit of the Vedanta 189

CHAPTER XIX

The Spirit of the Vedanta (*continued*) . . 203

CHAPTER XX

The Spirit of the Vedanta (*concluded*) . . 214

Epilogue 232

Appendix 251

Index 257

PROLOGUE

An Indian writer whose pen has played a not inconsiderable part in the social and political ferments which have stirred the waters of Indian life during recent years, has written much on the meaning of the word "nationality". He has defined it as "the individuality of a people". One race of men, he argues, is differentiated from another by peculiarities analogous to those which distinguish one individual from another. Such peculiarities are physical, mental and social. They are due to certain inexplicable and prehistoric conditions in the race-structure. "We cannot explain the how, much less can we explain the why of these peculiarities; all that we can say of them is that they are there, in the very constitution of these different peoples." The peculiarities of physiological structure are the most obvious; but they are not the most important. The most powerful of race peculiarities are to be found in the thought-structure and the social-structure of the different peoples. It is "the structural formation of the thought-life" of a people leading them "to view themselves, view the world, and approach the eternal world-problems, from different standpoints, resulting in differences in their literatures, arts, philosophies and religions", that are "the essential elements of different race-consciousness . . . and constitute the original elements of difference in the different types of civilisation ".[1]

Is there, then, an Indian People? And if so, is it differentiated from other peoples by peculiarities of the kind set forth above? I have written elsewhere of the medley of races, civilisations and religions found within the confines of the Indian continent, and of the wide differences—physiological, mental and social—between them.[2] Mr. Pal does not ignore the composite character of the population; and while he argues that a common national life lies before the India of the future, he admits that the Hindu, the Parsi, the Buddhist, the Moslem and the Christian Communities in India will have "to work out the common national problem along their respective traditional and historic lines". As a Hindu, he looks at the problem of "the attainment of the common national Ideal" from the Hindu point of view, leaving it to others to do the same from their respective standpoints. He might have justified his own attitude on other grounds; for there are powerful historical reasons, which have been set forth in an earlier volume,[3] for regarding the civilisation, the culture and the religion of the Hindus as those which are essentially and distinctively Indian. And it is in the main the thought-structure of Hindu India that I myself seek to interpret in the following pages.

Mr. Pal does not confine the peculiarities of peoples to differences which are more or less trivial. He assigns to different races something which corresponds to the soul of the individual. "Every nation", he writes, "has a particular world-idea of its own, and develops under the

[1] The proposition set forth above is to be found running through a whole series of writings and speeches by Mr. Bepin Chandra Pal, a number of which was collected and published under the title of "The New Spirit" in 1907.

[2] In "India: A Bird's-eye View". [3] *Ibid.*

influence of its special environment, particular institutions and politics for the due realisation of this world-idea." The fundamental conception of the Vedanta philosophy, namely, the unity of all life involving as its logical conclusion the identity of God and Man, is then stated to be the world-idea of the Hindu race. "The one central fact in Indian history—indeed the one everlasting and prehistoric fact in the life-story of our people—is this peculiar Hindu spirit-consciousness. . . . The corner-stone of the new Indian nation, as it was of the old Hindu race, must be this supreme consciousness of the Self." Without some acquaintance with the Vedanta philosophy this "central fact in Indian history" is scarcely intelligible; and I shall attempt an explanation of it later on. For the present I take as an example of "the peculiar thought-structure" of the Hindu race an episode from the more familiar sphere of recent political activity.

No Indian name has become better known to the British public in recent years than that of M. K. Gandhi, for the movement which he led, and for which in March 1922 he was convicted of sedition, produced widespread disorder throughout the Indian continent and gave rise to grave apprehensions in Great Britain. Mr. Gandhi never attempted to disguise the object which he had in view. He stated quite frankly that what he desired and hoped to do was to paralyse the Government. It is not, however, with his object that I am here concerned; but with his methods—and with his methods themselves only in so far as they provide an illustration of the peculiar thought-structure of the Hindu race. From the very beginning of his crusade he insisted that suffering and renunciation were the weapons with which those who served under his banner must fight. "He who runs may see", he declared in an open letter to H.R.H. the Duke of Connaught, "that this is a religious purifying movement"; and addressing himself on another occasion to the students of Bengal, he said in the course of a speech delivered in Calcutta: "I am not ashamed to repeat before you who seem to be nurtured in modern traditions—who seem to be filled with the writing of modern writers—that this is a religious battle. I am not ashamed to repeat before you that this is an attempt to revolutionise the political outlook—that this is an attempt to spiritualise our politics."

It was natural enough that when the result of the movement which he had inaugurated was seen to be a succession of outbreaks of mob violence, his appeals to soul-force and his denunciation of physical force should excite the derision of his opponents. But quite apart from this, the plan of his campaign was one which was puzzling to the Western mind. An anonymous writer in the *Englishman* newspaper, who professed his faith in the methods of Mr. Gandhi, stated that conversations which he had held with English people, as also the comments which he had read in the English Press, satisfied him that Europeans did not in the least realise what was meant by *Satyagraha*—the word chosen by Mr. Gandhi to indicate the nature of the movement of which he was the author. He explained that the reason why Mr. Gandhi wanted those who desired to join him "to give up connection with the Government, and worldly affairs, and the lust after money and mechanical contrivances, is because these things interfere with single-mindedness". And he added: "*Satyagraha* is soul-force exerted by a multitude of people all wishing hard for what they desire. In order to be in a position to wish hard they must divest themselves of their worldly possessions and of their earthbound desires."

The idea is certainly one with which the Western mind is little familiar. Not so the Indian mind, however, for the idea is a product of the thought-structure of the Hindu race, and rests upon an Indian belief of immemorial antiquity, namely, that power can be acquired by the practice of renunciation and austerities. The ancient literature of India is strewn with examples of the efficacy of self-mortification as a means of acquiring power. A famous figure who appears in the Vedas, in both the great epics, the Mahabharata and the Ramayana, as also in the Purânas is the hero of a story which may, perhaps, be described as the classic example of this practice. The figure is Visvamitra, a king, and the story is that of a fierce and sustained conflict between him and Vasishta, a Brahman. It can be recalled in a few words. The cupidity of Visvamitra was excited by a "cow of plenty" in the possession of Vasishta, which he determined to acquire. Failing to obtain the animal by force, he abandoned his kingdom and retired to the Himâlayas, where he lived the life of an ascetic, subjecting himself to the severest austerities. His earliest reward came in the shape of an armoury of celestial weapons presented to him by the great god Mahadeva. With these he hurried back to the conflict with Vasishta, but was again defeated by the powerful priest and returned to the Himâlayas and his self-imposed austerities with a view to acquiring further reserves of soul-force. We need not follow him through the thousand-year periods of self-mortification which he indulged in, obtaining with each successive period greater power, and being offered by the gods steadily increasing rewards. In the end the "cow of plenty", which had been the source of all the trouble, pales into insignificance before the prodigious developments arising out of Visvamitra's sustained practice of intense austerities, and it becomes a question of the continued existence of the universe. The supernatural power acquired by him does, indeed, become a menace to gods and men, so much so that the former proceed to Brahma to lay before him the critical state of affairs with which they find themselves confronted. " The great *muni* Visvamitra ", they declare, " has been allured and provoked in various ways, but still advances in his sanctity. If his wish is not conceded, he will destroy the three worlds by the force of his austerity. All the regions of the universe are confounded, no light anywhere shines ; all the oceans are tossed, and the mountains crumble, the earth quakes and the wind blows confusedly." The heavenly deputation is successful in impressing Brahma with a sense of the urgency of the matter, and, accompanied by the heavenly host he himself approaches the terrible ascetic and, pronouncing a blessing upon him, hails him as *Brahman-rishi.* Visvamitra the king having thus compelled the gods to grant him the supreme rank of Brahmanhood, desists from the course which through successive millenniums he had been following to the danger of the universe.

It will be seen that, viewed in the light of Indian thought, Mr. Gandhi's doctrine of soul-force, which to many Westerners appeared to be a meaningless fad, becomes not only intelligible, but perfectly natural. There are, indeed, striking points of resemblance between the story of King Visvamitra and that of Mr. Gandhi. The original cause of Visvamitra's campaign was a comparatively small thing, namely, Vasishta's " cow of plenty". Similarly, the original cause of Mr. Gandhi's campaign was a comparatively small thing, namely, a legislative enactment known as the Rowlatt Act. And just as in the former case the " cow of plenty " lost all importance in face of the shattering developments to which Visvamitra's action gave rise, so in the latter case did the Rowlatt Act lose all importance in face of the convulsion which Mr. Gandhi's action produced.

Here, then, is an illustration of one of the peculiarities of the thought - structure of the Hindu race—reliance upon renunciation rather than upon action. I have given it as an introduction to what follows. Other such peculiarities will emerge as my theme unfolds ; and it will become apparent that out of the clash between the thought-structure of the Hindu race and that of the British, has arisen some at least of the heat which in recent times has characterised the relations between the two peoples.

CHAPTER I

AN UNIQUE EXPERIMENT

An Indian gentleman expressed the opinion recently that instruction appeals more to the head and heart of a boy when it is conveyed through a medium in which he is fitted by tradition and environment to express his own thoughts; and that education imparted through an alien tongue becomes parrot-like cramming rather than intelligent understanding.[1] At first sight this appears to be a truism which scarcely requires stating. But in India this is not so.

A stranger visiting the colleges and high schools of that country with any such thought in the back of his mind would be startled at what he saw—still more at what he heard. In the colleges he would see the lecture-rooms packed with Indian young men. On the platform he would see, more often than not, an Indian lecturer. But what he would hear, whether the subject being taught was mathematics or history, philosophy or physics, or any other of the subjects which found a place in the college curriculum, would be a discourse in English. In the high schools he would find small Indian boys from the countryside struggling to pick up the rudiments of what is known in Europe as a liberal education, through the medium of a language quite clearly

[1] Mr. Bibhutibhuson Datta, in evidence before the Calcutta University Commission of 1917.

foreign to teacher and taught alike, which he might or might not recognise as English. If his interest was sufficiently aroused by this strange experience to cause him to investigate the nature of the education given in this novel way, he would discover that it was almost confined to a literary course of a strictly Western type; and that its most conspicuous achievement had been the production of vast numbers of persons on the model of the English city clerk—so far, at any rate, as intellectual equipment and deportment are concerned. The spiritual man, as he would discover, has been passed by, since we have thought it necessary to assume in the matter of religion an attitude of strict neutrality, and have shrunk from the task of instructing the Muhammadan in the tenets of Islam, or of guiding the Hindu through the intricate mazes of Sanâtana Dharma—"the Eternal Religion".

In marked contrast to the rigid uniformity of the educational courses which he would find being monotonously repeated in every part of the continent, would be the striking diversity of type which he would notice amongst those thronging the class-rooms and lecture-halls; and he would naturally be led to make inquiries as to the nature of the material upon which this surprising experiment in education was being made. Such inquiries would lead him to certain general conclusions. In the first place, that it was vast in quantity and markedly diversified in kind, a human mass of many millions—320,000,000 in 1921—in composition the reverse of homogeneous. In the second place, that there lay behind a considerable portion of it a distinctive civilisation and culture of immense antiquity. In the third place, that there was deep woven in its texture a powerful religious tendency of great age in the case of the greater part of it, that is to say, the

Hindu segment, and of fierce militancy in the case of the other great fraction, namely, the Muhammadan. In the fourth place, that it was notable for the bewildering variety of languages in which it was accustomed to express itself, and lastly, that it was as to approximately 92 per cent of the whole, totally illiterate even in its own tongues.

The experiment of giving to these peoples an exotic education through the medium of a foreign language is certainly one which possesses unusual features. And if it has in the main achieved a remarkable measure of success, there are necessarily some respects in which it has met with failure. The use of a foreign tongue as the medium of instruction is attended with obvious drawbacks, of which one sees many examples. These are aggravated by the fact that the Indian of to-day is the descendant of a people who evolved a vast mnemonic literature—whose scriptures were not committed to writing but stored in the chambers of the mind and handed down orally from one generation to another. He has inherited, consequently, an extreme facility for memorising, and it is scarcely to be wondered at that the Indian boy, who from the age of twelve onwards is expected to acquire all that he has to learn through the medium of English, should fall back instinctively upon his undeniable powers of memory to carry him through his formidable task. What happens only too often under these circumstances is illustrated by the answer given not long ago at an examination to the following question—" Explain the meaning of the word psychology ". The answer given in one paper was —" The science of mind ornamental phenomena ". It was doubtless this aptitude for committing to memory the uncomprehended notes dictated in the class-room, that Dr. Pramathanath Banerji had in mind when he stated in evidence before the Calcutta University Commission of 1917, that the employment of English as the medium of instruction "teaches our boys to attach importance to words rather than to thoughts, to forms rather than to substances".

I have myself visited a very large number of high schools in Bengal, and when doing so have made a practice of asking the boys a few simple questions. More often than not they have not understood what I have said to them, and the question has had to be repeated to them by their teacher. Equally often I have failed to understand their replies. This, though disappointing, is not really surprising, in spite of the fact that during the last two years of his school life the Indian boy often devotes as much as twenty-six hours a week to a study of English, a greater portion of time, as was pointed out by the members of the Calcutta University Commission, than is allotted to any single subject in any secondary system in any country with which they were acquainted. The cause of it is explained by an experienced educationalist, who tells us that while at the head of a training college in Eastern Bengal, he has repeatedly come across graduates who before their admission had never spoken to an Englishman in their lives. Under these circumstances he found nothing to astonish him in the fact that Indian students found it "impossible to understand Englishman's English at once, or to pick up the correct intonation of the language themselves".[1] A training college, it is to be noted in passing, is an institution for turning out *teachers*, who on leaving it are employed in educating their fellow-men.

Another experienced principal of a college has asserted that neither does the Indian university

[1] Mr. E. E. Biss.

student possess an adequate command of English on his entrance to the university nor, in the case of the majority, does he acquire it in the course of his university training. "The papers of M.A. candidates", he says, "show that quite a large proportion even of those who have spent six years at colleges, still express themselves with great difficulty in English and often commit gross grammatical blunders." And his conclusion is that "the system by which all instruction after the elementary stage is given through the medium of an alien tongue, has failed hopelessly".[1]

The various expedients which have been adopted to remedy this deficiency do not appear to have been altogether happy. The immense amount of time devoted to the teaching of English in the high schools has certainly proved out of all proportion to the results obtained; and it is at least arguable that the addition to the college curriculum of a compulsory course of English *literature* has in many cases tended to confuse, rather than to clarify the student's ideas as to the nature of the medium through which he is expected to express his thoughts. What, for example, is likely to be the effect upon the mind of the average Indian boy of a request made to him by an examiner to annotate such a sentence as—"He yaf nat of that text a pulled hen that seith that hunters been nat hooly men"?[2] Still more, what is likely to be its effect upon his knowledge of English as a spoken language? Or again, would the boy from an Indian village be likely to add to his working knowledge of the language by considering briefly—as on one occasion he was actually asked to do—"the various features which render 'Samson Agonistes'

[1] Mr. J. R. Barrow.

[2] This was a question which was actually set in an examination in the south of India some few years ago.

important (i.) as a work of art, and (ii.) as a personal revelation" ?

This necessity for concentrating upon the teaching of English has led, moreover, to an unfortunate neglect of the student's own language. Whether or not the candidate for entrance to the university possessed a reasonable knowledge of his own tongue and literature, became a matter of comparative indifference. It is true that the regulations required that he should be tested in composition in his vernacular; but the number of books prescribed for reading as models of style was limited to six, and questions on the subject-matter of the books so prescribed, or on the history of vernacular literature, were definitely ruled out; while it was also laid down that no lectures need be delivered in the colleges on vernacular composition. This surely showed a strange disregard for what one would have imagined should have been an essential in the education of an Indian boy. It so struck the members of the Calcutta University Commission, who expressed the opinion that there was "something unsound in a system of education which leaves a young man at the conclusion of his course unable to speak or write his own mother tongue fluently and correctly".[1]

And, quite apart from any question of the medium of instruction, the whole system of education is completely divorced from Indian culture and tradition. The high school and undergraduate courses are essentially Western courses, unrelated to Indian life as it was lived before the advent of the British. They are rigidly mechanical, and altogether lack that intimate relationship between teacher and taught which was an outstanding feature of the indigenous system. The university training of the

[1] Vol. v. of the Report.

Indian student " is almost wholly unrelated to the real thoughts and aspirations of his mind ".[1] An example at once occurs to one. The intellectual life of India has always been remarkable for the high place which it has accorded to philosophy; yet under the existing system the Indian student who takes philosophy as a subject for his bachelor degree, leaves the university without so much as hearing any mention of the six systems which have sprung from Indian soil, or of Bâdarâyaṉa, the compiler of the Vedanta Sûtras, or of giants among the commentators such as Sankara or Ramanuja.

Greatest paradox of all, this unexpected state of affairs has been brought about in the main by the efforts of Indians themselves. It was from Indians that came the demand for Western knowledge and a Western medium of expression; and it has been from Indians that the steady trend of the education given, towards a purely literary type, has derived its momentum. In Bengal the University Commission of 1917 found a population of 45,000,000 producing approximately the same number of students preparing for university degrees—26,000—as the same population in the United Kingdom. " But since in Bengal only about one in ten can read and write, the proportion of the educated classes of Bengal who are taking full-time university courses is almost ten times as great as in the United Kingdom." [2] The Commission was struck by other contrasts between conditions in Bengal and in Great Britain. In the latter country education was many-sided. By far the greater number of students was engaged upon vocational courses, a comparatively small proportion devoting itself to purely literary studies. Bengal, on the other hand, was " unlike any other civilised country,

[1] Calcutta University Commission of 1917. [2] *Ibid.*

in that so high a proportion of its educated classes set before them a university degree as the natural goal of ambition ", a goal which they sought by means of " studies which are almost purely literary in character, and which therefore provide scarcely any direct professional training ".[1] In Great Britain the variety of courses was marked by the existence of no less than eighteen universities varying widely in type. In Bengal, on the other hand, was one vast university—numerically the largest in the world —with 27,000 students of all grades, and an annual quota of candidates for its matriculation examination exceeding 16,000. The whole student community was brought under the control of this one great mechanism, " followed in each subject the same courses of study, read the same books and underwent the same examinations ". In India as a whole they found 133 English Arts Colleges with an attendance of 50,000 and 8149 secondary schools of a Western type with 1,212,000 pupils.[2] The flowering of the educational tree was, indeed, such that they found it difficult "to find any parallel to it in any part of the world ".

How did this surprising state of affairs arise ? The answer to that question must be sought in the history of the origin and evolution of the modern system of education during the past hundred years.

[1] Report of the Calcutta University Commission of 1917.
[2] Figures for 1918.

CHAPTER II

ORIGIN AND GROWTH OF THE SYSTEM

THE system of education, which has been briefly described in the preceding chapter, was certainly not planned by the early British administrators under the East India Company. Warren Hastings looked forward to a great flowering of Indian culture under the security afforded by British administration. He himself founded an indigenous educational institution for the benefit of the Muhammadans, which was known as the Calcutta Madrassa. And when, in 1813, a provision was included in the India Act of that year requiring the Directors of the Company to spend a specified sum annually on education, they rejected the idea of establishing colleges of a Western type and spent the money on the promotion of Oriental learning. The movement which was to end by bringing about the state of affairs which exists to-day was to come from a different quarter. Actually it derived its momentum from two very different sources—the zeal of a group of educationalists interested in movements for the advancement of secular learning, and the enthusiasm of the Christian missionaries.

There are in and near Calcutta to-day, monuments in stone directing the attention of the visitor to the beginnings of both these movements. One is the statue of an English tradesman, one David Hare a watchmaker by profession, which is to be seen in the grounds of a High School in the heart of Calcutta which still bears his name. The other is an imposing building standing on the right bank of the Hughli river, some miles above the city, opposite the park of Barrackpore. This latter was founded in 1818, in what was then Danish territory, by a famous trio of Baptist missionaries—Carey, Marshman and Ward—and is still a flourishing educational institution, known as the Serampore College.

David Hare was one of those persons disabled by temperament from accepting the dogma of religion, but compelled by his heart to lead an essentially Christian life. An Indian contemporary, babu Govinchandra Datta, declared in the words of Thackeray, that he knew not what Hare's doctrine was, "but his life was that of a veritable Christian". On the other hand, the *Friend of India*, the newspaper of the Serampore missionaries, after speaking in an obituary notice in June 1842 in terms of high praise of his philanthropic encouragement of education added—"At the same time it must be confessed with deep regret that his inveterate hostility to the Gospel produced an unhappy effect on the minds of the Native youths who were so largely under his influence, by indisposing their minds to all inquiry after religious truth and inducing a general scepticism, the melancholy consequences of which will long continue to be apparent in the opinions and conduct of the present generation of enlightened Natives". That this forecast proved only too true will become apparent hereafter;[1] though it would be unfair to lay upon the shoulders of David Hare sole responsibility for the wave of irreligion which a little

[1] See Chapter V.

later overtook the student community of Bengal. It was the inevitable result of pouring new wine into old bottles; and in so far as it could be attributed to persons, should be laid at the door of a prominent teacher in the Hindu College, Mr. H. L. Derozio, a free-thinker, who exercised a great influence over the students, whom he encouraged to discuss freely all subjects, social, moral and religious, rather than at that of David Hare.

Hare who had settled in Calcutta in the year 1800 retired from business in 1816. On the tombstone raised to his memory which still stands in College Square, it is stated that "he adopted for his own the country of his sojourn and cheerfully devoted the remainder of his life with unwearying zeal and benevolence to one pervading and darling object, on which he spared no personal trouble, money or influence, viz. the education and moral improvement of the Natives of Bengal". In pursuance of this object he studied the Bengali language, but finding it deficient in works of modern learning, he conceived the idea of founding an educational institution which should communicate to the rising generation a knowledge of Western literature and science. Fired with this ambition he sought the society of wealthy and cultured men of the city, and amongst them made the acquaintance of a great Hindu reformer, Raja Ram Mohan Roy, who, painfully conscious of the low ebb which the moral and intellectual culture of his own country had reached, was aiming independently at the same goal. The two joined forces, and in 1817 the Hindu College came into being. The object of the institution was set forth in the forefront of the rules drawn up by the directors, as being—"the tuition of the sons of respectable Hindoos in the English and Indian language, and in the literature and science of Europe and Asia".

The missionaries were little behind the secularists in furthering the advance of education on modern lines. Their object was necessarily a different one. For them education was important in the main as a means of conveying to Indians the teaching of the Christian religion. The earnest band of workers at Serampore produced first editions of the New Testament in more than thirty Oriental languages and dialects. And the famous trio of Serampore were followed in due course by Alexander Duff, scholar, missionary and statesman, who in 1830, with the cordial assistance of Ram Mohan Roy, founded a school and college from which have sprung the Scottish Churches' school and college of the present day.

These movements had their influence upon the Government. Raja Ram Mohan Roy himself urged upon Lord Amherst, the Governor-General, the desirability of adopting the study of Western sciences through the medium of the English language. In a letter in which he set forth his views on the subject he expressed his belief that the perpetuation of the Sanskrit system, far from serving to enlighten his countrymen, would keep them in darkness, and declared his confidence that "as the improvement of the native population" was the object of the Government, it would "subsequently promise a more liberal and enlightened system of instruction, embracing mathematics, natural philosophy, chemistry, anatomy and other useful sciences".[1]

Circumstances were so shaping themselves as to favour the adoption of these views. The India Act of 1833 provided for the addition of a legal member to the Governor-General's Council, and the first person to hold the new office, Macaulay, was also appointed Chairman of a body known

[1] The letter is given in full in "A Biographical Sketch of David Hare", by Peary Chand Mittra, published in Calcutta in 1877.

as the Committee of Public Instruction which had been created in 1823. A distinguished man of letters himself, Macaulay poured scorn upon Oriental learning. His view was stated tersely in a minute drawn up as a member of the Government in 1835—a minute which has since become famous as the turning-point in the controversy between the Orientalists and the Western school. A single shelf of a good European library he held to be worth the whole native literature of India and Arabia. And he concluded a lengthy analysis of the educational position by declaring that unless the system was changed, he must sever his connection with the Committee of Public Instruction.

In Lord William Bentinck, who had succeeded Lord Amherst as Governor-General, he found a warm supporter; and orders were issued the same year that the funds at the disposal of Government for educational purposes, should be expended in imparting instruction in European languages and sciences through the medium of English. Raja Ram Mohan Roy had died in England in 1833, the very year in which the India Act leading to this decision had been passed. But the seed which he had sown had borne fruit, and the victory of the Western school was hailed with satisfaction by a little band of Hindu reformers—prominent among whom was a Brahman gentleman, babu Ramtanu Lahiri—which was engaged upon schemes for the wide diffusion of knowledge. Journals were published, the *Gyanuneshun* or "Search after Knowledge", and the *Bengal Spectator*, and a club entitled the "Society for the Acquisition of General Knowledge" was formed.

June of the same year saw the foundation of the Calcutta Medical College, the success of which was made possible by the courage of one Madusudan Gupta who had been educated at Hare's school, in defying custom which forbade the touching of the dead by the higher castes, and with the assistance of a few courageous pupils, undertaking the dissection of a human body. Thus the process of pouring new wine into old bottles was in full swing, and received further impetus by the supersession of Persian as the language of the Courts in 1837, and by an announcement of Lord Hardinge in 1844, that for the future preference would be given, in all appointments under Government, to men who had received a Western education.

The highest official sanction was accorded to the trend of educational policy sketched above, by Sir Charles Wood's famous despatch of 1854, which decreed the creation of a Department of Public Instruction in every province, and aimed at a wide extension of effort by private enterprise, by inaugurating a system of grants-in-aid to all institutions reaching a specified standard. It urged the establishment of provincial universities and the institution of vocational courses on a generous scale which would "teach the natives of India the marvellous results of the employment of labour and capital, rouse them to emulate us in the development of the vast resources of their country, and gradually, but certainly, confer upon them all the advantages which accompany the healthy increase of wealth and commerce".

It was, however, one thing for Government to map out the educational course, but quite a different thing for it to guide the movement along it. The subsequent history of the movement shows indeed that it speedily attained a momentum of its own which the authorities were powerless to control. The comprehensive expectations set forth in the despatch of 1854 were not realised. The symmetry of the plan was upset, for while the practical courses, with the possible exception of medicine, never attained more than a stunted growth, the literary courses in their exuberant flowering drained the tree of its sap. That this was due to inherited characteristics on the part of the people is clear enough. It was inevitable that a people whose traditional systems of learning were almost exclusively literary and religious in character—as were those of the Muhammadans and the Hindus alike—should tend to concentrate upon purely literary studies. And this tendency was fostered by the particular type of university which was set up. The affiliating university which came into existence in 1857 was little more than an examining board. And by 1882, when the results of the measures taken in accordance with the policy of 1854 came under the examination of a Commission, "the university degree had become the accepted object of ambition, the passport to distinction in the public services, and in the learned professions ".[1] Moreover, academic distinctions of this kind—degrees and certificates—had acquired a definite social value, the man in possession of them being rated at a higher figure in the marriage market.

The Commission of 1882 was impressed with another respect in which the system lacked symmetry. It found it top-heavy. While the middle classes of the people had developed a perfect passion for secondary and higher education, primary education had fallen into the cold shades of neglect. The Commission sought to remedy these glaring defects. It made proposals which it believed were well designed to bring about a large expansion in elementary education, and in the sphere of higher education to check the wild race for academic distinctions and to divert some part of the rapidly swelling stream of students into channels of a more practical character.

[1] Report of the Calcutta University Commission of 1917–19.

Nothing could better illustrate the extent to which the system was now racing along under its own momentum, uninfluenced by attempts on the part of the authorities to guide it, than the complete failure of the laudable efforts of the Commission of 1882. The proposals which were made for the creation of courses in the high schools "intended to fit youths for commercial or non-literary pursuits" remained barren, while during the next twenty years there was a decrease in the expansion of primary relatively to secondary education; the preponderant development of secondary education was intensified, and the growth of the higher types of secondary schools was proportionately far greater than the growth of the more elementary type. And at the apex of the system there was a rapid expansion in the number of colleges which depended mainly or wholly on fees, colleges that throve as "coaching institutions rather than places of learning", colleges which gave English education without the aid of Englishmen, and whose students rarely came into contact with any one who spoke as his native tongue the language in which all their studies were conducted.[1] Some improvements in the system were effected as a result of the labours of yet another Commission in 1902; but the Commission of that year proved as powerless as the Commission of 1882, to divert the constantly growing stream of Western-educated students from the literary courses which they insisted on pursuing.

Such, in brief outline, is the history of the rise of the educational system which has taken root in Indian soil as a result of the contact between India and the Western World. And such is its nature at the close of a century of growth. That it constitutes an experiment of an

[1] Report of the Calcutta University Commission of 1917–19.

unprecedented character will hardly be disputed, for it aims at moulding a congeries of peoples vast in numbers, varied in type, the inheritors, in the case of the majority of ideals and traditions reaching back into a remote antiquity, upon a model which is the creation of a people whose genius is the product of a widely different history and environment. It is easy to point to its shortcomings in detail, while as a whole it lends itself to obvious satire. A humorist ignorant of the history of its rise and growth might think himself justified in asking us to picture a similar experiment of which we ourselves were the subjects. Great Britain in the days of her own internal disorders taken charge of gradually by an alien people; her young men, or such of them as desired to proceed beyond the primary school standard, obliged to learn an alien tongue taught indifferently by persons with a very defective knowledge of it themselves; and then to proceed to alien universities established upon English soil, where were taught through the medium of the foreign tongue, by methods to which they were not accustomed, subjects which were altogether strange to their upbringing and wholly unconnected with their own history, traditions, home life, civilisation and culture.

The answer to such an attack is, of course, provided by the history of the movement which has been briefly sketched and which shows that it was the people themselves who pressed for a Western education, and that since the vernaculars did not possess the vocabulary necessary for the teaching of modern science, there was no practical alternative to the use of English as the medium of instruction. To which might be added that the value of English as the *lingua franca* of a continent inhabited by peoples speaking a great variety of tongues, is sufficiently proved by the fact that the proceedings of conferences of all kinds held by Indians from all parts of the continent, are conducted as a matter of course in English; that such success as has been achieved in welding the peoples of India into a nation has been due to the unifying influence of English ideas and the English language; and, finally, that by these means alone could the splendid attainments of the Western World—its lofty ideals in the sphere of morals as illustrated in particular by its exaltation of the great principle of liberty, and its far-reaching achievements in the domain of human knowledge as exemplified by the towering edifice of modern science—have been made accessible to the Indian peoples.

The answer goes a long way towards justifying the educational system which has grown up, but not, I think, the whole way. Not even Macaulay, the great protagonist of the Western School, had contemplated quite so drastic a rejection of everything Indian as has actually taken place. He aimed, it is true, at training up a class of persons "Indian in blood and colour, but English in taste, in opinions, in morals and in intellect", who should become the interpreters between the British and the millions of India subject to British rule; but he also expected that such a body of Indians would "refine the vernacular dialects of the country" and, by enriching them with the terms of science borrowed from the nomenclature of the West, "render them by degrees fit vehicles for conveying knowledge to the great mass of the population".[1] Has, then, this expectation been fulfilled? Have the vernaculars of India shown a capacity for development to the extent of bearing the burden of the increasingly complex civilisations of the modern world? Or is the

[1] Minute of February 2, 1835.

adoption by India of an alien speech as her chief medium of expression, necessary to her survival in the struggle for existence amongst the nations of the modern world ?

Nor is it a mere question of the adoption of this or that language that is involved, for language is the raiment in which man clothes his thought, and the one reacts upon the other—the thought upon the language and *vice versa.* In the first flush of their enthusiasm for the things of the West when, despising their own vernacular and rejecting their own classical languages, they adopted English as their primary medium of expression, there were those amongst the new class of modern educated persons in Bengal who lost their Indian individuality. The choice of language is, in fact, but one aspect of a much larger question—the question whether India has the will to persist as a distinctive type among the races of the world, or whether she will be content to merge her individuality in the virile type which has been evolved in the Western hemisphere ?

A factor of no little importance militating against this latter possibility is the persistence in the villages, amongst the masses of the people, of a stolid conservatism which has offered a vigorous resistance to the impact of the West. Will the modern educated middle classes end by uprooting the masses of the people from the intellectual and cultural soil from which they have sprung ? Or will the former, invigorated by a generous infusion of the moral and intellectual sap of the West, seek to graft themselves upon the ancient tree-trunk of the East ? It is to a consideration of this question that the following pages are to a large extent devoted. And since the introduction of the Western system of education in Bengal has been the most powerful factor in modifying the Indian type, it will be convenient in the first place, to search for any indications which there may be of a tendency amongst the Western-educated classes to engraft themselves upon the parent stem. And if, with this object in view, we examine the developments of the past century, we shall discover side by side with the growth of the Western educational movement a less obtrusive, but none the less clearly perceptible effort among some, at least, of those who were growing up amidst the new intellectual environment, to find in their mother-tongue a medium capable of giving expression to the new ideas.

CHAPTER III

THE FLOWERING OF AN INDIAN LANGUAGE

WHEN the foundations of the present educational system were being laid, Bengali literature was admittedly at a low ebb. Such literature as there was at the beginning of the nineteenth century was in verse rather than in prose, and was the possession of the masses rather than of the classes. The Committee of Public Instruction, which at the time of Macaulay's Minute was divided in opinion on the question of Western education *versus* Oriental learning, was unanimously of opinion that " the vernacular languages contained neither the literary nor scientific information necessary for a liberal education ". Not only was Bengali inadequate to the needs of the times, it was also looked down upon by cultured Bengalis themselves ; and it is on record that a suggestion made by an Englishman, Mr. Adam, that some at least of the lectures to be delivered at the newly established educational institutions might be given in Bengali, was vetoed by the Indian members of his committee on the ground that, " anything said or written in the vernacular tongue would be despised in consequence of the medium through which it was conveyed ".[1] The languages of culture were Sanskrit, Arabic and Persian, and of the first Raja Ram Mohan Roy—himself a Sanskrit

[1] See " Twelve Men of Bengal ", by F. B. Bradley Birt.

scholar of repute—had written to Lord Amherst that it was "so difficult that almost a lifetime is necessary for its acquisition". There were cogent reasons, then, at that time for the employment of English as the medium of instruction in higher education.

There were influences at work, however, which were destined to lift the Bengali language out of the trough into which it had fallen. The Serampore missionaries, headed by William Carey, threw themselves enthusiastically into the task of acquiring a thorough mastery of the vernacular, with the object of translating the Bible and bringing the fruits of Western learning to the people of India through its agency. From the side of Government came the establishment by Lord Wellesley, in the year 1800, of the Fort William College for the training of civil servants, with a vernacular department, which was placed in charge of Carey himself. With him were associated a number of pundits whose scholarship in the classical languages of India was profound. The immediate effect of these developments was to give to the language of Bengal a curious hybrid character; the ultimate effect was to make of it a language described by Mr. J. D. Anderson as "one of the great expressive languages of the world, capable of being the vehicle of as great things as any speech of men".

The English enthusiasts rendered an immense service to the vernacular and attained to a high degree of proficiency in it. But they displayed a quite natural tendency to import into it the syntactical constructions of their own tongue, while the pundits similarly overweighted it with the highly developed idiom and figures of speech of the classical languages. The result has been summed up by Rai Dinesh Chandra Sen Bahadur in a recent course of lectures on Bengali Prose

Style—" Bengali prose in the hands of the pundits was a fantastic thing, unintelligible, foolish and full of unmeaning, vain pedantry "; and with reference to the introduction of foreign idiom—" our language for a quarter of a century lay hopelessly entangled in the figures of foreign rhetoric and their involved syntactical constructions ".

Nevertheless an impetus had been given which fired the imagination of the cultured classes. By the middle of the century there were pioneers in this new field of modern Bengali producing works on which their successors were able to build. The name of Dr. Rajendralal Mitra stands out among the pioneers, and that of K. M. Banerji, who compiled an encyclopaedia, the "Vidyakalpadrûma", and of Ramkamal Sen, who published a dictionary of over 1500 pages, containing Bengali equivalents of 5300 English words.[1] Opinion was no longer so contemptuous of the vernacular as it had been. At the third anniversary meeting held to commemorate the life of David Hare in 1845, one of the speakers, babu Akshay Kumar Datta, delivered his address in Bengali, a proceeding which called forth the warm approval of babu Kisori Chandra Mitra, who followed him. The address, he declared, interesting as it was, was all the more so because it was in Bengali. He admitted that it was the fashion amongst their educated fellow-countrymen to decry their own tongue. But this was a prejudice which he thought was wearing out, and he prophesied that " the necessity and importance of cultivating the Bengali language—the language of our country, the language of our infancy, the language in which our earliest ideas and associations are intwined—will ere long be recognised by all ".[2]

[1] " Bengali Prose Style ", by Rai D. C. Sen Bahadur.
[2] See " A Biographical Sketch of David Hare ", by Peary Chand Mitra.

Another influence was the vernacular press. The first Indian newspaper was the short-lived *Bengal Gazette*, started by a Bengali Brahman, Gangadhar Bhattacharji, in 1816. It was soon followed by an organ of the Serampore missionaries. The most notable of the early vernacular newspapers, however, was the *Probhakar*, under the editorship first of Isvar Chandra Gupta and later of others. It was in the columns of this paper that a number of writers, who were to play a decisive part in moulding the language, made their bow to the public — Bankim Chandra Chatterji, the most famous of the novelists of Bengal; Dinabandhu Mitra, the father of Bengali drama, and Dwarkanath Adhikari.[1] Another notable paper, in that it gave a new refinement to Bengali journalism, was the *Sama Prakas*, founded in 1858 largely by the efforts of a Sanskrit scholar Pundit Isvar Chandra Vidyasagar. Where the pundits of Fort William College had failed Vidyasagar succeeded, for into the warp of Bengali prose he wove a woof of Sanskrit which, far from rendering it foolishly grandiloquent, gave to it " a new status and a classic dignity ".[2] Nor was Bengali only to assimilate the grace and dignity of Sanskrit; it was also to acquire the vigour of English. Men whose names stand out as artificers giving to the language this quality are Akshay Kumar Datta and Bankim Chandra Chatterji, the former adapting it to become the medium of scientifie treatises, the latter of vigorous and rich romance.

Bankim Chandra Chatterji set up another landmark in the history of Bengali journalism when in 1872 he founded a magazine under the title of *Banga Darsan*, through whose pages not

[1] " A Hundred Years of the Bengali Press ", by P. N. Bose and H. W. N. Moreno.

[2] Rai D. C. Sen Bahadur.

only his own novels, but the works of a brilliant band of writers were given to the public. It has been said of him that he taught the people of Bengal to read Bengali for pleasure; and we have the evidence of Dr. Rabindra Nath Tagore, who at a later date was himself to be awarded the Nobel prize for literature, to this effect. He has told us in his reminiscences how, when he was himself a young man, Bankim's *Banga Darsan* "took the Bengali heart by storm"; and he has given a graphic account of the deep impression which such writings made upon his own mind. "It was bad enough to have to wait till the next monthly number was out, but to be kept waiting further till my elders had done with it was simply intolerable!"[1] And second only to the interest excited by Bankim's novels was that aroused by the historical articles of Dr. Ramdas Sen and the scientific articles of prominent writers.[2] The day foreseen by Macaulay when he spoke of the vernacular refined and enriched so as to render it a fit vehicle for conveying knowledge to the great mass of the population had surely come. Yet for many years still was the child from the Indian countryside, who aspired to a high school education, to spend hour after hour in puzzled study of the English idiom, that might have been spent to so much greater advantage in learning, in the medium of expression natural to him, not to memorise but to think.

It is plain from the official literature from Macaulay's Minute onwards, that Government has adhered steadfastly to its aim of rendering the vernaculars fit media for the imparting of modern learning. The excessive use which has been made of English and the neglect of the vernaculars under the system of State education, must be

[1] "My Reminiscences", by Rabindra Nath Tagore.
[2] See "A Hundred Years of the Bengali Press".

attributed to the general trend of opinion amongst the Western-educated Indian intelligentsia which, in its new-found zeal for everything Western, often displayed a tendency during the nineteenth century to cut itself adrift as completely as possible from its own past. All the more significant, consequently, is a change in this respect which has recently made itself felt. The evidence tendered to the Calcutta University Commission of 1917 showed the existence of a profound difference of opinion on the question of the continued employment of English as the medium of instruction, even during the university courses, and though the opinion of the majority still favoured this practice, there were many Indians amongst the minority who expressed the view that "the forcing of an alien language only serves to dry up, at their very sources, the very fountain springs of national power and thus impoverishes the nation on the side of initiative and originality".[1]

The Commission recommended a reduction of the use of English as a medium of instruction in the High Schools, but, considering that there was an overwhelming mass of opinion pointing to its use as the chief medium in the case of university education, advised its retention for all courses after the matriculation stage. Generally speaking, there was discernible amongst the Indian witnesses a distinct move of opinion in the direction of a progressive use of the vernacular as the medium of instruction and the retention of English as a compulsory second language. And when in 1922 the Calcutta University decided on the introduction of the vernacular as the medium of instruction and examination in the secondary schools, an Indian publicist declared that the change received the whole-hearted support of every shade of Bengali opinion, and added that there

[1] Mr. Bibhutibhuson Datta.

was a very strong body of educated opinion which would welcome the introduction of a similar change in the colleges.[1]

The significance of this change of view is due to the fact that it has taken place in that section of the Indian public which, throughout the century of its growth, has been the champion of the Western system. The system, partly because it is the State system, and partly because it has been the most powerful factor in the Indian renaissance ; and its adherents because they have provided the inspiration and driving force of the movement, occupy a position on the Indian stage which is apt to monopolise attention. It would nevertheless be a mistake, as I have already hinted, to suppose that the Western system has been universally accepted. Away in quiet and secluded places sheltered from the noise and bustle of the modern world the indigenous system flourishes. Scattered widely over the face of the land is a network of Sanskrit tôls, where the ancient learning of India is studied and taught by the ancient methods of the East. That the system of old still appeals to the heart of India is shown by the appearance in recent years of educational institutions which, while welcoming the learning of the West, have swung back in greater or less degree to the ideals of the East. Of these I shall have something to say later on. First let me conduct the reader to a famous centre of indigenous learning where still burns with pure flame the spirit of the immemorial East.

[1] In the *Englishman* of August 10, 1922.

CHAPTER IV

NAVADVÎPA AND ITS ASSOCIATIONS

WE had been floating down the waters of the sacred Bhagirathi and on an afternoon in late August we dropped anchor close to the right bank of the river, where the ancient town of Navadvîpa lay bedded like a jewel in a setting of green. Local legend carries the history of Navadvîpa back to Buddhist times ; but its fame as the greatest centre of Hindu learning in Bengal dates from the fifteenth century A.D., when one, Vasudeva Sarvabhauma, stole the lamp of learning so jealously guarded by the pundits of Mithilâ and, travelling by devious ways, carried it at length to Navadvîpa, where he kindled the fire which burns brightly upon her altars at the present day.

The task was no easy one. Jealous of her reputation the great masters of logic (*Nyâya*) who controlled the university of Mithilâ, forbade their students carrying away with them aught in the shape of written word beyond their own diplomas. With a single-minded determination, which deserved and won success, Vasudeva committed to memory the entire Tattva - cintâmaṇi and the metrical portion of the Kusumâñjalî. Having in due course reached Navadvîpa, he transcribed these two works from memory and established the first of the great academies of Logic for which the town was subsequently to become famous. Among his pupils were four men of outstanding eminence, Raghunâtha Siromani, the highest authority on modern logic; Raghunandana, the founder of the Bengal School of Hindu Law; Krishnânanda Agamvâgîsa, the first expounder of Tantras in Bengal; and Chaitanya, whose name is revered throughout Bengal to-day as the most famous exponent of Bengali Vaishnavism.

It was the first of these four scholars who deprived Mithilâ of her reputation by compelling Pundit Paksadhara Misra, to whose tôl he had gained admittance in the guise of a pupil, publicly to admit defeat in argument at his hands, and thus secured for Navadvîpa a charter to confer degrees. The university dates from the year of Raghunâtha's triumph—A.D. 1503.[1]

* * * * * *

It very soon became evident that the official description of my visit as private was a *misnomer.* The streets, which were narrow and picturesque, were packed with people, and on the roofs of the houses, at no great height in most cases, were crowds of gaily dressed women. As we drove slowly through the town these latter rained down flowers and rice upon us and greeted us with the curious ululation known as *hooloo*—a long-drawn note with a tremor in it caused by the rapid movement of the tongue from side to side of the open mouth. On all sides dense masses of dusky faces welcomed us, the white robes of many contrasting with the dark bodies of those who spurned raiment. All shades of brown were there, the pale and glistening copper of the pure Aryan standing out markedly against the surrounding background of duskier hue. So we reached the

[1] For the above brief sketch of the rise of the University of Navadvîpa I am indebted to a monograph entitled "Logic in the University of Nadia", by the late Mahâmahopadhyaya Satis Chandra Vidyabhusana, M.A.

hall of the Anglo-Sanskrit library, where we were formally received by the members of the Municipal Board, and by representatives of the pundits. Here was assuredly the very antithesis of the modern world. It was back down the centuries that the gaze of Navadvîpa was set—from the future she turned shuddering away.

Navadvîpa, declared the city fathers in an address of deep pathos, had been, once upon a time, the chief centre of Sanskrit learning in Bengal, the place where Lord Gauranga (Chaitanya) was born and preached his doctrine of love, the soil whence sprang teachers of world-wide fame, and last but not least, the capital of a mighty line of Hindu kings. " But now ", they added, " it has been shorn of all its former glory, having only the traditions of its scholarship living in the memory, like the vibrations of some sweet music when its soft and feeling tunes have died." With similar pessimism the pundits conjured up a vision of their city as a vast and deserted hall, whose empty spaces were haunted only by the ghostly memories of a shining but irrevocable past. The new was clearly pressing heavily upon the old—and the old was sullenly resentful.

Outside in the town itself and in the tôls I found a less oppressive atmosphere. Of these latter I visited a number, handling old manuscripts—notably one by the father of S̱rî Chaitanya—and listening to the discourses of the pundits. The scene that lingers most vividly in my memory is one set in the dim evening light in the Chaitanya Chatuspathi, where my attention was suddenly caught and riveted by an overwhelming and altogether irresistible sense of familiarity. Where had I seen all this before ? I was searching darkly through the chambers of my mind for an explanation, when it unexpectedly welled up into consciousness. Here was being enacted before my eyes one of those scenes described with such graphic effect in the pages of the New Testament. I give the description as I wrote it at the time.

Ascending by a narrow winding stairway, we came to an upper room. This was long and narrow, and barely furnished with a wooden table and a few chairs. At the table was seated a venerable pundit with a countenance which might have been taken straight from a stained-glass window; and grouped round the table were twelve pupils. A soft twilight filtered through the lattice windows, showing up only the salient objects in the room. At one end of the table a tall and massive wooden candlestick stood on the floor, its solitary flame forming a point of light which showed up against, rather than illumined, the surrounding dusk. The effect was striking, the tense faces of the disciples at that end of the table being lit up and their white garments showing sharply against the gloom of the dark panelled walls. The eyes of the twelve were fixed upon the face of the master as he expounded to them the canon of the Sanskrit law. Now and then he would pause, and a question would be put and answered. The scene was that of the *guru* and *chela* of ancient India. It might equally have been that of the Master and the disciple of Galilee. It could not conceivably have been that of professor and student of twentieth-century Indo-Anglia.

* * * * * *

It is impossible to leave Navadvîpa without making passing reference to the emotional value which Chaitanya gave to worship. It is a subject which is not strictly relevant to the matter immediately under consideration; yet it helps to emphasise certain aspects of the Eastern temperament which cannot be ignored.

Like the other pundits of Navadvîpa of his day, Bishwambhar, son of Jaganâth Misra Purandar and of Shachi, proud of his intellectual attainments despised *bhakti*, or devotion, as a sign of weakness. A change of a marked character, however, took place in him as a result of his meeting with one Ishvar Puri, a Vaishnava monk, and he became henceforth an ardent *bhakta*. In the year A.D. 1509, at the age of twenty-four, he was initiated as a sannyasi under the name of Krishna-Chaitanya. From the description given in Krishnadas's biography known as the Chaitanya-charit-amrita, it is clear that Chaitanya underwent one of those curious psychological changes of which history provides many examples, from Saul of Tarsus to the Welsh revivalists. With him worship of Krishna became a religious frenzy. Processions, headed by him and his fellow-devotee Nityananda, went dancing and singing through the streets, thus giving rise to the *nâm-kîrtan* (chanting God's name), which became a distinctive feature of the Vaishnava creed. An abandoned adoration of God incarnate as S̱rî Krishna became the obsession alike of his waking and his sleeping hours. We are told how on his first glimpse of the image in the temple of Jaganâth at Puri he fell down on the temple floor in a deep swoon, in which he remained until the third quarter of the day when he awoke "and rose up shouting 'Hari! Hari!'" His biographer, indeed, pictures him and his companions as perpetually working themselves by means of song and dance into a state of religious ecstasy. "With perspiration, thrill, tears of joy, shout and roar, they turned and turned, touching the Master's feet now and then"; and of Chaitanya himself he writes that "while he was singing all passions swept over him, now he stood still, now trembled, now shed tears of joy or uttered broken words, now he fainted. At times he fell down on the ground, at which his mother, Shachi, wept, saying, 'Methinks Nimai's body has been shattered'." [1]

His enthusiasm was contagious. One of his earliest exploits on arrival at Puri was the defeat in argument, and the eventual conversion of a famous dialectician, Sarvabhauma by name. The latter "supported his own position, using refutation, feint, pressure, and other logical devices. But the Master answered them all and established his own view"; and instructing him later in the chief means of cultivating faith, chanted Hari's name. "Hari's name, Hari's name, Hari's name alone, in the Kâlî era there is no other means of salvation, no other, indeed, no other."

Leaving Puri and travelling to the south, he converted the countryside wholesale. "Crowds gathered to see him; the very sight of his marvellous beauty and devotion made them Vaishnavas. They danced with uplifted arms, chanting Krishna's name in deep emotion." Some allowance must doubtless be made for the enthusiasm of his biographer, especially when he tells us that "He (Chaitanya) refuted and proved faulty all the doctrines of the logicians, mîmâṃsâkas, illusionists, and the followers of Sâṅkhya, Patanjali, Smṛiti, Purâna and Veda", and everywhere established the dogmas of Vaishnavism, which none could refute. But unless the whole of the Chaitanya-charita-amrita is a work of fiction, there is ample testimony in its pages to the existence among the people of a deep-seated capacity for religious devotion, and of a strongly developed emotional temperament—a conclusion to which one is equally inevitably led by one's own observation at the present day.

A careful description is given in the Chaitanya-

[1] From the translation of "Madhya Lîlâ", the second book of the Chaitanya-charit-amrita, by Jadunath Sarkar, M.A.

charita-amrita of Chaitanya's dance in the temple of Jaganâth. "With the whole party", we are told, "he went to Jaganâth's temple and began to chant. After the burning of evening incense he began a saṅkîrtan. . . . Four parties sang on four sides, while in their midst danced Shachi's darling (Chaitanya). Eight *dholes* and thirty-two cymbals were played on. All shouted 'Hari! Hari!' and cheered. The blissful sound of kîrtan penetrated through the fourteen regions to the *Brahmanda*." Other details of the dancing and singing are given by the biographer, who concludes his description with the following comment: "The people of Puri swam in a sea of delight as they beheld such grand dancing, devotion and saṅkîrtan. The king himself, on hearing of the splendour of the kîrtan, ascended the terrace of his palace with his court to gaze at it."

It was neither at Navadvîpa nor at Puri that I myself witnessed a dance such as that described above. The descendants of Chaitanya's companion Nityananda have settled in the State of Tripura, where they are held in honour as the leaders of the religious life of the State. The principles of Vaishnavism have taken firm hold of the surrounding peoples, and it was within the walls of the Ujaiyanta palace at Agartolla that I witnessed on two occasions the dramatic intensity of the Vaishnava dance. After a preliminary episode representing Ṣrî Krishna among the Gopis of Brindaban, the girls playing the part of the latter withdrew, and the floor was occupied by thirty-eight men wearing nothing but white dhotis and paggris of pink cotton, their dark bodies being ornamented only with light wreaths of flowers hung round the neck. Conspicuous among them were eight men with drums, some of which were flat with a large surface and others of the more familiar oblong variety. These men led the dance.

The proceedings began quietly with measured beats upon the drums, accompanied by the clapping of hands and stamping of feet on the part of the remaining thirty dancers. Soon the rhythmic steps and turns were accompanied by a chant. Movement became more forceful, the chanting swelled in volume, the stamping and hand-clapping became fiercer. Individuals stepped into the centre of the circle and gave special turns. One was beginning to be caught up in the spirit of the dance and carried away by the growing energy and rapidity of the movement, when there was a dramatic *dénouement.* With a motion as rapid as it was unexpected, each of the dancers whipped from the folds of his dhoti a pair of brazen cymbals. From now on the dance became a storm of primal energy. Where there had hitherto been force there was now frenzy. Thirty pairs of cymbals clanged and clashed until the atmosphere vibrated and trembled like an angry ocean of sound. A harsh metallic jar dominated everything. The thrup of the drums served only to mark the terrific din of the cymbals. The shouting of the dancers was heard only dimly, as it struggled impotently against the nerve-shattering crash—heard like the wail of lost souls growing fainter and fainter as it succumbed to what had now become a consuming orgy of noise. A moment came when it seemed that jangled nerves could bear no more; that some wild unimaginable climax *must* be reached; that a final rending crash *must* put an end to this tempestuous triumph of noise. It came, quite suddenly, with a crash like the splitting asunder of the universe. And as silence descended upon the world and one's tautened nerves relaxed, it was as though the world itself, exhausted by its age-long race through space, had suddenly come to rest. We had been given a glimpse of an emotional reservoir which may remain latent, but which most assuredly will not dry up under any conceivable veneer of foreign workmanship.

CHAPTER V

THE NEW WINE OF THE WEST

The episodes of which I have written, looked at in retrospect, bear something of the character of lantern pictures thrown upon the screen of one's consciousness. At the moment of experiencing them they are vivid, brilliantly illumined, and sharply focussed. Later, when one is back on the broad highway of Indo-Anglia,[1] they tend to fade like the dissolving views of the lantern. But they leave behind them a subtle impress. The broad highway of Indo-Anglia, which before seemed so natural and so substantial, no longer looks quite the same. Sometimes it assumes almost the nature of a mirage obscuring the underlying landscape upon which it rests. How then did it obtain the degree of solidity which at first sight it appears to possess? For a reply to that question it is necessary to consider the conditions which were prevalent at the time when the tide of Western civilisation first flowed in force over the shores of the Indian continent.

India was then passing through a period of exhaustion, consequent upon the disruption of the Moghul Empire. Her national vitality was at a low ebb. She was not in a fit state to meet

[1] I use this word to denote Western-educated India. Anglo-India would, perhaps, be the more obvious term; but this word has already been appropriated and, in accordance with instructions issued by a former Secretary of State applied to the descendants of mixed European and Indian marriages.

a sudden and powerful influx of new ideas critically and with discrimination. A few strong characters stood out as exceptions, notably Raja Ram Mohan Roy and Dewan Ramkamal Sen, who welcomed what they perceived to be good in the civilisation of the West for its own sake, and who doubtless believed that a synthesis of all that was best in the thought and practice of East and West was both desirable and possible. But it is significant that these men grew up before the introduction of a definite system of English education. Raja Ram Mohan Roy was born in A.D. 1772 and died in A.D. 1833. The Hindu College with its secular curriculum came into existence under rationalist auspices in 1817, and Lord Macaulay's famous Minute was penned in 1835. Thereafter the new wine of Western learning was poured with disastrous results into the old bottles of Hinduism; and there is no doubt that it went to the heads of young Bengal.

By the middle of the nineteenth century a period of intellectual anarchy had set in, which swept the rising generation before it like a craft which has snapped its moorings. Westernism became the fashion of the day—and Westernism demanded of its votaries that they should cry down the civilisation of their own country. The more ardent their admiration for everything Western, the more vehement became their denunciation of everything Eastern. The ancient learning was despised; ancient custom and tradition were thrust aside; ancient religion was decried as an outworn superstition. The ancient foundations upon which the complex structure of Hindu society had been built up were undermined; and the new generation of iconoclasts found little enough with which to underpin the edifice which they were so recklessly depriving of its own foundations.

A graphic description of this state of affairs has been given by a Bengali gentleman who was himself a college student at this critical period in the history of Bengal. "Sanskrit, Persian and Arabic," he declares, "held in such supreme reverence but a few years before as the only source of wisdom, were in consequence of such teachings, looked upon with supreme contempt." They came to be regarded as "barbarous, unwholesome, unfashionable". The young men of the day sought for inspiration in "the wide unclean waters of inferior works of English fiction. For history, especially Indian history, they had an unnameable horror." And following hard upon this new spirit of contempt for their own past, came religious scepticism, which ate its way into the moral fibre of young Bengal with all the virulence of a corroding acid. "The ancient scriptures of the country, the famous records of the spiritual experiences of the great men of numerous Hindu sects, had long since been discredited. The Vedas and Upanishads were sealed books. All that we knew of the immortal Mahabharata, Ramayana, or the Bhagavad Gîtâ, was from the execrable translations into popular Bengali, which no respectable young man was supposed to read. The whole religious literature of ancient India presented an endless void. Our young reformers studied Paine's 'Age of Reason' to get fresh ideas on the subject of religion." And the result is painted with an unsparing hand. "All faith in morality and religion every day became weaker and tended to decay. The advancing tide of a very mixed civilisation, with as much evil as good in it, the flood of fashionable carnality threatened to carry everything before it." [1]

[1] The Rev. P. C. Mazumdar in his introduction to the "Life and Teachings of Keshub Chandra Sen".

With a certain section of the newly educated the adoption of all the less reputable habits of the youth of Europe became an obsession, and the open defiance of the traditions of Hinduism a point of honour. Babu Raj Narain Bose, a well-known Bengali gentleman of the nineteenth century, mentions in his autobiography that " it was a common belief of the alumni of the college, that the drinking of wine was one of the concomitants of civilisation ", and he adds that in 1884 he himself was attacked by a dangerous illness, the seeds of which had been sown by excessive drinking. Bengali gentlemen have told me that when they were children the young men of the day used to boast of their liking for beef and to jeer openly at those who protested against this outrage upon their feelings. " Intemperate drinking and licentiousness of thought, taste and character were fearfully rampant. Infidelity, indifference to religion and point - blank atheism were unblushingly professed. Education had degenerated or never developed into anything higher than a frivolous pursuit of rhetoric and dilettantism."[1]

Such descriptions, coming as they do from the pens of men who wrote of what they themselves saw and experienced, leave little room for doubt as to the state of affairs. Young Bengal was rapidly becoming both de-nationalised and demoralised. Still it must be borne in mind that however prominent a place young Bengal occupied in the public eye, it constituted but a minute fraction of the population. It was like the foam caught by the wind on the surface of the sea. Beneath the surface still rolled the deep placid waters of Indian life. And it is probable that the reaction against Westernism would have been as sudden and as violent as the original craze for

[1] The Rev. P. C. Mazumdar.

it, had it not been for two things—the economic pressure which drove the middle classes to seek employment in government service, and in the professions for which a Western education had become a necessity; and secondly, the rise of certain men of outstanding personality and character, who took up the threads where they had been dropped by Raja Ram Mohan Roy and his companions—men of vision who saw the need of a rational synthesis of the best that Europe and Asia had to give and who strove, consequently, to weave into the tapestry of Indian life such threads from the spindles of the West as would enrich, without bringing about a complete alteration of outline in the pattern upon the Eastern loom. Among such men stands out the commanding figure of Keshub Chandra Sen.

Born in 1838, he was educated at the Hindu College and the Metropolitan School, and at the age of twenty-one entered the Bank of Bengal as a clerk on Rs.25 a month. He met with rapid promotion, and a successful career was undoubtedly open to him in the service of that institution if he chose to pursue it. There was every encouragement for him to do so. He had before him the example of his grandfather, Ramkamal Sen, a truly remarkable man, who by sheer force of character and ability had raised himself from the humble position of an assistant type-setter on Rs.8 a month in the employment of the Asiatic Society of Bengal, to that of a member of the Council of the Society and of Dewan of the Bank of Bengal on a salary of Rs.2000 a month. But worldly success possessed no attractions for Keshub Chandra Sen, and he soon gave up the post which he held, in order to devote his life to the service of his fellow-men. He was one of those men whose whole being is inspired by a missionary zeal, and in the circumstances of the times in which he lived he found unlimited scope for his activities.

During the latter part of his student days he had probed deep into the study of mental and moral philosophy, and it was scarcely to be wondered at that a man of so inquiring a turn of mind, living in such times, should have failed to find complete satisfaction in old traditions and an ancient creed. The strength of his character and the robustness of his faith were shown by his refusal to give way to the tendencies of the times, or to rest satisfied until he had discovered something to fill the void. At first he fell back, as Gautama Buddha did and as so many of his countrymen have done throughout the centuries, upon a life of asceticism and meditation. But action was the mainspring of his life, and before long he was up and doing. It is not necessary for my purpose to dwell upon the actual events of his career as an active preacher—how in 1857 he founded a religious association for the discussion of the all-absorbing questions of life ; how he was thus brought into contact with Devendra Nath Tagore and led by him to join the Brahmo Samaj ; how his zeal for social reform and his strong iconoclastic tendencies carried him away from the more conservative elements in the Brahmo Samaj and severed the close ties which had bound him to his patron ; or how finally, after having been left in his turn by many of his own associates, he achieved the crowning event of his life by founding the Church of the New Dispensation.

All these crowded years of history are familiar to every student of the times, and I am not so much concerned to narrate history as to record an impression. And I have referred to them here mainly because they bear striking witness to his indifference to the opinions of others, when once he was convinced that his own action was inspired by God — in other words, to the tremendous strength of his faith. He was, indeed, pre-eminently a man who lived by faith, a man whose whole life was dominated by an intuitive knowledge that he had a mission to perform, and who exercised over his fellow-men the influence which outstanding personality inspired by a steadfast singleness of purpose and a contagious enthusiasm, can always command.

He does not seem to have been a highly-finished orator, capable of delighting an audience of dilettantes with polished periods of artistic rhetoric. Yet he was undoubtedly able to sway and dominate vast assemblies by his power of speech—speech pouring forth in torrents of rugged eloquence, speech surging up spontaneously from the depths of his innermost being, speech stamping him not as an artist, but as a seer—a man inspired with a message for the world, and compelled by unseen forces to deliver it. He was not, in all probability, a man of outstanding eminence considered exclusively from the point of view of intellectuality. His intellect was not of that type which loves to build up elaborate systems of philosophy based upon pure reason. His intellectual life was passed in a warm atmosphere of emotion rather than in the chill regions of undiluted logic. He must certainly be judged to have been lacking in powers of organisation; and there is some excuse for assuming at first sight that his actions were not infrequently dictated by caprice. Reflection upon the more marked characteristics of his temperament, however, and particularly upon the extent to which his whole life was guided by prayer and the response received by him to his prayers, suggests that what might at first be mistaken for impulse was in reality in his case inspiration.

Such a mind is always sensitive to new thought

impressions, and the mind of Keshub Chandra Sen undoubtedly reacted like a delicate instrument to the invigorating streams of thought which at that time were pouring in upon India from all sides. This sensitiveness of mind, with its consequent power of rapid assimilation, is responsible for a certain difficulty in the way of grasping the precise nature of his religious beliefs. That he was a theist is beyond question, and as I have already pointed out, he was a profound believer in the efficacy of prayer. He has himself left it on record that the first lesson of the scriptures of his life was prayer. And he prayed fervently and without ceasing. From the first he tells us he had recourse to "that supplication before God which is greater than Veda or Vedanta, Koran or Purâna". But his theism was peculiarly free from dogma. There is truth, he held, in all religions. Later, under the influence, probably, of Ram Krishna Paramahaṃsha, whom he held in great respect, this eclecticism underwent a further development. From the position that there is truth in all religions, he advanced to the position that all religions are true.

Further indication of his sensitiveness to new ideas is provided by the zeal with which he embraced the cause of social reform. He imbibed the teachings of Christianity with avidity, studying closely the works of Dean Stanley, Robertson, Liddon and Seeley; and he was profoundly moved by the stress which the teaching of Christ laid upon the ethics of life. And it is in this particular connection that his responsiveness to fresh ideas, stands out in strong contrast to the conservatism of the older elements in the Brahmo Samaj under the leadership of Devendra Nath Tagore. There can be little doubt, I think, that the latter seriously feared that spiritual religion would be sacrificed to the new passion for social reform; and with Keshub Chandra Sen's enthusiasm for reform becoming steadily greater, it was inevitable that a split in the ranks of the Samaj should occur. His determination to embark on a crusade was confirmed by his visit to England in 1870, where he met many of the intellectual giants of the day—Dean Stanley, Max Müller, Gladstone and John Stuart Mill—and where he found the women of the country taking an active and a prominent part in public life. And it was only in keeping with his character and temperament, that he should return to India to throw himself with renewed zeal into the task of emancipating his countrymen from the network of social restrictions imposed on them by long centuries of tradition.

No single document, perhaps, gives a clearer conspectus of his aims and achievements in this direction than the act passed in 1872 at his instance for legalising Brahmo marriages. It abolished early marriage, made polygamy penal, and sanctioned widow and inter-caste marriages. It was a bold measure, and it required a man of unusual courage to carry it through for, as Pundit Siva Nath Sastri observed, it was one of the principal causes that alienated the sympathies of their orthodox countrymen from the reformers. But Keshub Chandra Sen was convinced that he was acting in obedience to the Divine Will, and when once he was satisfied on that point, he never wavered.

This brief sketch of the life and character of Keshub Chandra Sen, imperfect though it be, will suffice perhaps to indicate the influence which he exercised in stemming the tide of profligacy and irreligion which was sweeping over the educated classes of his day, and in retarding the inevitable reaction against the source whence that tide had sprung—the mode of life, the new learning—particularly that derived from discoveries in natural science—and above all the free thought of the West. For he, more than any man perhaps, showed by precept and by example that the gulf between Europe and Asia might be bridged without the sacrifice of anything that was fundamental in the race-genius or the race-culture of either. While he was capable of assimilating much that seemed to him to be good in the ideals and practice of the West, he remained always a true Indian. He was too great a character to become a mere mimic of others, and he was too great a soul to cherish that false pride of race which blinds a man to the virtues of all peoples other than his own. He showed how East and West might be complementary rather than antagonistic to one another, and his life was an incitement to those who might not be willing to go so far as he did in casting aside the restraints and trammels of an ancient and venerable social tradition, at least to follow him in the spirit if not in the actual letter of his teaching.

It was, then, due in large measure to the influence exerted by the lives of men like Keshub Chandra Sen that the violence of the swing back of the pendulum was moderated, and that the possibility of a synthesis of the best features of two distinct civilisations raised itself upon the surface of the troubled waters of Indian life. The question whether that possibility can be realised is the absorbing problem of to-day. The answer to it depends to a large extent upon the nature and ultimate extent of the reaction against the West which is in progress at the present time; and it is this which gives the present position and its tendencies so profound an interest and importance.

There were, of course, at all times critics of the

demoralisation of society which marked the middle of the nineteenth century. The laxity and depravity of the times were scathingly commented on by Dinabandhu Mitra, a contemporary and associate of Bankim Chandra Chatterji, in a famous novel entitled "Sadhabar Ekadashi", a story so realistic in its treatment of the subject that an attempt to reprint it in recent times called forth a temporary prohibition order from the authority in Calcutta charged with censorship powers, on the ground that its circulation was inimical to good morals.

But a protest against the manners of the times need not necessarily have been of a revivalist nature. This latter characteristic is much more apparent in other and more marked phases of the reaction and not least, certainly, in the sphere of education. There are, indeed, many indications of a reaction against the exclusively Western system of education which has been described, and they deserve careful consideration.

CHAPTER VI

AT THE CROSS-ROADS

I HAVE described a visit to the tôls of Navadvîpa in Chapter IV., and have pointed out that in spite of the rapidity with which English high schools and colleges have become multiplied, it would be a grave mistake to suppose that the indigenous system of education is defunct. No accurate estimate of the number of indigenous institutions in existence is possible, but it is certainly large. The number of private tôls is known to be upwards of 1500 in Bengal alone; and the returns used in the compilation of the seventh quinquennial review of the progress of education in India (1912–17) show the existence of nearly 38,000 private institutions, the majority of which consists of tôls and pathshalas, madrassas and maktabs, and it is probable that there are many which find no mention in the returns.[1]

In spite, too, of the demand for medical educa-

[1] Economic pressure, especially in the case of private institutions devoted to indigenous classical learning, is said to be making itself felt; and in the quinquennial review for 1917–22, published since the above was written, the number of private institutions of all kinds in British India is estimated to be about 35,000, with an attendance of 640,000. With reference to the tôls and madrassas of Assam, Mr. J. R. Cunningham, C.I.E., writes that Hindus and Muhammadans who are in close touch with the more modern civilisation, though they may be drawn by sentiment towards the old institutions, feel nevertheless that the day of tôls and madrassas is past, "and that the tempering of modern life and learning with the ancient wisdom can be best achieved, so far as it can be achieved by educational means, by bringing the old and the new together in the higher institutions of learning with a view to interaction and the survival of the best in both".

tion on Western lines, the wide extent to which indigenous systems are practised is instructive. Here again no statistics are available, but, as a result of a very careful inquiry, it was ascertained that a very large proportion of the total number of persons practising medicine in Bengal was made up of *Kavirajes* and *Hakims.* And the inquiry left little room for doubt that, quite apart from the fact that the village *kaviraj* was the chief medical resource of the bulk of the population, the orthodox *kaviraj* and *hakim* were held in high esteem by the better classes, and were not infrequently preferred by them to the Western practitioner.

The method of instruction in vogue among the *kavirajes* is characterised by one of the most distinctive features of the ancient educational system of the Indo-Aryan people. Every *kaviraj* of repute gathers round him a little band of disciples who receive free board, lodging and instruction at his hands. And it is notable that when representative *kavirajes* were asked how best Government could assist with a view to improving the teaching of Ayurveda, they deprecated the establishment of institutions on Western lines on two main grounds, firstly, that this would mean the setting up of courses of instruction available only on the payment of fees—an idea altogether repugnant to the orthodox *kaviraj*; and secondly, that it would imply the addition of a course in Western science resulting in a hybrid product half-*kaviraj*, half-doctor, in whom the people would have little faith. As one eminent *kaviraj* put it, " a mixture of the *kaviraj* and of the doctor is not at all wanted in the country. It cannot be said with propriety that an allopathic practitioner would supplement his knowledge with that in Ayurveda. Why, then, should Ayurveda be supplemented by Allopath ? "

But more significant than the persistence of indigenous institutions are the signs of a revulsion against the exclusively Western type of institution among those who have themselves been brought up in it. A notable feature of the political ferment in Bengal at the time of the partition was the establishment of national schools wholly Indian in management and altogether free from foreign control. It may be true that these institutions were the direct outcome of a desire on the part of those who were then ranged against Government to provide for persons who were expelled from Government and Government-aided schools, or whose animosity against the British made attendance at such schools distasteful, rather than of any genuine revolt against the Western system of education which they stood for. But it would be rash to assume that this latter sentiment was not present as well, and it defined itself more clearly later on with the formation in Madras of a society for the promotion of national education, and again in the course of the controversies that arose out of the storm of political unrest that swept over the land at the close of the Great War.

Dissatisfaction with the educational system was by then apparent in different quarters. A demand for vocational courses was being made by the very classes which had been mainly responsible for the rigidly literary bias which the system had acquired. The driving force behind this demand, however, was not sentiment but the economic strain upon the middle classes. The colleges were turning out a supply of graduates and undergraduates in arts largely in excess of the demand, whence the agitation for courses of a more practical type. The demand for medical training in Bengal, for example, became clamorous and widespread. It was, indeed, necessity rather than predilection that was the determining factor in this movement. So much was admitted by one of the most prominent of the Indian-owned newspapers in Calcutta, the *Amrita Bazar Patrika*, which early in 1921 was bewailing the extent to which education was being dominated by economic necessities. The vast majority of Indian parents subjected themselves to real hardships in order to provide their boys with a Western education; and the tendency of the day to belittle academic education was to be explained in the main, by the disappointment caused by the failure of the boys to give a good return for the money invested in their education. The rush for the medical, engineering and other institutions giving technical education was the direct result of this disappointment.[1]

But apart from the economic aspect of the question Western education was condemned as such by extreme nationalist opinion; and if this sentiment was visible in the attack upon the schools and colleges in 1907, it was violently in evidence in the campaign against the Government led by Mr. Gandhi in 1921 and 1922, when students were persuaded to leave their schools and colleges *en masse*. In the heat of the political battle reason was ousted by political prejudice and passion. "English learning", declaimed Mr. Jitendralal Banerji, "may be good; English culture may be good; their philosophy may be good; their government, their law, everything may be good; but each one of these but helps to rivet the fetters of our servitude. Therefore I say to the English, good as these things may be, Take them away; take them away beyond the seas, far off to your Western home, so that we and our generation may have nothing to do with them

[1] See an article entitled "Western Civilisation and Western Rule" in the *Amrita Bazar Patrika* of January 7, 1921.

—may not be accursed with the contamination either of your goodness or of your evil ".[1]

Few, even under stress of intense political excitement, would go so far as Mr. Jitendralal Banerji. Nevertheless it would be a mistake wholly to discount such sentiments as the froth and bubble upon waters lashed to fury by a political storm. There are many Indians who are far from hostile to the British connection, who ardently desire to see a more distinctively Indian orientation given to the education imparted to their people. The views of such persons were voiced by Sir Rashbehary Ghose in the course of a speech delivered in 1911, in support of the establishment of a Hindu university. " Education ", he said, " must have its roots deep down in national sentiment and tradition. . . . We are the heirs of an ancient civilisation, and the true office of education ought to be the encouragement of a gradual and spontaneous growth of the ideals which have given a definite mould to our culture and our institutions. . . . In our curriculum, therefore, Hindu ethics and metaphysics will occupy a foremost place, the Western system being used only for purposes of contrast and illustration. Special attention will also be paid to a knowledge of the country, its literature, its arts, its philosophy and its history." Similar views have been repeated frequently of late. Mr. S. Srinivasa Iyengar, C.I.E., presiding at an annual educational conference in Madras in May 1921, declared that it was the conviction of the educated community that the Western system of education had been barren of results, and he traced this alleged failure to the fact that those who were responsible for its direction and control had ignored India's racial psychology, history, literature and religion, and patriotic ideals and

[1] In a speech in Calcutta on February 10, 1921.

aspirations. A year later another Indian publicist, while protesting against undiscriminating condemnation of the Calcutta university, laid stress upon what he regarded as its main defects, and asserted that, apart altogether from political considerations, an education directed by men of an alien race, however noble their motives, must inevitably be out of touch with the inner soul of the people. "This education", was his verdict, "has not been able to build up the new culture on our real life."[1] Opinion has moved far since the days of Ram Mohan Roy and David Hare.

A closely reasoned statement of the view set forth above is to be found in a paper by Dr. Rabindra Nath Tagore, published by the Society for the Promotion of National Education in Madras in 1919, with the title of "The Centre of Indian Culture".

The burden of the theme is not that the learning of the West is valueless for the people of the East, but that under the existing system foreign education occupies all the available space in the Indian mind, and so "kills or hampers the great opportunity for the creation of a new thought power, by a new combination of truths". English education as now given is for the Indian mind "a kind of food which contains only one particular ingredient needful for its vitality, and even that not fresh, but dried and packed in tins. In our true food we must have co-ordination of all different ingredients—and most of these not as laboratory products, or in a desiccated condition, but as organic things similar to our own living tissues." The crux of the whole matter lies in the last few words of the above quotation. One comes across the same sentiment clothed in different words over and over again. "It is

[1] In an article contributed anonymously to the *Englishman* in June 1922.

hopeless to cater for some clamorous demand of the moment by endeavouring to fashion the history of one people on the model of another—however flourishing the latter may be. . . . For India to force herself along European lines of growth would not make her Europe, but only a distorted India." [1]

He deals forcefully with the question of language which he regards as a factor of paramount importance in the whole educational problem. His experience as a teacher goes to show that many pupils are naturally deficient in the power of learning languages. And given this premise, it is difficult to resist his conclusion that it is an appalling waste of national material to cut off all higher educational facilities from the thousands of pupils who have no gift for acquiring a foreign tongue, but who possess the intellect and the desire to learn. Or again that even in the case of those who possess an average ability for acquiring a foreign tongue, "the knocking at the gate and turning of the key take away the best part of their life".

Looked at from a somewhat different point of view the use of English inevitably tends to turn the Indian mind Westwards for its source of inspiration; and, indeed, the education given in the universities "takes it for granted that it is for cultivating a hopeless desert", and that language, mental outlook and knowledge must be imported bodily from across the sea. "And this makes our education so nebulously distant and unreal, so detached from all our associations of life, so terribly costly to us in time, health and means and yet so meagre of results." The emphasis here given to the weight of the incubus laid upon the educated classes in having to imbibe

[1] "The Message of the Forest", by Dr. R. N. Tagore, in the *Modern Review* for May 1919.

their education through the medium of a foreign tongue, acquires additional significance by comparison with the views of fifty years ago, when it was the fashion of the educated classes to regard the use of the Bengali tongue as undignified, and when—as I have been told—men like Michael Madhusudan Datta boasted that they even dreamed in English.

The difficulty so often paraded of the multiplicity of tongues in India, is shown to be the product of superficial thinking. It is due to a habit of thinking of India as one thinks of one of the countries of Europe, whereas one should think of her as one thinks of Europe herself with a common civilisation and an intellectual unity which is not based upon uniformity of language. Just as in Europe there was a time in the early days of her culture when she had Latin as the one language of her learning, so in India, in the corresponding stage of her evolution, there was one common language of culture, namely, Sanskrit. But in Europe the perfection of her mental unfolding came later. "When the great European countries found their individual languages, then only the true federation of cultures became possible in the West, and the very differences of the channels made the commerce of ideas in Europe so richly copious and so variedly active." And if this diversity of tongues proved to be no obstacle, but on the contrary a stimulus to the growth of a distinctive culture and civilisation in Europe, why should it not act in the same way in India ?

In his views on the language question Dr. Rabindra Nath Tagore is, as I have already shown, voicing a considerable and growing volume of opinion. For many years past an association called the Council of Indian Education, which was formed in Madras in 1900, has urged that the vernaculars should be the media of instruction in non-language subjects in secondary education; and in 1915 a resolution was moved in the Imperial Legislative Council by the Hon. Mr. Rama Rayaningar recommending that steps should be taken for making the vernaculars the media of instruction, and the study of English as a *second language* compulsory in all secondary schools. Elsewhere the matter has been carried further, for in the State of Hyderabad definite steps were taken four years later to put this suggestion into operation.

Amongst the officials of the State was a little group of men with whom the belief had steadily been growing that if modern education was to reach the masses, it must be imparted to them through their own mother-tongue. Prominent among them were Nawab Hyder Nawaz Jung Bahadur, the able Financial Minister of the State, and the Director of Public Instruction, Nawab Masood Jung Bahadur, a grandson of the famous founder of Aligarh. By the exertions of these men, carried on with the warm approval of His Exalted Highness the Nizam, the foundations of a teaching and examining university under the title of the Osmania University were laid, the outstanding feature of which was the employment of Urdu as the medium of instruction. The initial difficulty, namely, the lack of suitable text-books, was vigorously tackled from the start by the establishment of a Bureau of Translation with a staff of qualified translators under the direction of a noted scholar and writer; and to such good purpose has the Bureau worked that the translation of over one hundred and thirty volumes on such varying subjects as history, philosophy, economics, mathematics, physics, chemistry and law has already been successfully accomplished. Other features of the scheme which are worthy of note are the acceptance of a school leaving-certificate in respect of certain of the subjects required for matriculation, and the compulsory teaching of English as a second language throughout the high school and college courses and of theology or ethics throughout the latter.

Great progress has been made during the half-dozen years of the university's existence. Fourteen high schools are at work preparing boys for the Osmania College, where 700 students are already undergoing undergraduate courses in buildings temporarily assigned to it; and preparations are in hand for a large expansion in the near future. A site of 1400 acres has been selected for permanent buildings, and a sum approaching a crore of rupees is to be provided by Government for their erection. High schools affiliated to the university are to be established at the headquarters of every district throughout the State, and arrangements are being made to accommodate 2000 university students, it being estimated that this figure will be reached within the next six years. In brief, the goal which the State has set before itself is, in the words of the Nizam, the creation of a national seat of learning, " where full advantage may be taken of all that is best in the ancient and modern systems of physical, intellectual and spiritual culture ".[1]

All these things are straws which show which way the wind is blowing, and the growing desire on the part of many to see religious instruction become once more an integral part of the educational course, is a finger-board pointing in the same direction. The most marked development along these lines is the establishment of denominational universities at Benares and Aligarh.

[1] From His Exalted Highness's *Firman* authorising the establishment of the university.

But these two institutions, though the best known, are by no means the only examples of the kind. Other striking enterprises which bear witness to the kind of unrest of mind of which I have been writing are to be found in the Hindu Academy of Daulatpur in the district of Khulna in Bengal, in the educational activities of the Arya Samaj in the United Provinces and the Punjab, and in the school founded by Dr. Rabindra Nath Tagore at Bholpur in Western Bengal, which has recently developed into a university known as the Visva Bharati. Of this latter institution I shall have something to say later on; in the meantime let me conduct the reader to a rural district in Bengal, where on the banks of the Bhairab river, in the heart of the countryside, stand the buildings of the Hindu Academy of Daulatpur.

CHAPTER VII

A RE-ORIENTATION OF AIM ?

THE whole of the teaching staff and the majority of the six hundred students attending the classes at Daulatpur reside in hostels of various types, the most striking of which is a group of thatched cottages built in the immemorial style of rural Bengal. In addition to the hostels and the laboratories and class-rooms, there is a guest-house and a temple.

The idea of the institution was explained to me by the little band of enthusiastic workers, to whom it owed its existence, on the occasion of an informal visit. They told me how, nearly twenty years before, they had been struck with the grave defects of an educational system under which the teaching was wholly divorced from religion. Was it not possible, they asked themselves, to bring about a harmonious combination of the Religion and Philosophy of the East with the Arts and Sciences of the West ? And for the answer they pointed to the buildings all round ; the chemical and physical laboratories much of whose equipment had been manufactured upon the spot ; the simple hostels half seen amid clusters of typical Bengali trees ; the playing fields, and the temple on the floor of whose quiet and shaded portico a Sanskrit pundit was expounding the ṣastras to an eager but reverent group of boys. The whole scene was a crystallisation of the idea with which they had started, "the combination", to use their own words, "of secular education with moral and religious training based on the highest ideals of life expounded by the Hindu Acharyas of old".

In practice the two distinctive types of education, the Eastern and the Western, flourish side by side, the former being represented by a chatuspathi and the latter by a college affiliated to the Calcutta University. The chatuspathi is conducted in strict accordance with ancient Hindu ideals. Instruction and, in the case of resident students, board and lodging, are provided free of charge. Classes in grammar, literature, Hindu law, Mîmâmsâ and Vedanta are held by the acharya and competent pundits in the court of the temple. Its students have no part in the college; it is a purely indigenous institution. It exercises a marked influence, however, upon the college, for the temple is the point at which the two systems meet.

It is stated in the trust-deed that "a symbol of God Dadhibaman (Vishnu) was installed in this Institution on the 13th Magh 1310 (February 1, 1904). We dedicate this Institution and all property connected herewith to him. Henceforth He will have His seat in this Institution and will be the proprietor of all its property, both present and future, and also of all its work." And it is in the presence of this symbol of the Eternal installed in the shrine of the temple that teachers and students of the college and chatuspathi alike meet, and have expounded to them the dharmaṣastras of old.

My hosts were somewhat diffident in informing me of the exact extent of the religious instruction given. Much was left to the discretion of the acharya, they said. But in the report of a university inspector drawn up some years ago, I found it stated that instruction from the Manu-saṃhitâ given by the acharya was compulsory in the case of all Hindu students; and the same writer stated that he could himself bear witness that "a beautiful prayer for the fruitfulness of the day's labour and the happiness and prosperity of the Motherland, chanted simultaneously throughout the whole college at the beginning and the end of each day's work, produces a permanent impression, even upon an uninitiated onlooker".

The influence upon the college of the Eastern tradition as represented by the chatuspathi and the temple, is apparent even on a cursory inspection. It attracts one's attention in the library where the "Encyclopaedia Britannica" shares a shelf appropriately enough with the compendious "Ṣabdakalpadrûma", and "Journals of the Chemical Society" stand side by side with the "Rigveda Saṃhitâ". The college time-table follows Indian rather than European custom, the classes being held between 6 A.M. and 10 A.M., and again in the afternoon after a long break in the middle of the day.

As one passed from its class-rooms to its simple hostels one became aware of a distinctive atmosphere, and standing in converse with the earnest band of workers in the shadow of the temple portico, the hush of the tropic noon scarcely broken by the soft murmur of the Bhairab river pursuing its eternal journey from the mountains to the sea, with the restful features of the acharya and his fellow-pundits outlined against the gloom which brooded like a softly draped figure of Night behind the open door of the inner shrine, it was easy to believe that the hope of its founders had been realised—that the college had, indeed, "grown under the shade of the temple", and that the teachers and students had found "in their pursuit of knowledge the Worship of God".

A more drastic break with Western tradition, and a more complete return to that of the East than is provided by Daulatpur, is to be found in the educational activities of the Arya Samaj. The early history of the founder of the Samaj, Mulshankar, now known as Swami Dayanand Saraswati, bears a striking resemblance to the story of the early years of Gautama Buddha.[1]

Like the famous scion of the Sakya clan he brooded deeply upon the problems of life, and equally with him he failed to find satisfaction in the creed current among his family and immediate neighbours. As in the case of Gautama so in the case of Mulshankar, his parents sought to distract him from his melancholy meditations by pressing upon him the joys and duties of married life. Less amenable than Gautama, he refused his assent to the marriage arranged for him, and when at length, at the age of twenty, the importunity of his father seemed likely to overcome his resistance, he, like Gautama, went forth from his home on the same quest, discarding all for the saffron robe of the wandering ascetic, possessed of but one idea—the discovery of the hidden portals giving egress from the bewildering thaumatrope of human existence which for more than two millenniums, has weighed so heavily upon the soul of India. This was in the year 1845.

For fifteen years Mulshankar led the life of a homeless wanderer, travelling far and wide, and questioning pundits and sadhus in his search after truth. Nowhere did he find satisfaction. The learning of the day seemed to him like the ashes of a dead fire. The intellectual vigour of the great sages of old had burned itself out ; the teachers of to-day were the slaves of dogma, intellectually and spiritually bankrupt. One sage

[1] See chapter vi. of my " Lands of the Thunderbolt ".

only did he find towards the end of his long search at whose feet he was content to sit—a sannyasi of the same order as Dayanand himself, Swami Virjananda Saraswati, whom he encountered at holy Mathura, the reputed birthplace of Srî Krishna. For more than two years these two kindred spirits lived as guru and chela, and when the time came for them to part Virjananda asked of his pupil in payment of the fee customary on such occasions in ancient times, that he would wage unceasing warfare against the dogma and the idolatry of the Purânic faith and establish education in accordance with the great Brahmanic tradition of pre-Buddhist days.

The pledge was readily given, for Dayanand had emerged from his long probation a stern iconoclast. He lashed the theologians of a decadent church with the fiery zeal of a protestant reformer. The six systems and the eighteen Purânas he cast aside. For him salvation lay in the worship and service of the One God, the Creator of the Vedas and of the World; and for his country in the rejection of the mythology and idolatry of the vast mass of theological literature which had laid its parasitic grip upon the Vedic tree, and an unconditional return to the teaching of the Vedas in all its purity. Such was the founder of the Arya Samaj which first took form in Bombay in 1875, and received its final constitution two years later in Lahore. He himself stated quite categorically that he entertained not the least idea of founding a new religion or sect. His sole object was to lead men back to the repository of all knowledge and religious truth—the original Vedas, the Word of God Himself.

The whole history of the Arya Samaj is of extraordinary interest, particularly for the light which it throws on the present-day tendencies of the Indian consciousness to assert itself. But I am mainly concerned here with its educational activities, which in themselves are typical of the aim and guiding principle of this powerful movement for the restoration and rejuvenation of the spirit of primitive Hinduism. Every Arya is required to subscribe to ten principles which constitute the creed of the Samaj. Of these the eighth lays down that ignorance must be dispelled and knowledge diffused, and in proof of the zeal with which the application of this principle has been pursued, it is claimed by the Samaj that in the United Provinces and the Punjab, at any rate, its educational work is second in extent to that of Government alone. It possesses two colleges which may be taken as typical of its educational ideal, the Dayanand Anglo-Vedic College at Lahore, and the famous Gurukul near Hardwar. Its other institutions are primary and secondary schools of various types, and a certain number of establishments modelled on the Hardwar Gurukul.

The reasons which led to the establishment of these institutions are set forth in the first report of the Dayanand Anglo-Vedic college. After admitting that Western education had stimulated intellectual activity, and had produced some men of whom the country might feel proud, the report goes on to point out that such education has nevertheless produced a deplorable schism in society. An educated class has been created which is without precedent in any country on earth, a class wholly divorced in mental outlook from the vast mass of the people. National education demands among other things adequate study of the national language and literature, and in particular of classical Sanskrit, " wherein lie deep buried and crystallised the fruits of whole lives spent in secluded meditation upon the nature of soul, of virtue, of creation, of matter and, so far as can be vouchsafed to man, of the Creator". And it is stated that the primary object of the founders of the college is to "weld together the educated and uneducated classes by encouraging the study of the national language and vernaculars; to spread a knowledge of moral and spiritual truths by insisting on the study of classical Sanskrit; to encourage sound acquaintance with English literature; and to afford a stimulus to the material progress of the country by spreading a knowledge of the physical and applied sciences". What is aimed at here is clearly a rational synthesis between the learning of East and West, and it has been claimed for it that while it has created an atmosphere of Hindu nationalism, it has at the same time turned out graduates who are playing a leading part in the public and private life of the country.[1]

Nevertheless it failed to satisfy a considerable volume of opinion within the Samaj itself, which demanded a much more drastic severance with Western tradition, and which was responsible for the establishment in the year 1902 of the famous Gurukul near Hardwar.

The avowed aim of its founder, Mr. Munshi Ram, is the revival of the ancient practice of Brahmacharya; the resuscitation of ancient Indian philosophy and literature, and the building up of a Hindu literature which shall absorb all that is best in Occidental thought; the production of preachers of the Vedic religion and of a culture in which the loftiest elements of the civilisation of East and West shall be harmoniously blended. He took as his model the famous universities of ancient India—Taxila, Sridhanya Katak, Nalanda, Odantapuri and Vikramasila—

[1] Speech by Lala Lajpat Rai delivered in London in June 1915. See "The Arya Samaj" by the Speaker, to which I am mainly indebted for the facts and the quotations here given concerning the educational activities of the Samaj.

and at a spot not far removed from Hardwar, where the holy Ganges issues from the heart of the majestic Himâlayas, sheltered from the restless activities of man, amid such surroundings as throughout the ages have been sought and prized by the sages of India, he has succeeded, according to Mr. Myron Phelps, an American writer, whose account of the Gurukul is endorsed by its founder, in creating an atmosphere "saturated with the Vedas and the Upanishads". Mr. Munshi Ram has himself described how, when he was searching for a suitable site, he was offered the gift of a large tract of land, chiefly jungle. No one who has appreciated the part played by Nature in the shaping of the thought and culture of India in the past, could doubt the satisfaction with which this gift was accepted. For now, as then, the soul of India feels irresistibly the urge towards Nature. She still delights to linger in reverent prayer in softly lighted glades of the silent forest, as in the hushed aisles of a cathedral not built by hands; now, as then, she listens for the "still small voice" calling to her from the infinite soul of the world, in the eternal murmur of her glorious rivers, hallowed by the adoration of generation upon generation of the great and unceasing migration of mankind across the toil-worn sands of time; she still sees in her mountains—immutable and sublime—the divine handiwork of the unseen, but ever-present architect. And amid such surroundings she still seeks a place of spiritual reconcilement, where the finite may approach the infinite, a meeting-place between the soul of man and the soul of the world, a vast temple of nature where, if anywhere, the Eternal manifests itself to man as God immanent—omnipotent, omniscient, yet lovingly accessible.

A boy enters the Gurukul at the age of seven or eight, when he takes a vow of poverty, chastity and obedience for sixteen years, during which time he remains in almost complete isolation from the outside world. Though the parents are permitted to visit the institution at intervals, the inmates are only allowed to return to their homes, during the period of their education, under circumstances of a very special and urgent nature. Discipline is strict and life regular. The day begins at 4 A.M., and prayer and worship are offered morning and evening. The former consists of the individual repetition of Sanskrit texts and the latter of the fire oblation prescribed by the Vedas. Much time is also given to moral, ethical and religious instruction. The medium of instruction is Hindi; but great attention is paid to Sanskrit and English. By the age of seventeen or eighteen the boys read, write and speak the former fluently, and are giving much time to the study of Indian philosophy and logic, while the latter is a compulsory subject from the sixth to the fourteenth year. Physical culture and games also occupy a regular and important place in the curriculum.

While the outstanding feature of the Gurukul is its rejection of the purely Western system of education which has taken root under official auspices and encouragement, and its reversion to a system more in keeping with the traditions and genius of the Hindu people, Western learning has by no means been discarded. And in the estimate of Mr. Myron Phelps, the boy at the end of his tenth year at the Gurukul is at least on a par in intellectual equipment with the student who has reached the intermediate standard in other colleges.

It was inevitable, perhaps, that the loyalty of the Arya Samaj to British rule should be questioned. In the Punjab exception was taken to its political activities—or those of some of its prominent members—both in the disturbances which occurred in 1907 and again in 1919. Controversy has raged over the question. It has been hotly attacked and as hotly defended. The question of its loyalty or otherwise to British rule, however, is irrelevant in the connection in which its activities have been examined here. From this point of view its main interest lies in the fact that its educational activities are the outcome of a revolt against the domination of an alien ideal. And it is interesting to note that Mr. Munshi Ram himself has adhered faithfully to the path of life laid down in the ancient scriptures of the race as the ideal one for the twice-born castes; for in 1917 he brought to a close the period of his life devoted to active pursuits—the second of the four stages described in the Institutes of Manu—and since that time, under the name of Swami Shraddhananda, has lived the life of a sannyasi. And if his recent association with the *shuddhi* movement, the object of which is the restoration to the fold of Hinduism of the Muhammadan descendants of converted Hindus, has involved him in activities which are hardly in accord with the isolation from the world required of the strict Sannyasi, this must be attributed to his zeal for the Arya Samaj as an active missionary body.

Such institutions as the Hindu Academy at Daulatpur and the Gurukul at Hardwar provide striking illustrations of the swing back to Indian tradition which has been noticeable in many quarters in recent times. A reaction of the same kind is to be observed, as I have already indicated, in the strongholds of the Western system themselves. The Western-educated Indian of to-day no longer looks upon his country's past with the contempt of his predecessor of fifty years ago. On the contrary, his tendency is, rather, unduly to exalt it. At the second Oriental Conference—

itself an indication of the rapidly growing interest of Indians in their own past—the Vice-Chancellor of the Calcutta University, the late Sir Asutosh Mukherji, C.S.I., took pride in the fact that the University had been " the first in academic circles to recognise the supreme value of oriental studies by the foundation of a chair in ancient Indian history and culture, by the establishment of a new department for advanced instruction and research in that fascinating domain, and by the institution of a special degree for the encouragement of meritorious students ". And an examination of the work of the department of post-graduate studies, which came into existence towards the close of 1917, is sufficient to show how eager is now the desire among Western-educated Indians themselves, to probe into that vast storehouse of ancient lore which Macaulay dismissed with a gesture as a contemptible collection of crude puerilities and fantastic superstitions.

With the inauguration of the department there was brought together, under the shadow of the university, a staff of fifty scholars devoted exclusively to teaching and research in various branches of ancient Indian learning. Sanskrit, the sorry vehicle less than a century before of history, physics, theology and metaphysics, for which Macaulay could find no epithet other than " absurd ", was now divided up into ten great groups of subjects under the charge of twenty university teachers. Fourteen more devoted their time and abilities to ancient Indian history and culture, ten to Pali, and six to Islamic studies, Arabic and Persian. A chair of Indian Fine Arts was created and a famous Indian artist, Dr. Abanindra Nath Tagore, appointed to it. The scientific study of Indian vernaculars was undertaken, and a scheme inaugurated for the institution of a special degree therein. In 1922 the

Indian Vice-Chancellor of the University which in 1861 had withdrawn from the candidates for its entrance examination the right of answering in their own tongue, and which in 1864 had gone a step further and removed the vernaculars from its B.A. courses altogether, spoke with enthusiasm of " that great department of Indian vernaculars which is a special feature of our university, and which should constitute its chief glory in the eyes of all patriotic and public-spirited citizens ".[1] He went on to declare with obvious satisfaction that for the first time in the history of higher education in British India an attempt had been made to impart instruction to students in " Indian Epigraphy, Indian Fine Arts, Indian Iconography, Indian Coinage, Indian Palaeography, Indian Architecture, Indian Economic Life, Indian Social Life, Indian Administration, Indian Religions, Indian Astronomy, Indian Mathematics and Indian Race Origins ". And, gazing back down the vanishing vista of the past over the century of growth of the educational system, he pronounced his verdict upon it; the attempt to modernise the East by the importation of Western culture to the complete supersession of Indian ideals had proved a failure; the Indian universities had not succeeded in taking root in the life of the nation because they had been exotics. And he concluded with a profession of the faith that was in him: " Western civilisation, however valuable as a factor in the progress of mankind, should not supersede, much less be permitted to destroy, the vital elements of our civilisation ".

Nor was it in the Calcutta University only that there were indications of a quickening interest on the part of Western-educated Indians in their country's past. In northern Bengal a

[1] Address by the late Sir Asutosh Mukherji, C.S.I., at the annual convocation of the Calcutta University, March 18, 1922.

little body of Indian gentlemen had formed themselves in 1910 into a society for the promotion of systematic archaeological research. The field of their labours was a wide tract of country known in Sanskrit literature as Varendra, the home of the great Pala dynasty which rose to power towards the close of the eighth century A.D., and which made of its kingdom a great centre of Buddhist culture. When in November 1919 I had the pleasure of opening the admirable museum which was one of the first-fruits of the society's activities, it contained a collection of nearly 1350 Sanskrit manuscripts, gold, silver and copper coins; some of the earliest copper-plate records hitherto discovered in India; a number of images in metal, and a collection of several hundred specimens of sculpture in stone.

All this is significant. It is the repetition in India of a process through which the British people themselves passed before the wonderful flowering of English literature and learning took place. It is sometimes forgotten that just as India of the nineteenth century felt the necessity of a foreign language as its vehicle of learning, so did Great Britain in the sixteenth and preceding centuries experience the same necessity. For centuries English occupied the same position as did the vernaculars of India at the beginning of the nineteenth century. In cultured circles it was regarded with contempt as the jargon of the people. "If a man would commune with great minds," as a recent writer has reminded us, "whether of the past in their writings or of the present by cultured speech, he must have Latin. Would he be a churchman, an administrator, a diplomatist? He must speak fluently, he must read and write with ease, the international tongue. . . . Would he be a man of science, of medicine, of law, of letters? Again he must have Latin, for there were not the books in English. Without Latin he could neither learn nor teach."[1] But silently and even unperceived perhaps, at the time, the soul of England was preparing to blossom forth in raiment of its own, and the dialects of those centuries "barbarous and most unstable", have since become the mother-tongue of 180,000,000 people, and of all the languages of Europe, the most widely spoken in the other continents of the world. Englishmen can scarcely view with anything but sympathy, then, such attempts of modern India as have been described above, to strike root once more in her own intellectual soil. Such sympathy would have been deeper and wider spread, had it not been for the fact that in the sphere of politics the resurgent spirit of India has at times been perverted along channels which have led to rebellious movements against the existing order. A notable case in point was the revolutionary movement in Bengal which was responsible for a formidable volume of political crime during at least a decade from 1907 onwards, and which has lately made a sinister reappearance upon the scene of its former activities. There is no sadder chapter in the history of modern India than that which recounts the callous perversion of the emotional enthusiasm of a number of the young men of Bengal by the organisers of this criminal conspiracy. A study of it will be found illuminating.

[1] Mr. H. W. Household, in the *Hibbert Journal* for April 1923.

CHAPTER VIII

PERVERTED PATRIOTISM

In January 1918 a Committee assembled in Calcutta under the chairmanship of the Hon. Mr. Justice Rowlatt, judge of the King's Bench Division of His Majesty's High Court of Justice, to investigate and report on the nature and extent of the criminal conspiracies connected with the revolutionary movement in India. Their report was submitted to Government on April the 15th, the conclusion which they had arrived at being that all the conspiracies which they had investigated were directed towards one and the same objective, the overthrow by force of British rule in India. Speaking of Bengal in particular they expressed the opinion that the revolutionary outrages with which they were concerned were all " the outcome of a widespread but essentially single movement of perverted religion and equally perverted patriotism ".

This movement had broken out in anarchical form in Bengal in 1906, and during the succeeding ten years had been characterised by a long series of outrages including an appreciable number of assassinations.

Between 1906 and 1917 twenty-one police officers had been murdered in the Presidency besides a public prosecutor, the headmasters of two schools, two witnesses who had given evidence against members of the revolutionary party, and fifteen other persons who were believed to have given information to Government. In all, eighty-two persons in Bengal lost their lives during the period, and one hundred and twenty-one were wounded; while attempts were made upon the lives of a number of high officials, including a lieutenant-governor, a district judge, and a district magistrate. The fresh outbreak in 1923 was destined once again to stain the honour of Bengal with some peculiarly revolting crimes, of which the cold-blooded murder of an Indian post-master in Calcutta on August the 3rd, 1923, and the callous assassination of an English assistant in a Calcutta business house in broad daylight in the most fashionable thoroughfare in the European quarter of the city on January the 12th, 1924, provide outstanding examples. The latter crime was not rendered less shocking by the confession of the perpetrator that he had mistaken the murdered man for his intended victim—a high official. It was rendered all the more brutal by his attitude in the dock, and by his insolent declaration that he hoped that others would be found to complete his uncompleted task. What is the nature of the impulse which has prompted such revolting deeds?

Some part of the momentum has undoubtedly been derived from sources outside India. During the war some at least of the organisers of the conspiracy effected touch through tortuous channels with German agents; and a similar connection has been traced between the more recent developments of the movement and hostile elements in Russia. I am not so much concerned to trace the movement to its source, however, as to examine the methods by which the organisers of the movement—whoever they are and whatever their motives—have sought successfully to commend their programme of violent crime to appreciable numbers of young men, the sons of respectable and law-abiding parents. The mentality of such persons does, indeed, provide a psychological study of extreme interest. In the course of a jail inspection I was brought into personal contact with a number of young men charged with the murder of a police officer. They were all of the Hindu middle classes known as *badralôk.* They showed no disposition to deny the charge, but at the same time appeared to be oppressed by no sense of moral guilt. One at least appeared to cherish feelings of genuine regret that circumstances should have necessitated his being a party to the assassination of a person against whom he harboured no feelings of personal hatred. But he seemed to be troubled by no doubts as to the righteousness of his action.

Further light was thrown upon this aspect of the case by the literature of the movement, notably by a document in which was set forth an elaborate scheme for the organisation of the revolutionary forces. In the course of some introductory remarks it was stated that Salvation was the goal which every member of the league wished to reach. Mention was made of certain essentials to the winning of the goal. Salvation, it was stated, was not possible without the revival of the ancient Hindu spiritual culture in all its phases. The spiritual idea, it was explained, demanded the formation of national character on the basis of national education in indigenous institutions under independent Indian management. For this, political independence in its entirety was a pre-requisite. After this preliminary explanation the writer went on to describe the details of the organisation. Minute instructions to the active organisers of the league were drawn up under different heads such as training, the diffusion of literature, the formation of character, discipline, intelligence, finance and recruitment. The instructions under this latter head were significant. Among the agencies to be employed for securing recruits were schoolmasters and professors of colleges, philanthropic associations, religious institutions and associations, students' messes, hostels, reading clubs and so on. A digest of the subjects which should be discussed with the recruit was then given. This began with questions of a general nature calculated to arouse his interest. He was to be asked to consider the nature of man; his existence and the cause thereof; his origin and the reason for his life upon this earth; his relation and duty to the world and his environment. From these generalities he was to be brought to particulars. He was to be asked to consider the duties he owed to India. A picture was to be painted for him of "India past, India present, and India future in its three phases, political, religious and social". The future India was to be set up as the goal for which he was to strive.

Philosophical and religious literature was to be given to him to study. It was to be impressed upon him that religion should be his goal and moral scruples his guiding principles; that life was a mission and duty the highest law. "Each one of us", declared the writer, "is bound to purify his own soul as a temple, free it from egotism, set before himself, with a religious sense of its importance, the study of the problem of his own life, and search out what is the most striking and most urgent need of the men by whom he is surrounded." Finally, the man who was to become a genuine member of the league must become consumed with "a yearning for unity, moral and political, founded upon some great organic authoritative idea, the love of country, the worship of India, the sublime vision of the destiny in store for her, leading the Indians in holiness and truth ".

A study of the document of which the above is a very brief outline, left little doubt that success in recruiting was obtained by appealing to the idealism which is so marked a characteristic of the Indian mind. Innumerable examples could be given to show with what fidelity these instructions were carried out. A young man stated in explanation of how he became involved in the movement, that it was through a teacher in a certain high school. " In December he began to lecture me on religious and moral subjects, advised me to practise Bramacharya [the study of Brahman] and to give up play. He used to give me books to read on religious and moral subjects. By and by I was given to know by him that there was an Anushilan party whose aim was to do good to the country. At first I had no idea that this party also planned murders and dacoities; but gradually I came to know this."

This case provides a very good example of the insidious methods by which the seed was sown. The boy was advised to practise Bramacharya, *i.e.* the study of Brahman. To a Hindu boy the word Bramacharya is full of meaning. It brings vividly to his mind the rigid ordering of the life of the priestly caste laid down by the code of Manu—a life divided into the four definite stages of studentship with its study of the vedic system and its rigorous discipline, of family life with its duties as a householder, of retirement from the society of men with its mortification of the flesh; and finally of life divorced from home and all earthly ties devoted to the practice of asceticism. In other words, it brings to his mind something which is peculiarly Indian; something of which he, as an Indian, is the privileged inheritor. He is led to ponder upon the India of the past, and to contrast it with the India of the present, and it is an easy step from the contemplation of the past and present to speculation as to and hope for the future.

Other statements came to my notice which showed how responsive was the youth of Bengal to this subtle appeal.

"From my early life", wrote a young Bengali whose imagination had been captured by it, "I was of a religious turn of mind and was in the habit of nursing the sick and helping the poor. . . . I began to feel a peculiar despondency and was pondering over my life's mission, which I thought should be towards the amelioration of the condition of the poor and the needy, when I met A, with whom I had some conversation on the subject. After a few days I met him again and he gave expressions congenial to my religious tendencies and encouraged me in my line of thought. After some days more he gave me a book called 'Desher Kotha'[1] to read, which I did. On reading the book I got an excitement of mind, thinking of our past glories and the present deplorable condition of the people of this country. Suspecting nothing, I began to have closer intimacy with him and to have religious discourse with him at times. Gradually he began to insert ideas of anarchism into my religiously disposed mind, saying that religion and politics are inseparable and that our paramount duty should be to do good to the people of our country." The writer then tells how he was given another book to read entitled "Pathrabali",[2] by Vivekananda, and how he learned from it what self-sacrifice the author had made for the good of his country. Later he was asked if he had read the books of Bankim babu,

[1] The title signifies "all about the country", and the book deals with the economic condition of the country, with the object of casting the blame for all that is unfavourable upon British rule.

[2] Collection of letters by the great apostle of neo-vedantism.

and it was suggested to him that he should read "Ananda Math".[1] He did so, and his mentor then discussed it with him and pointed out the morals of the story and suggested that much good could be done to the country if only one desired.

A vast accumulation of evidence of a similar character pointed definitely to an earnest groping after an ideal by the impressionable young men who became entangled in the movement; though only too often the ideal was lost sight of in the dust stirred up by the perpetration of deeds of violence. Many episodes took place which showed that the weapon of violence was a two-edged one which recoiled upon those who employed it. It became apparent in many cases that a man who had once adopted the rôle of the highwayman in the interests of an ideal before long adopted it in the interests of himself. The economic pressure upon the educated middle classes of Bengal is severe; and among the revolutionaries themselves quarrels arising out of the misappropriation of party funds were frequent, showing that under this pressure degeneration set in, and that a man who had once stolen for an ideal was in danger of becoming little more than a common thief.

Nevertheless the ideal was there—the yearning for a revival of the ancient culture of the Hindu race, the natural corollary of the reaction against the excessive Westernisation of the country described in the foregoing chapters. This in itself provides an explanation of the exclusively Hindu character of the revolutionary movement in Bengal, for the ranks of the secret societies contained neither Moslem nor peasant, but were confined to the educated Hindu middle classes, *i.e.* those who were conscious of being the inheritors of a distinctive culture—that of the

[1] For the story of this remarkable book see Chapter X.

Indo-Aryan race.[1] The revolutionary movement in Bengal was *au fond* this yearning, expressing itself in terms of force. This at any rate is the interpretation placed on it by Indians themselves, who, while differing from the revolutionary party upon the question of methods, share with it a passionate admiration for the spiritual genius of their people and a longing for a renewed flowering of the ancient culture of their race. Such an interpretation of the anarchical movement in Bengal is vividly set forth in a memorandum in my possession, by an Indian gentleman who was placed by circumstances in a position in which he was in the confidence of some, at least, of those who were connected with the movement.[2] The following précis contains, I think, a fair presentation of the writer's views.

[1] This was of course before the defeat of Turkey in the World War brought the kilâfat movement into existence and excited Muhammadan sentiment against Great Britain.

[2] The author of the Memorandum was Mr. B. C. Chatterji, barrister-at-law.

CHAPTER IX

PANEGYRICS OF THE PAST

THE Memorandum of which I have spoken purports to be an explanation of "the storm that had been gathering in the heart of India for the best part of a decade, and would demand immediate attention at the close of the War". A desire for release from foreign tutelage is postulated, and the writer begins by tracing a history of the methods by which educated Indians have endeavoured to bring about, in the government of their country, "the principle of national liberty, which has for its outer embodiment in England the British Parliament".

First came the Indian National Congress, whose leaders made speeches, passed resolutions, and thought that by much importunity they might obtain their desire. "But the doom of this easy political doctrine was drawing near", and the partition of Bengal is cited as "a conclusive object-lesson in the impotence of that method of mendicancy by which Indians had been dreaming of securing self-government". The attitude of Government is depicted as a complete answer to those who sought to attain their ends by constitutional means. "The united voice of the whole nation rose and fell like the voice of one crying in the wilderness. None heeded it. The Viceroy persevered in his scheme of administrative division; and the English Parliament pronounced its benediction upon it. The political method of the Congress had been tried and failed—and the people fell upon bitterness."

Into these black depths of despair, we are next told, there suddenly fell a spark of light. Japan, an Eastern nation, had flung aside the tyranny of the West and had gloriously vindicated her right to unfettered independence by her victory over Russia. Henceforth a new hope—the hope of liberty and independence—burned with a bright flame in the soul of Bengal. A gifted prophet of this new creed arose in the person of Bepin Chandra Pal,[1] "who threw the whole strength and passion of his being into the work of proselytising his countrymen to the creed of his adoption". And hard upon the footsteps of Bepin Chandra Pal came Arabinda Ghose, who "aspired to work out for the whole continent that liberation of the human spirit which Bepin Chandra Pal was accomplishing in Bengal".

So far, then, the explanation of the ferment in Bengal is a sufficiently simple one. It discloses the not unfamiliar spectacle of a subject people girding against their impotence to influence the decisions, still less to control the actions of their alien rulers. But we now come to a contributory cause of a far more subtle and illusive character. Speaking of Arabinda Ghose, the writer declares in a fine passage that "the aspirations of Young India were in his writings, a divining intention of the spirit of liberty, the beating of whose wings was being heard over Asia; an exaltation, an urgency, a heartening call on his countrymen to serve and save the Motherland, an impassioned appeal to their manhood to reinstate her in the greatness that was hers. Had she not once been the High Priestess of the Orient? Had not her

[1] The author of the essays referred to in the Prologue, and now a member of the Indian Legislative Assembly.

civilisation left its ripple-mark on the furthermost limits of Asia? India still had a soul to save, which the parching drought of modern vulgarity threatened daily with death; she alone in a pharisaical world, where every one acclaimed God in speech and denied Him in fact, offered Him the worship of her heart; she alone yet gave birth to the choice spirits who cast aside the highest of earth's gifts in their enraptured pursuit of the life of life. Show us the country but India that could produce in the nineteenth century the Saint of Dakshineshwar.[1] The saving wisdom was still in the land which taught man how to know and realise his God—the wisdom which had been gathered and garnered in their forest homes by her priest-philosophers, the builders of the Vedas, the thinkers of the Upanishads, the greatest aristocrats of humanity that had ever been. But how should the culture of the soul survive in the land where a shifting materialism was asserting itself under the ægis of foreign rule? Had not the fools and the Philistines, whose name was legion—the monstrous products of a soulless education nourished on the rind of European thought—already begun to laugh at their country's past? And dared to condemn the wisdom of their ancestors? Was India to deform herself from a temple of God into one vast inglorious suburb of English civilisation? Even beauty, the vernal Goddess enshrined in her hymns and her poetry, was feeling the country chased by a hungry commercialism pouring out its flood of ugly and worthless wares owing naught to art or religion. This doom that impended over the land must be averted. India must save herself by ending the alien dominion which had not only impoverished her body, but was also

[1] Ramkrishna. For a description of this widely respected saint see Chapter XIX.

strangulating her soul. It was only in an independent India, with the reins of self-determination in her own hands, that the ideal could be re-enthroned in its integrity of high thinking and holy living, which cast on every man the obligation to cultivate throughout life the knowledge of Atman (Self and God), and of striving to realise in conduct the code of humanity that Gautama Buddha had enjoined. It was from the height of this vision of India to be that he called upon his countrymen to prepare themselves to be free, and *not* for the mere secularity of autonomy and wealth, the pseudo-divinities upon whose altars Europe has sacrificed her soul and would some day end by immolating her very physical existence."

Here we have clear intimation of something other than mere political unrest. The passage gives a vivid idea of the clash of two distinct cultures—those of the East and of the West. The idealism of the one is contrasted with what is pictured as the materialism of the other. The whole passage portrays a violent reaction against the tendencies of the nineteenth century, which have been described in the earlier chapters of this volume; and an appeal is made to instincts deep-rooted in the Hindu mind. The effect, according to the writer, was profound. "The nation felt a quickening in the beating of its heart, a stirring in its blood, the vibration of chords long silent in its race consciousness."

The apostles of the new movement were not slow to grasp the advantage of playing upon the religious side of the people's mind. Following in the wake of Bepin Chandra Pal and Arabinda Ghose there appeared a fiery prophet of the new nationalism in the person of Barindra Kumar Ghose, who breathed forth contempt and ridicule against the constitutionalists. What he demanded of India was men—" hundreds of thousands of them who are ready to wipe out with their blood the stain of her age-long subjection ". And the burden of Barindra Kumar Ghose's song also (if the writer's interpretation of his propaganda is correct) was that the soul of India was being strangled by the materialism of the West. Unless they bestirred themselves they would become a race of slaves. " And then ? Good-bye for ever to the India of Vâlmîki and Vyasa, of the Vedas and Vedanta, from whose sacred soil had sprung Lord Krishna and Gautama Buddha. Farewell Priestess of Asia, mistress of the eastern seas, temple of Nirvana to which pilgrims journeyed from Palestine and Cathay. . . . Come, then, with the vow of death that you may renew life. Remember the soil that your blood will manure shall bear the florescence of a new faith that shall redeem mankind, the fruitage of a new manhood that shall readjust the rights and wrongs of the world."

By temperament the people of Bengal are imaginative and highly emotional. Appeals to their pride of race were well calculated to sweep them off their feet. The fiery oratory of Barindra Kumar Ghose and his fellow-workers and the writings of an unrestrained press, which sprang into existence as the new movement spread, " smote on the heart of the people as on a giant's harp, awakening out of it a storm and a tumult such as Bengal had never known through the long centuries of her political serfdom ".

From this brief précis it will be seen that one of the factors which go to make up a complex whole is nationalism expressing itself in terms of religion. And in India, indeed, religion enters into politics as it does into most of the activities of man which in the West are usually described as secular. Not long ago at a large gathering of politicians in Bengal convened for the discussion of non-coöperation, the outstanding political controversy of the day, the speech of the principal speaker, babu Sarat Chandra Ghose, was described by one who heard it as "a discourse on the abstract truth of Hindu philosophy rather than a political address". Similarly, at an earlier date before the birth of the non-coöperation movement, Mr. C. R. Das, soon to become the leader of the extremists of Bengal, delivered an address from the presidential chair at the annual meeting of the Bengal provincial congress in 1917, which reflected views similar to these which have been set forth above.

Mr. Das spoke, indeed, with all the ardour of a missionary. He smote in pieces the golden calf which he set up as symbolical of the ideals of Europe, and with the fervour of a seer, he pointed the way to a promised land. His dominating note was hatred—and dread—of everything that savoured of the West. The industrialism, the commerce, the education, the very mode of life itself of Europe—all these were held up to opprobrium and denounced with undiscriminating bitterness. It was the pursuit of these false gods that had converted Bengal from a smiling land of happiness and plenty into a salt waste over which brooded stagnation and death. With a fine disregard of historical accuracy, the India of pre-British days was pictured in glowing colours as a land of happiness and prosperity. "We had corn in our granaries; our tanks supplied us with fish; and the eye was soothed and refreshed by the limpid blue of the sky and the green foliage of the trees. All day long the peasant toiled in the fields; and at eve, returning to his lamp-lit home, he sang the song of his heart." But these things were no more. "The granaries are empty of their golden wealth; the kine are dry and give no milk; and the fields once so green are dry and parched with thirst. What remains is the dream of former happiness and the languor and misery of insistent pain." How, he asked, had this fearful nakedness and desolation come about? The whole significance of the speech lay in the answer which he gave to this question. It was repeated over and over again in varying form throughout the discourse. "We had made aliens of our own people; we had forgotten the ideals of our heart. As I look back on the dim darkness of this distant century, the past seems peopled with vague and phantom shapes of terror; and I repeat again that the fault was ours. We had lost our manhood; and losing manhood we had lost all claim save the claim of life. Miserable as we were—our commerce, our manufacture, our industry—we sacrificed it all on the altar of the alien tradesman. The wheel and distaff broke in our household; we cut off our own hands and feet; we strangled fortune in her own cradle."

Word pictures of a golden age of peace and plenty before the advent of the British have become so common a property in the nationalist orator's rhetorical stock in trade, that some comment seems called for. Perhaps the best corrective for these strange historical aberrations is provided by the literature current amongst the peasantry itself. For centuries past there have been sung and handed down from father to son amongst the peasant population of Eastern Bengal a whole collection of ballads, the faithful record by village poets of episodes in the daily lives of the people. A number of these illuminating songs has recently been collected, edited and translated by Rai Bahadur Dinesh Chandra Sen, who has done so much to make better known to the world the literary treasures of Bengal. Amongst these ballads is the story of Kenaram, a famous robber chief. This interesting work, composed by the poetess Chandravati, is described by the editor of the collection as a historical account by one who knew them at first hand, of events in Bengal during the closing quarter of the sixteenth century. There is every reason to suppose, therefore, that it contains an accurate account of events in Mr. Das's golden age before the advent of the British.

The tale which it unfolds is that of a land racked and riven by anarchy, of deserted homesteads, and of a people harried and panic-stricken under a chaotic administration. " The people buried their wealth under the earth for fear of plunder ", sings the poetess. " The robbers strangled the wayfarers with nooses of rope. Many villages presented a scene of total desertion under the rule of the kajis." And with particular reference to the activities of Kenaram—" the very leaves of the trees shivered as if in fright : none dared to light a lamp in the evening lest it should attract notice to the house, nor dared to come outside after dark ". An interesting commentary, surely, upon Mr. Das's glowing picture of the peasant toiling in the fields all day and " at eve returning to his lamp-lit home " to sing the song of his heart.

Nor does this historical ballad bear out the contention of Mr. Das and his fellow-thinkers that famine is a product of British rule. " At this time ", declares Chandravati, the village poetess, " the district of Mymensingh was visited by one of the most cruel famines that had ever come upon Bengal." And she describes its horrors in graphic detail. " The homes of many families became scenes of terrible suffering, and men and women died by hundreds. . . . Husbands sold their wives and wives their children. All convention, all affection and feeling were gone, and men became like lower animals seeking the whole day long for something to live upon."

It would seem, therefore, that even before the advent of the British there were sombre interludes amid the golden days of brimming granaries and sweet content. Mr. Das's history would, indeed, profit by a perusal of the whole collection of these interesting ballads, even if in the process it lost something of its bold and picturesque originality.

Let me now return to Mr. Das's speech. From contemplation of the prostration of the countryside he turned his gaze upon the cities, and poured the vials of his wrath upon the commercialism of the age.

The industrialism of Europe was anathema—a thing accursed. "Christian Europe within the last two hundred years has forsaken Christ and set up the mammon of industrialism", and had trodden in pain the path of sorrow. Could they not heed the writing upon the wall? Must they too grope blindly after this grisly monster? "In our heart of hearts, this one thing we must remember for ever, that this industrialism never was and never will be art and part of our nature. . . . If we seek to establish industrialism in our land, we shall be laying down with our own hands the road to our destruction. Mills and factories—like some gigantic monster—will crush out the little of life that still feebly pulsates in our veins, and we shall whirl round with their huge wheels and be like some dead and soulless machine ourselves; and the rich capitalist operating at a distance will lick us dry of what little blood we still may have."

The Western system of education had been imposed like shackles upon the people. In the golden days of Āryâvarta education congenial to the people had been diffused in the household of the guru, in the institutions of domestic life, through *jatras* and *kathakathas*, in the songs from Ramayana and Chandi, in Saṅkîrtans, and in the *Bratas* and rituals of the women-folk. "But, like other ideals, our ideal of education also has become mean and impoverished. We have set up the huge structure of the University, . . . but this abnormal system has brought many evils in its train, and it will continue to be a source of evil in the days to come. For one thing, it has imparted an element of unnecessary anglicism into our manners and modes of life, so that in outer seeming it might almost appear as if the educated Bengali had little organic touch with the heart of his countrymen." This more than anything was destroying the genius of Bengal. It might be suited to other lands and other peoples, but for Bengal it was an empty simulacrum, a system without a soul, a lifeless image standing upon feet of clay, which must be broken and cast out of the national temple of learning. "To me it seems perfectly clear that if we want to lead our newly awakened consciousness in the paths of true knowledge, education will have to be diffused through the medium of our own vernacular and not through the unwholesome medium of English. The education which we now receive is a borrowed and imitated article; it does not co-operate with the national genius of our being, and hence it is powerless to enrich the life blood of our soul."

Even in their politics, the speaker declared there was no life or reality, merely mimicry of an alien system. They had borrowed the phrases and the formulæ of the West, and in doing so had neglected the one thing essential. They never looked to their country, never thought of Bengal, of their past national history or their present material condition. Hence their political agitation was unreal and unsubstantial, divorced from all intimate touch with the soul of the people. Down in the depths of their soul they, the educated people, had become anglicised. They read in English and thought in English. Their borrowed anglicism repelled the masses of their countrymen, who preferred the genuine article to the shoddy imitation. Thus in every aspect of their present life—in commerce, in industry, in education, in politics, in social custom—they found the taint of anglicism. "Mimic anglicism has become an obsession with us; we find its black footprint in every walk and endeavour of our life. We substitute meeting-houses for temples; we perform stage plays and sell pleasures in order to help charities; we hold lotteries in aid of orphanages; we give up the national and healthful games of our country and introduce all sorts of foreign importations. We have become hybrid in dress, in thought, in sentiment and culture, and are making frantic attempts even to be hybrids in blood."

Quotations might be multiplied, but enough has been said to show that the speaker had gone forth to preach a sermon and to point a moral. The state of the country to-day stood in sombre contrast with the Bengal of old. This calamity had been brought about because, in the dust which had been raised by the clash of ideals of East and West, the people had lost sight of their own divinities, and had cast their offerings upon the altars of strange gods. But the speaker did not stop here. He asked his audience to consider how it was that the people had been thus led astray, and having answered this question, he pointed to the signs which had been given that the scales were falling from their eyes, and while exhorting them to pay heed to these signs and portents, he himself assumed the rôle of prophet, and pointed the road to the promised land. How was it that they had succumbed to this passion for alien culture and foreign ideals? It was because when the English came to Bengal the people of the land were decadent. They were a people whose vital spark had burned low, whose Religion of Power had become a mockery of its former self—had lost its soul of beneficence in the repetition of empty formulæ and the observance of meaningless mummeries. As with religion, so with knowledge; the traditions of Navadvîpa's ancient glory and scholarship had become a mere name and memory. And so it had happened to them as it happens to all the weak. From pure inanition they had accepted the English Government, and with that the English race—their culture, their civilisation and their luxury. But the time had come when they must cast off the spell which had lain upon them. Already prophets of the race had arisen who had kindled once again the fires on the ancient altars. Bankim had come and had set up the image of their Mother in the Motherland. He had called unto the whole people, and had said, "Behold, this is our Mother, well-watered, well-fruited, cooled with the southern breeze, green with the growing corn; worship her and establish her in your homes". Time had passed. The trumpet of *Swadeshism* had begun to sound in 1903. The *Swadeshi* movement had come like a tempest; it had rushed along impetuously like some mighty flood, submerging them, sweeping them off their feet, but revitalising their lives. Under its reviving influence they had steeped themselves once again in that stream of culture and civilisation which had been flowing perennially through the heart of Bengal. They had been enabled once more to catch glimpses of the true continuity of their national history. The main problem for their consideration, therefore, was this—how to develop fully and adequately the newly awakened national life of Bengal? And assuming the rôle of priest and prophet, he pointed the road. In this critical period of nation building they must root out and cast aside the European ideal of indulgence, and must cleave fast to their native and ancient ideal of sacrifice. Problems of education and culture, of agriculture and commerce, must be dealt with in the light of their treatment in the past. The connection of these things with their ancient social system must be considered. And not this alone. They must consider also the precise relation in which all their thoughts, endeavours and activities stood, and still stand, with reference to the question of religion, for they would misread and misknow all things unless they kept this point steadily in view. They must accept only what was consonant with the genius of their being, and must reject and utterly cast aside what was foreign to their soul. What they formerly possessed, the permanent and perennial source of their strength, was still theirs. The stately and majestic rivers of Bengal which rushed impetuously towards the sea and the strength and might of which it was impossible to resist—they still flowed onwards in all their ancient majesty and might of strength. The august Himâlaya, ancient of days, still stood lifting up its brow towards Heaven. The great permanent features of earth upon which the life and soul of Bengal were founded—they were still there, permanent, immutable, majestic. Theirs the task to restore the life that had fled, to revivify the soul that was all but dead.

With the economic theories propounded by Mr. Das—viz. the superiority of the system of production which existed in all countries before the introduction of steam power—I am not here concerned. The real interest of the address lies in the insight which it gives into the working of the speaker's mind. That his whole outlook upon life is dominated by racial bitterness is plainly apparent: that the intention no less than the effect of his words must be to foster racial antagonism is scarcely open to doubt. Of course Mr. Das condemned the revolutionary crime which he described as the outer manifestation of the feeling of impatience and despair which had permeated the minds of the younger generation—impatience and despair born of the thwarting by the bureaucracy of a noble and overwhelming desire to serve their Motherland. Nevertheless, it was the doctrine set forth by Mr. Das and others before him, and the preaching of it, which were largely responsible for the illegitimate outlet which this pent-up energy sought. The people of Bengal are peculiarly susceptible to the influence of oratory. Appeals to their past greatness, couched in powerful and moving language, are capable of stirring their souls to their very depths. And naturally enough, perhaps, the darker shadows in the picture of Indian life as it existed when Great Britain took up her beneficent task find no place in these glittering but fanciful panegyrics of the past. The inhuman practice of suttee, in accordance with which, year after year, hundreds of unfortunate women were burned alive on their dead husbands' funeral pyres—a custom upheld by the priesthood as having been ordained by the earliest scriptures of the race—finds no mention in them. Neither does the scourge of the Thugs, by whom murder by strangulation followed by robbery was reduced to a fine art under the religious sanction of the goddess Bhawani; nor yet the equally heinous practice of infanticide, which in some parts of the country was responsible for the wholesale slaughter of female children. Still less does the fact that it was a British Viceroy who brought suttee to an end; that it was British initiative that brought to justice in the brief space of six years two thousand Thugs, and so ridded the land of one of its most cruel afflictions; or that it was, once again, British action which purged India of the cancer of infanticide.[1] Forgotten are the mutilations and other forms of torture inflicted as punishments at the individual caprice of those who administered what passed for a system of criminal justice, before the British established a new and merciful reign of law; forgotten is the devouring sword of the Pindharis who swept over the land, leaving in their train the smouldering ashes of perished homesteads, the anguish of tortured and ravished humanity, side by side with the lifeless bodies of the victims of their blood lust. For these twentieth-century audiences hypnotised by the persuasive oratory of Mr. Das and his colleagues, these things might never have been. For them the India of pre-British days was a golden land of peace and plenty: the India of to-day a sick and stricken land, lying pale and wan under the deadening shadow of the West.

[1] A startling illustration of the magnitude of this evil before the intervention of the British is provided by the case of the Chauhan Thakurs, a numerous and important Rajput clan in the district of Mainpuri in the United Provinces. When in 1842 serious steps were taken by the authorities to deal with the evil, it was found by Mr. Unwin, the officer concerned with the matter, that there was not a single female child alive amongst the Chauhan Thakurs in the district. Within a year 156 girls were enumerated, and by 1847 this number had risen to 299.

CHAPTER X

"ANANDA MATH"

THE revivalist character of the extremist movements of recent years has been emphasised in the foregoing chapters. A survey of the literature of the revolutionary movement in Bengal discloses overwhelming evidence of the religious sanction with which its chief organisers sought to endow it. Revolutionary documents such as letters, orders, proclamations and pamphlets were commonly headed with the Hindu invocation "OM!" And with this mystic syllable were frequently to be found associated the words "Bande Mâtaram".

The first of these two invocations is associated in the mind of every Hindu with the distinctive philosophy of his race. The opening sentence of the "Khândogya Upanishad" runs as follows, "Let a man meditate on the syllable OM". By concentrating his thoughts on this syllable he gradually excluded from his consciousness all other subjects. He underwent a process of mental hypnotism until the chambers of his mind were emptied of everything except the syllable OM. The syllable then became the symbol of a transcendent idea, the omnipresence of the Highest Self or Brahman. Recognition of the Universal Self entailed acceptance of the central doctrine of the Vedanta philosophy, namely, the identity of the Self in man with Brahman, the

Universal Self or Absolute. To a true Hindu, therefore, the syllable Om was a reminder of the belief (a Hindu would say knowledge) which was the special possession of his race—the supreme fact of Hindu national life according to Mr. B. C. Pal, which should constantly be borne in mind by the modern nation-builder in India.

But in India philosophy and religion have always gone hand in hand; and if the syllable Om placed upon the nationalist movement the seal of the particular philosophy of the race, the cry "Bande Mâtaram!" likewise gave it a religio-patriotic sanction. "This new nationalism which Bande Mâtaram reveals", said Mr. B. C. Pal, "is not a mere civic or economic or political ideal. It is a religion." The salutation "I reverence the Mother!" or, as it is more generally translated, "Hail, Mother!" derives its significance from the circumstances of its origin. The invocation was put into the mouth of one of the characters in his book, "Ananda Math", by Bankim Chandra Chatterji, the most famous and most popular of the novelists of Bengal, of whom mention has been made in an earlier chapter. I have given an instance in Chapter VIII. of the use which was made of this book by the members of the revolutionary organisations for inculcating their ideas into the minds of the impressionable young Bengalis whom they sought to recruit. So closely, indeed, did the revolutionary parties in Bengal follow the ideas contained in this romantic story, that one could ask for no better introduction to an understanding of the movement than is provided by the novel itself.

An indication of the position occupied by Bankim Chandra Chatterji in the world of letters in Bengal has been given in Chapter III. Until his day Sanskrit reigned supreme. Bengali was for the most part looked down upon by cultured society as a vulgar dialect altogether unworthy of its pen. From this position it was raised by Bankim Chandra Chatterji to that of a living language capable of giving expression to great and moving thoughts and ideas. *Banga Darsan*, the Bengali periodical which he founded in 1872, became a focus for the literary talent of the day. Dinabandhu Mitra the dramatist, Hemchandra Banerji the poet, Ramdas Sen the antiquarian, Krishna Kamal Bhattacharya and Akshoy Chandra Sarkar were among those who contributed to its pages. But prominent even among the contributions of these men were those of Bankim himself—his novels and his scathing criticisms of current literature. In his capacity of literary critic he made use of the pages of *Banga Darsan* to purge the Bengali tongue of those weaknesses and mannerisms which had hitherto marked it; and he discharged the duty which he had set himself with a remorseless pen. His novels were read with surprised delight by his fellow-countrymen. They have been described by Mr. R. W. Frazer in his "Literary History of India" as a revelation for the Western reader of the inward spirit of Indian life and thought. The same writer has assigned to him the position of the first creative genius modern India has produced. He has been compared by his admirers to Sir Walter Scott, particularly in regard to the intense patriotism which runs through his writings. And it is to be noted that his patriotism is deeply tinged with religion. "He perceived that the strongest sentiment of the Indian as well as the most pronounced element in Eastern civilisation is the religious sentiment", and he was led "not only to imbue patriotic sentiments with religion, but also to conceive nationality itself under the category of religion."[1] Another writer refers to

[1] Nares Chandra Sen-Gupta.

the magic charm of his pen which imparted to the Bengali language a unique life and vigour, and adds that " during the latter days of his life he devoted himself to religion and religious literature, the inevitable *dénouement* of an Oriental's life-story ". He was a staunch upholder of the British connection—for some time he was in Government service—and the mission which he set before himself was that of bringing about " a synthesis of the ideals of the East and the West in the life of the Indian ".[1] Violence was abhorrent to him. " Revolutions ", he wrote in his preface to the first edition of " Ananda Math ", " are very generally processes of self-torture and rebels are suicides. The English have saved Bengal from anarchy. These truths are elucidated in this work." It was a curious irony of fate, surely, that it should have been upon this very book that the revolutionaries should have drawn so deeply for inspiration.

The story, which is described by Mr. Nares Chandra Sen-Gupta as " a parable of patriotism ", is founded upon fact. It purports to be a narration of events in a certain phase of the disorders which attended the dissolution of the Moghul empire. In the early seventies of the eighteenth century northern Bengal was infested with roving bands of marauders who roamed over the country in the guise of ascetics, committing widespread depredations. Frequent mention is made of their lawless activities in the letters of Warren Hastings, and so prominent did they become that the episodes for which they were responsible came to be known as the sannyasi rebellion. It is from the sannyasi rebellion that Bankim Chandra Chatterji has drawn the material which he has woven into the romance entitled " Ananda Math ". The sannyasis appear in it

[1] Nares Chandra Sen-Gupta.

under the title of *the children*. Children of whom? Of the Motherland which is mysteriously identified with the great Goddess of the Hindus in her many aspects, Jagaddhatri, Kâlî, Durga. Indeed the intention which is read into the story by the nationalists of Bengal, if we may accept Mr. B. C. Pal as a trustworthy exponent of their views, is the interpretation of Kâlî and her different manifestations and forms such as Jagaddhatri, Durga, Bhawani, etc., as symbolic of the Motherland and the Nation spirit.[1]

The story opens in a year of famine with a vivid description of the plight of the people brought about by want and disease. Mahendra Singha, the landlord of a village once rich and prosperous, now desolate and almost deserted, decides to make an attempt to reach the nearest big town with Kalyani and Sukumari, his wife and daughter. They set off on foot in the month of Jaistha (May-June). " The sun was furious and the earth like a furnace. The wind spread fire all round, the sky looked like a canopy of heated copper and the grains of street dust were like sparks of fire." [2] While Mahendra is hunting round for food and water in a deserted village where they purpose spending the first night, his wife and daughter are carried off by a band of common outlaws and hidden in the depth of a dense forest. The outlaws quarrel over the division of the trinkets which they have taken from her, and during the fight which ensues she escapes with her child into the darkness of the forest. Overwrought and exhausted she loses consciousness, and on awaking from her swoon, finds herself in a room in a ruined monastery and in the presence of a venerable and saintly

[1] See "The New Spirit", a selection from the writings and speeches of B. C. Pal.

[2] This and the ensuing quotations are from the translation by Mr. Nares Chandra Sen-Gupta.

man with flowing hair and beard who thus addresses her, "Mother, this is a place of the gods, you need not be afraid". He learns from her the story of her adventures and promises to try to obtain news of her husband, and with this object in view seeks out from a band of armed men hidden in the recesses of the forest a young man, Bhavananda.

The latter finds Mahendra and guides him to the monastery—Ananda Math, the abbey of bliss—engaging him in conversation on the way and singing a song which interests but puzzles Mahendra. "Hail! Mother!" sings Bhavananda. "Who is the Mother?" asks Mahendra. Bhavananda makes no reply but sings another verse. "It is the country and no mortal mother," cries Mahendra. "We own no other mother," retorts Bhavananda. Mahendra then understands that it is of the Motherland that Bhavananda sings, and asks him to repeat the song. He perceived that as he sang his companion wept, and he asked in wonder who he was? "We are the *children,*" replied Bhavananda. "Whose children are you?" he persists. "Our Mother's." In due course they reach the abbey, and Mahendra is taken charge of by Satyananda, the venerable ascetic who has already given asylum to Kalyani and her daughter.

Before conducting him to them, however, he takes him to different temples in the abbey precincts, in which he shows him different images. He is first shown Jagaddhatri, and is told to perceive in her the Mother as she was. Next he is taken to a dark chamber where he sees a fearful figure. Trembling, he cries, "This is Kâlî!" and it is explained to him that this is the Mother as she is to-day. In the last shrine he sees a female figure more glorious than Lakshmi or Saraswati, in whose company she is seated, to whom the whole universe is depicted as paying homage. This, he learns, represents the Mother as she would be. At the sight of this last image Mahendra becomes greatly moved, and asks when they will see the Mother in this glorious form. " When all the children of the Mother learn to call her so," he is informed. He is then conducted to his wife and child. There is no need to dwell upon the author's description of their meeting; what is of importance is that Kalyani and he agree that wife and child shall return home, so that Mahendra may be free " to take the glorious and heavenly vow of service to the Motherland ".

A series of exciting episodes which may be passed over briefly are next described. Three of the characters, Satyananda, Kalyani and Sukumari, meet with mishaps. The two latter are rescued by two of the *children*, Bhavananda and Jivananda respectively. The former places Kalyani in safety in a neighbouring town; the latter takes the child to his sister Nimi, living in a cottage in the seclusion of the forest in company with Jivananda's wife Santi, who figures later in the story. Satyananda is taken captive by a company of Government troops and incarcerated. News of this latter happening spreads rapidly and brings the *children* in large numbers to the abbey. Here they are addressed by a *child*, Jnanananda, who adjures them to go forth and rescue Satyananda, " who has pledged his life for the revival of the True Religion and whom we look upon as an incarnation of Vishnu ". They sally forth " with slow and solemn steps chanting Harinâm aloud ", overcome the resistance of the guard and restore Satyananda to freedom.

On his return to the abbey Satyananda has a long talk with Mahendra, whom he desires to initiate into the Society of the *children.* The conversation is of importance, because it can be interpreted as giving the sanction of religion to deeds of violence. He explains to Mahendra that the *children* are all Vaishnavas. The latter objects that the avoidance of all bloodshed is considered the highest virtue among Vaishnavas, while the *children* fight and take life. Satyananda then points out that Mahendra is thinking only of the creed of Chaitanya.[1] The ideal of true Vaishnavism is the chastisement of wrongdoers and the salvation of Mother Earth. Chaitanya's Vaishnavism is only half the true faith. Its God is only Love; but the true God is not Love alone, but also Infinite Power. "Chaitanya's Vishnu is all Love; our Vishnu is all Power. We are all of us Vaishnavas, but the creed of either is only half of the whole creed." Mahendra asks for further explanation, and is reminded that the Deity consists of three guṇas (qualities)—sattva, rajas and tamas.[2] These three guṇas, he is told, have to be propitiated by distinct modes of worship. "From sattva springs God's mercy and Love, and this is to be propitiated by Love. That is what the followers of Chaitanya do. From rajas springs his Power. This has got to be propitiated by fight, by slaying the enemies of the gods. This is what we do. From tamas the Lord takes what form he chooses, and has to be worshipped with garlands, *sandal* and so on. This is what the ordinary man does." "Then the *children* are only a religious community?" asks Mahendra in conclusion. "Quite so," replies Satyananda, "we do not want sovereignty; we only want to kill these Mussulmans,[3] root and branch, because they have become the enemies of God."

Mahendra is then taken to the temple of the

[1] For some account of Chaitanya see Chapter IV.
[2] See p. 120 forward.
[3] The events recorded in the book took place during the latter days of Muhammadan rule in India.

"Mother as she would be", and, in company with another candidate who is discovered praying before the goddess, takes the vow of the *children*. They swear to renounce family and riches, to conquer all passion and "never even to share a seat with a woman", to fight for the true religion, and as children of one mother to give up caste. They then sing the hymn to the Mother and are initiated in due form.

The second candidate for initiation mentioned above turns out to be Santi, Jivananda's wife, in disguise. She is brought into the story in this way to emphasise the importance attached by the *children* to the vow of chastity. After initiation she reveals her identity to Satyananda, and later to Jivananda himself. The part she plays in the remainder of the story is an illustration of how a woman, setting aside all earthly relations with her husband, may yet live with him in intimate spiritual union. At the conclusion of the last victorious fight of the *children* described in the book we are given a picture of Jivananda and Santi discussing their future. "We can no more be householders," said Santi; "we shall be ascetics like this for ever and keep the vow of virginity. Come, let us now go about visiting the shrines."

"What, when we have done that ?" inquires Jivananda.

"After that we shall build ourselves a hut on the Himâlayas, worship God and ask for the blessing that good may be our Mother's share."

Jivananda's acceptance of a life of renunciation is made known with an appropriate simplicity. "Then the two arose and departed hand in hand —to eternity it would seem—in the dead of that moonlight night."

The lesson of chastity, which the author seeks to enforce by the example of Santi and Jivananda, is repeated with additional emphasis in the case of Bhavananda. It will be remembered that Kalyani was rescued by Bhavananda and placed in safety in a neighbouring town. A visit paid her by him, at which he confesses his love for her, provides material for a dramatic scene. On hearing his confession she asks him what of his vow to the *children* ? " In the fire of thy beauty the creed gets burned to ashes," he replies. Kalyani says, " I have heard from your lips that it is a rule of the *children's* creed that he who is swayed by passion has got to expiate his sin by death. Is it true ? " He admits it, and begs her to remember him when he is dead. Kalyani dismisses him with scorn, telling him that she will remember him when he is dead " as a sinner, and as one who has transgressed his vow ". Bhavananda is killed soon afterwards plunging into the forefront of a fight between the *children* and a company of Government troops to expiate his sin.

I have given some prominence to these episodes because, as I shall show later, they provided a lofty ideal for the Bengali revolutionaries—an ideal which, however criminal were their methods and however sordid many of their actions, was still to be caught sight of like a ray of sunlight breaking through the clouds of a dark and menacing sky. It is unnecessary for my purpose to do more than touch very briefly upon the remainder of the story. Two battles between the *children* and the troops are described, from each of which the *children* emerge victorious.

The scene after victory is thus depicted : " On that night that part of the country rang with shouts of Harinâm. . . . Everybody said, 'the Moslems have been defeated and the country has come back to the Hindus ; cry Hari ! Hari ! ' "

The conclusion of the book is designed by the

author to show that the advent of the British and their rule for a time is necessary to the re-establishment of the True Religion, and provide him with an opportunity of dissociating himself from the lawless deeds of the *children*. Satyananda, who had returned to the abbey after the battle, is roused from meditation by a mysterious ascetic of high authority, who bids him now desist from the struggle and accompany him to the seclusion of the Himâlayas. Satyananda objects that the task is but half done. Mussulman rule has been brought to an end, but the power of the Hindus has not yet been established. The saint replies that Hindu rule will not yet be established, for it is necessary for the good of India that the English should first hold sway. Satyananda still objects, and the saint explains further. " You have won victories with the proceeds of robbery. A vice never leads to good consequences, and you may never expect to save your country by a sinful procedure." Moreover, the advent of the English with their Western knowledge is essential to the re-establishment of the true faith. True Hinduism is based on knowledge, and not on action. Knowledge is of two kinds, subjective and objective, and until the latter is acquired the former, which is the essential part of the true faith, cannot flourish. Objective knowledge has long passed away from India ; the English will bring it back. They will spread it throughout the land, and India will then be able to comprehend subjective truths once more. But " till the Hindus are great again in knowledge, virtue and power, till then English rule will remain undisturbed ".

In the end Satyananda is persuaded, and hand in hand they pass out of the scene of active strife.

It will be seen from the foregoing summary that the essence of the story is a Hindu revival, necessitating the overthrow of the enemies of

Hinduism—at the time of the events narrated, Mussulman rule—which was to be achieved by a body of men pledged by solemn vows to the service of the Motherland. It provided the revolutionaries with an ideal which made a strong appeal to their imagination, and with the framework of an organisation admirably designed to meet the circumstances of their case. For the Mussulman rule of the novel they substituted British rule, and by so doing they ignored the conclusions drawn by Bankim Chandra Chatterji at the close of his book on two points—the benefits of British rule, and the fallacy underlying the assumption that the attainment of any particular end justified the employment of any means. It is an interesting fact that the conclusions arrived at by the author of "Ananda Math" on these two points were accepted in many cases by prominent revolutionaries; but only after terms of imprisonment or restraint, during which they had opportunities for reflection uninfluenced by the appeal to their emotional nature made by revolutionary oratory and literature, or by the glamour of the idea of a great Hindu revival to be brought about by successful revolution. In other respects the secret societies modelled themselves closely upon the society of the *children* of "Ananda Math".

"Bande Mâtaram!" the battle cry of the *children*, became the war cry not only of the revolutionary societies, but of the whole of nationalist Bengal, which differed from the societies in method only, and not in aim. One of the most desperate of the gangs of Bengali revolutionaries, that of Jotindra Nath Mukherji, two of whom were killed in an encounter with the police in the district of Balasore in 1915, adopted the names of the chief characters in "Ananda Math". As was the case with the *children*, the members of the Dacca Anushilan Samiti were required to pledge themselves to lives of continence and moral rectitude. "Come, sons of India, casting aside desire for pleasure, luxury, wealth and worldly attachment, come forward to devote yourselves to the worship of the Mother." So runs an appeal entitled "A call" and headed with the invocation "OM: Bande Mâtaram!" which made its appearance in the summer of 1913. More striking still, one of the four vows taken by the members of the Dacca Anushilan Samiti was almost identical with the vow of austerity and renunciation administered to Mahendra by Satyananda. That part of it which pledged the initiate to a life of rigorous continence was drafted with much greater elaboration than is the case in the novel, and gave a list of the acts which were to be eschewed with a wealth of detail which could not have been set forth in a novel without gravely offending against accepted canons of decorum. It concluded with these words: "If I flinch from this solemn vow or in any way act contrarily, the curse of God, of Mother and the mighty sages will destroy me ere long". The vow was administered before the image or picture of Kâlî and a binding religious sanction was thus given to it.

It was, indeed, no empty undertaking, for in the case of a breach of its provisions the penalty was exacted, and the culprit died as did Bhavananda for his conduct towards Kalyani. I can recall no less than four specific cases which were brought directly to my notice of members of a society thus meeting with summary justice at the hands of their fellows. Against this it would be possible to set the case of a man who was alleged to have caused the assassination of a fellow-member, who had become aware of certain grave offences against morality of which he himself had been guilty. But I am not so much concerned with the frequent and serious lapses from an ideal of which individual members of the secret societies were guilty, as with the search after the existence of an ideal itself in the background of an admittedly criminal movement. The view which I have put forward that there was an ideal—that of a Hindu revival—receives added testimony from the persistence with which the organisers of the movement sought to give not merely their aims, but their methods also, the sanction of the Hindu scriptures. And in the "Bhagavad Gîtâ", the most widely treasured, perhaps, of all the sacred books of the Hindus, they found material which, torn from its context, could be made to wear the appearance of giving sanction to deeds of violence. No study of the psychology of the movement would be complete without some examination of the use to which the organisers of the conspiracy were able to put this sacred volume; and in order to make this clear some account of the book and its meaning is a necessary preliminary.

CHAPTER XI

THE SONG OF THE LORD

THE "Bhagavad Gîtâ" seems to have been composed at a time when Indian thought was experiencing a desire for a reconciliation between the idealistic teaching of its recognised exponents and the stubborn facts of everyday existence, and was disturbed and perplexed by the difficulty which it experienced in effecting one. The ills of human existence—and, indeed, that existence itself—were due to karma (activity); and in theory, at any rate, there was a perfectly simple antidote in abstention from all activity or, in other words, in renunciation of the world. And it was renunciation that the exponents of Indian thought, consequently, preached.

If the premises were accepted the conclusion was obviously unassailable; equally obviously the remedy was incapable of universal application. There was the adamantine institution of caste with its restrictions and its obligations. How, for example, was the man of the kshatriya caste, the warrior whose duty (dharma) it was to fight, to avoid a life of action? It was this problem which the author of the "Bhagavad Gîtâ" attempted to solve. There were other reconciliations to be attempted. The conception of God as a shadowy and dimly apprehended abstraction remote from anything known to human experience, a veiled enigma whose nature was hidden from the understanding of the ordinary man in a bewildering maze of metaphysical verbiage, an insentient, inexorable existence uninfluenced by, and wholly indifferent to the affairs of men groping their way blindly from life to life in an endless and hopeless cycle of birth and death, may have sufficed for the sannyasi who sought salvation along the passionless path of inaction and renunciation. But the man of action required something less elusive to turn to in his hour of need, and acting upon the innate tendency of mankind to anthropomorphise, he evolved a personal God. Here again the author of the "Bhagavad Gîtâ" essayed the impossible task of reconciling two such widely differing conceptions of the supreme Being. No such attempt could hope to be wholly successful, and it is not surprising to find in the "Gîtâ" a somewhat confusing juxtaposition of contradictory ideas. The Hindu mind, however, is remarkable for its toleration and flexibility, and this characteristic of the "Song of the Lord" has never presented the same difficulty to the Indian mind as it has to the more methodical and exacting mind of the European. A mind that can convince itself not merely that there is truth in all religions, but that all religions are true,[1] is not likely to be troubled by the inconsistencies contained in the "Gîtâ".

The poem occurs in the 6th book of the Mahabharata and is a description of a kshatriya episode. There are two characters of major and two of minor importance in the story. The latter are Dhritarashtra, the head of two princely houses, the Pandavas and the Kurus, who with their armies are arrayed against one another in battle; and Sanjaya, a messenger who brings the old king news from the scene of action. The two

[1] As did Keshub Chandra Sen, for example: see Chapter V.

characters of major importance are the warrior prince Arjuna, the second of the Pandavas, and Krishna, an incarnation of Vishnu, who acts as his charioteer. The scene is laid upon the field of Kurukshetra, where the opposing forces are drawn up. Struck with a sudden pang of remorse at the prospect of the slaughter of his relatives in the ranks of the opposing army, Arjuna stays his hand and appeals to Krishna for instruction. The latter replies in seventeen discourses, interrupted only by occasional questions put by Arjuna.[1] It is this dialogue retailed by the messenger Sanjaya to the old king Dhritarashtra that constitutes the " Bhagavad Gîtâ ". And in these discourses, presented to the reader as having been delivered on the field of Kurukshetra more than two thousand years ago, is summed up a profound philosophy, the contribution of Indian thought towards the solution of those problems which for all time have exercised most deeply the mind of speculative man—of thought so penetrating and so appealing that it has winged its way triumphant down the flights of time and lives with unimpaired vitality enshrined in the heart and intellect of her sons to-day.

The picture of Arjuna, the famous representative of the warrior caste, smitten suddenly with anguish at the prospect of the task which lies before him, torn between the promptings of an awakened conscience and the requirements of the duty imposed upon him by circumstances and by caste, is one which at once attracts attention and excites sympathy, for it portrays a dilemma in which few men have not found themselves at one time or another when a decision has had to be taken between two alternative courses, the advantages and disadvantages of which appear

[1] The whole book consists of eighteen discourses, but Krishna does not begin his reply to the questions put by Arjuna until the second.

to be evenly balanced. Krishna experiences no difficulty in pointing the right way. "Smiling, as it were", he enters into the explanation contained in the second discourse. The teaching here is based on the cosmogony of the Sâṅkhya system, which recognises two eternal and, in a sense, independent verities, spirit (purusha) and matter or Nature (prakṟiti). Sentience is exclusively a quality of the latter, which is made up of three constituents called guṉas (usually translated by the word qualities), namely, sattva, rajas and tamas, which may be rendered for want of better words, goodness, desire and indifference.[1] As long as the three guṉas are in a state of equilibrium, consciousness is latent. It becomes manifest when, in some unexplained way, a union takes place between purusha and prakṟiti, resulting in a disturbance of the state of equilibrium of the guṉas. In other words, the phenomenal universe, or world of experience, is inherent in prakṟiti, but only becomes manifest in conjunction with purusha. It follows from a true understanding of the real nature of these two verities that the real man (purusha) is absolved from the consequences of his actions in that they appertain to prakṟiti only. This is brought out in the discourses which Krishna delivers.

The eternal nature of that which is real in man is set forth with an emphasis which recalls the teaching of Buddhism upon the meaninglessness of the word creation. "Nor at any time verily was I not, nor these princes of men nor verily shall we ever cease to be hereafter." The dweller in the body is defined in accordance with the teaching of the Vedanta philosophy. Human beings are but embodiments of the Eternal.

[1] Mrs. Besant, in her translation of the "Bhagavad Gitâ", explains the word guṉa as an attribute or form of energy. Sattva she translates rhythm, harmony or purity; rajas, motion, activity or passion; and tamas, inertia, darkness or stupidity.

"Know That to be indestructible by whom all This is pervaded," declares Krishna; "That" being the essence of the universe or God and "This" being the universe as it appears to man. The eternal nature and the indestructibility of "That" is affirmed over and over again. "Nor can any Work the destruction of that imperishable One. . . . He is not born nor doth he die; nor having been, ceaseth he any more to be; unborn, perpetual, eternal and ancient, he is not slain when the body is slaughtered."

It follows from this that, when a man in his ignorance imagines that he has slain another, he has in reality but caused him to change his form, for his body is as a garment which is put on and taken off without affecting the essential nature of the wearer. But this is not all, for "he who regardeth the dweller in the body as a slayer and he who thinketh he is slain both of them are ignorant. He slayeth not, nor is he slain." It may be said that the one follows from the other, that if no one has been slain there can have been no slayer. But more than this is involved in the statement that "he who regardeth the dweller in the body as a slayer" is ignorant. Looking at the matter for a moment from the point of view of ordinary experience; when a man A is slain by a person B, who is it or what is it that has done the slaying? the answer is not in doubt; it is B who has done the slaying and who is responsible for the deed. But looked at from the point of view of the Sâṅkhya system, this is not so. The deed is the outcome of the moods of Nature (prakṛiti), "for helpless is every one driven to action by the moods (guṇas) of Nature (prakṛiti)".[1] These have been made active, it is true, by a mysterious union between spirit (purusha) and Nature (prakṛiti), but for

[1] "Bhagavad Gîtâ", iii. 5.

the character of the deed the former is in no way responsible. "All actions are wrought by the qualities (guṇas) of Nature (prakṛiti) only. The self deluded by egoism thinketh 'I am the doer'."[1]

Arjuna is not convinced. If it is thought by Krishna that knowledge is superior to action, why does he urge him to terrible deeds? "With these perplexing words Thou only confusest my understanding; therefore tell me with certainty the one way by which I may reach bliss."[2] And Krishna replies once more that there is a twofold path, that of salvation by knowledge of the Sâṅkhyas and that of salvation by action of the Yogis; and that of these two paths the way of action is the best—at least, we may presume, for the ordinary man. But in order to lead to salvation, action must be performed with a single end in view—the discharge of duty. A man cannot escape the duty imposed upon him by his caste. "Bound by thine own duty, born of thine own nature, that which from delusion thou desirest not to do even that helplessly thou shalt perform."[3] But he can and should avoid action which is not assigned to him in the course of his own duty. "Better is one's own duty though destitute of merits than the well-executed duty of another. He who doeth the duty laid down for him by his own nature incurreth not sin."[4] Even so a man's duty must be performed in a spirit of lofty altruism. He must act because it is his duty, *and for no other reason.* Action performed with a view to results is fatal and binds the doer to the ever-revolving cycle of existence. "Better death in the discharge of one's own duty; the duty of another is full of danger."[5] This is the great lesson repeated over and over again throughout the discourses. "Thy business is

[1] "Bhagavad Gîtâ", iii. 27. [2] *Ibid.* iii. 2.
[3] *Ibid.* xviii. 60. [4] *Ibid.* xviii. 47. [5] *Ibid.* iii. 35.

with the action only, never with its fruits";[1] and again, "He that performeth such action as is duty independently of the fruit of action, he is an ascetic. Hoping for naught his mind and self controlled, having abandoned all greed, performing action by the body alone, he doth not commit sin."[2]

The similarity of the teaching here to that of Buddhism is immediately apparent. It is desire, attachment to life that has to be eradicated. If this is successfully accomplished, the real man, the shackles of this world thrown off, exists in a state of complete harmony unaffected by pleasure or pain, and from this lofty altitude of serenity gazes down unmoved at the actions in which his physical nature is engaged. He has, in fact, reached the state of the arahat of Buddhism.

But it is in its attempt to meet the craving of humanity for a personal God that the author of the "Gîtâ" parts company with the founder of Buddhism. The teaching so far set forth is mainly philosophical, and is based on existing systems—the Sâṅkhya and Vedanta. But throughout the discourse ideas which are purely religious compete with those which are purely philosophical. It is as if below the surface of the author's mind there was being waged a continuous struggle between the cold reasoning of his intellect and the passionate craving of his emotional nature. An early indication of the theism which later becomes so marked a feature of the poem is met with in the 7th verse of the second discourse, when Arjuna, perplexed as to his duty, cries out, "I ask thee which may be the better—that tell me decisively. I am thy disciple suppliant to Thee; teach me." In the seventh discourse Krishna himself begins to reveal himself as the one God. "All this world, deluded by these

[1] "Bhagavad Gîtâ", ii. 47. [2] *Ibid.* vi. 1; and iv. 21.

natures made by the three qualities (guṇas) knoweth not Me above these imperishable. This divine illusion of Mine, caused by the qualities (guṇas), is hard to pierce; they who come to Me they cross over this illusion."[1] And in the ninth discourse his godhead is fully proclaimed. "I the Father of the Universe . . . give heat; I hold back and send forth the rain; immortality and also death. Even if the most sinful worship Me with undivided heart, he too must be accounted righteous. Know thou for certain that my devotee perisheth never. On Me fix thy mind; be devoted to Me, sacrifice to Me; prostrate thyself before Me."[2] But perhaps the most pronouncedly theistic passage of all is that in the fourth discourse, in which there is a definite statement of God made man. "Whenever there is decay of righteousness, O Bharata, and there is exaltation of unrighteousness, then I myself come forth for the protection of the good, for the destruction of evil-doers; for the sake of firmly establishing righteousness I am born from age to age."[3] Finally, in the eleventh discourse Arjuna prays Krishna that he may see him in his form omnipotent, and being given for a space the divine vision, he perceives him as God all-marvellous, boundless, with face turned everywhere, shining with the splendour of a thousand suns. As infinite form he is pictured with "mouths, eyes, arms, breasts multitudinous", radiant and rainbow-hued with shining vast-orbed eyes; filling entirely "the earth, the heavens and all the regions that are stretched between", at once glorious and terrible. It is interesting to find here infinite form and infinite power represented by the same symbolism which is invariably employed by the Indian artist for the same purpose.

[1] "Bhagavad Gītā", vii. 13 and 14.
[2] *Ibid.* ix. 17, 19, 30, 31 and 34.
[3] *Ibid.* iv. 7 and 8.

The supreme Being thus portrayed is something very different from the unconditioned Absolute, the Brahman of the Vedanta. The conception of a "beginningless supreme Eternal, called neither being nor non-being",[1] is not wholly lost sight of; but while referred to as the ultimate it is not delineated in the sharp clear outline in which it is depicted by the firm touch of Sankara and other apostles of idealistic monism, and it tends to become merged in the conception of God as Lord of all. Throughout the "Gîtâ", indeed, the unmanifest Absolute takes second place to the manifest God. Nor is the central teaching, that salvation can be acquired by works, accepted by the extreme monistic school; and in his commentary Sankara declares of this doctrine that "it is not possible to imagine, even in a dream, that the man who knows the Self can have anything to do with karma-yoga (the rule of action), so opposed to right knowledge and entirely based on illusory knowledge".[2] Yet for the ordinary man it bridged adequately the gulf which yawned between the teaching of the philosophy of his race and the practice of his daily life.

* * * * * *

Such, in brief, is the "Song of the Lord". Its popularity in revolutionary circles, when the reason for that popularity is considered, provides one of the most tragic of the many examples with which the history of mankind abounds, of religious zeal perverted to irreligious ends.

More than a dozen copies of the "Gîtâ" were found among the effects of the Dacca Anushilan Samiti when the Society was first proscribed and its premises searched in 1908; and there was evidence to show that special "Gîtâ" classes were

[1] "Bhagavad Gîtâ", xiii. 12.

[2] Quoted by Dorothea Jane Stephen in "Early Indian Thought," p. 125.

regularly held there. The *Juguntur* newspaper, the most violent, perhaps, of all the revolutionary organs which had sooner or later to be suppressed, had as its motto the verse from the poem which declares the repeated incarnation of God for the protection of the good and the destruction of evil-doers ; and members of the Society were required to take its vows with a sword and copy of the "Gîtâ" on the head, while the observance of certain ceremonies in which the "Gîtâ" played an essential part was customary when some revolutionary enterprise was about to be undertaken.

It will be seen from the brief résumé of the "Gîtâ" which I have given, how easily the teaching of certain of its texts can be represented as giving support to criminal action in the interests of a perverted patriotism. The stress which is laid upon the relative unimportance of human life and its inevitable transitoriness, is used to accustom the novice to the relative unimportance of giving and taking life ; while the constant exhortation to Arjuna to fight, is held to apply to every one striving for the restoration of righteousness upon earth, *i.e.* the revival of the Hindu religion. It is easy to understand the play which can be made with a text such as the following: "Slain thou wilt obtain Heaven ; victorious thou wilt enjoy the earth ; therefore stand up, O Son of Kunti, resolute to fight ".[1] Thus, for example, the late Bal Gangadhar Tilak, "The most practical teaching of the 'Gîtâ', and one for which it is of abiding interest and value to the men of the world with whom life is a series of struggles, is not to give way to any morbid sentimentality when duty demands sternness and the boldness to face terrible things ". Whatever may have been the

[1] "Bhagavad Gîtâ ", ii. 37.

intention, the effect of such teaching upon the impressionable youths of Bengal is conclusively demonstrated by the indifference with which members of the revolutionary party committed the most deadly of all sins, the killing of a Brahman. Basanta Kumar Chatterji was a Brahman; but he was also a successful police officer, and he was murdered without the smallest compunction. It is, perhaps, hardly necessary to point out that one, at least, of the essential doctrines of the "Gîtâ" is severely ignored by the self-appointed gurus of the revolutionary organisations, namely, that of caste dharma. Arjuna is exhorted to fight because it is his caste duty to do so, and the most solemn warning is pronounced against the man of one caste arrogating to himself the duties of a member of another caste. It is safe to assert that verses 43-47 of the eighteenth discourse, which define the duty of the great castes and adjure a man to restrict his action accordingly, find no mention in the "Gîtâ" classes of the revolutionaries, nor the 35th verse of the third discourse which declares that the duty of another is full of danger. That such a misconstruction of so universally treasured a scripture should be possible in so religious a country is surprising. It is to be feared that it must be attributed in no small measure to the disappearance of all religious instruction from the schools, due to the assumption of a strict religious neutrality on the part of Government.

The mass of material bearing upon this aspect of the revolutionary movement is so great that one might with ease devote a whole volume to its analysis. To do so, however, would be to alter completely the character and scope of this book, and I shall content myself with a reference to one more piece of revolutionary literature only. This last example is a pamphlet entitled "Bhawani Mandir", which is believed to have been written by Arabinda Ghose, whose fervid writings were steeped in idealism, and who did more than any one to breathe into the sinister spectre of anarchy the vitalising influence of religion. The author starts by declaring that a temple is to be erected in the Himâlayas and consecrated to Bhawani, the Mother. To all the children of the Mother the call is sent forth to help in the sacred work. Who is Bhawani, one naturally inquires? The author proceeds to explain, couching his explanation in the metaphysical language which appeals so strongly to the Indian mind. "In the unending revolutions of the world, as the wheel of the eternal turns mightily in its courses, the Infinite Energy, which streams forth from the Eternal and sets the wheel to work, looms up in the vision of man in various aspects and infinite forms. Each aspect creates and marks an age. . . . This Infinite Energy is Bhawani. She also is Durga. She is Kâlî, She is Radha the beloved, She is Lakshmi. She is our Mother and creatress of us all. In the present age the Mother is manifested as the mother of Strength."

The lesson that the writer seeks to impart is the need in which his countrymen stand of energy, strength, force. All else they possess—knowledge, love, enthusiasm; but in the present era these things will avail them nothing unless they have added to them Strength. "The deeper we look the more we shall be convinced that the one thing wanting which we must strive to acquire before all others is strength—strength physical, strength mental, strength moral, but above all strength spiritual, which is the one inexhaustible and imperishable source of all others."

Next we are given a glimpse of that pride of race which is so resentful of alien domination, and which was so potent a factor in driving those possessed of it to the revolver and the bomb. "India cannot perish, our race cannot become extinct, because among all the divisions of mankind it is to India that is reserved the highest and most splendid destiny, the most essential to the future of the human race. It is she who must send forth from herself the future religion of the entire world, the Eternal religion which is to harmonise all religion, science and philosophies, and make mankind one soul. . . . It was to initiate this great work, the greatest and most wonderful work ever given to a race, that Bhagavân Ramkrishna came and Vivekananda preached." But if she is to fulfil her destiny she must acquire strength. Now is the time. First, then, a temple must be built to Bhawani, the source of strength. And attached to the temple there must be a new order of karma-yogis, who will renounce all in order to work for the Mother. And the work of the order must be based upon knowledge as upon a rock—the knowledge enshrined in the mighty formula of the Vedanta, the ancient gospel which when vivified by Karma and Bhakti, delivers man out of all fear and all weakness.

And by doing these things what is it that will be achieved? The writer puts the answer into the mouth of Bhawani herself. "You will be helping to create a nation, to consolidate an age, to Aryanise a world. And that nation is your own, that age is the age of yourselves and your children, that world is no fragment of land bounded by seas and hills, but the whole earth with her teeming millions."

Upon the warm and emotional temperament of the young Bengali such appeals had the effect of deep draughts of intoxicating nectar. They were swept off their feet and carried headlong down the road to disaster by an overwhelming surge of religious fervour. The working of the process is well illustrated by a petition which I received from a disillusioned member of one of the Bengal societies early in the year 1919. Incidentally it gives point to the statement made earlier, that the conclusions of the author of "Ananda Math" were not infrequently accepted by members of the revolutionary party who had had leisure for quiet reflection amid surroundings removed from the influence of the societies themselves. After admitting that he had acted in a way prejudicial to the public safety and had therefore been rightly interned, he stated that while in internment, "being able to think calmly and considerately over the true situation . . . he has his eyes opened, and holds that the overthrow of British rule in India . . . is neither desirable nor feasible, . . . and that even if there was any chance of success by such unconstitutional, extreme, nay, unrighteous and outrageous measures (as those of the revolutionary party), India of all countries of the world should never, with that great mission of hers—the spiritual uplift of the world—take to them". It is clear from the whole tenor of the petition that the author is one of those spiritually-minded persons of whom India provides so many examples, whose whole interest in life is devoted to religion. He tells how he gave up his connection with the revolutionary party before his arrest, "not because he did not support the party's aims and objects, but because, goaded by his soul-inspiration, he devoted his life for the realisation of God, the Eternal Truth". And he explains how his religious aspirations were made use of by the organisers of revolution to enlist him in their ranks. "Curiously enough, your petitioner was led to believe that by the emancipation of India, which of course could only be got, according to the established doctrine, by revolutionary works, the Hindu religion could break its binding fetters and again flourish in its past glories, vivified and brightened a thousandfold, and triumph over the world, and thus bring about the world's spiritual transformation."

This is the tragedy of this melancholy but sinister movement—that it has been so largely sustained by "perverted patriotism and equally perverted religion". The young man convicted of murdering Amrita Lall Roy, the officer in charge of the Sankaritolla post-office in Calcutta, on August the 3rd, 1923, described the man at whose bidding he acted as "a God-fearing man and a man of learning". It is this blind faith of the recruits to the secret societies in the holiness of the organisers of the movement that gives to it so poignant a pathos.

CHAPTER XII

CHARACTERISTICS OF INDIAN ART

In the last few chapters I have traced much of the bitterness and the violence which have characterised political movements in India in recent years, to a reaction against the Westernisation of the country and the consequent loss of that individuality of race to the value of which educated India has been gradually awakened. It is natural that this resurgent spirit should be most strongly in evidence in the field of politics, for in India as elsewhere it is the politician who attracts the limelight to himself. Nevertheless a man need not be a politician to be a Nationalist in the sense in which the word is defined by Mr. B. C. Pal; and the nationalism of a man who is not a politician is a thing of greater significance than that of the man who is. Dr. Rabindra Nath Tagore, for example, is a poet, and for vast numbers of Indians he stands for the very embodiment of the National Ideal. He speaks to India not so much of the tyranny and injustice—the favourite catch-cries of a certain school of politicians—of a foreign administration, as of the genius which is her own. And his ability to quicken the pulse of an Indian audience is derived from his power of stirring in its innermost being memories of a dimly apprehended past, and of bringing to life a consciousness of an almost forgotten heritage. " The soul of ancient India is mirrored in his writings", declares Professor Radhakrishnan; and if his appeal is in different terms to that of the politician or of the revolutionary, it draws its inspiration from the same source and it leads to the same goal. The secret of his power is to be found in the extent to which in an age of cosmopolitanism he identifies himself with all that is fundamentally and essentially Indian. The Indian view of him is summed up concisely by Professor Radhakrishnan in a brief preface to his volume on the poet's philosophy: "In interpreting the philosophy and message of Sir Rabindra Nath Tagore we are interpreting the Indian ideal of philosophy, religion and art of which his work is the outcome and the expression. We do not know whether it is Rabindra Nath's own heart or the heart of India that is beating here. In his work India finds the lost word she was seeking."[1] In other words, it is, in India, his championship of Indian culture and his ability to display it before the world as a thing compelling the respect and homage of other nations, more than his mere skill in literature, that has won for him the commanding position which he occupies in public estimation.

Less apparent at first sight, but equally striking when it is appreciated, is the same spirit of revolt against Western domination which is to be found stirring in the sphere of art. The renaissance which is visible here is the outcome of the struggle of the Indian spirit after survival in a fiercely competitive age. It is once more a manifestation of the clash of two ideals.

It is difficult to make this clear without first attempting to describe the fundamental difference between the art of India and that of the Western world—a difference which is only too often ignored or misunderstood. I am not here

[1] "The Philosophy of Rabindra Nath Tagore."

referring so much to difference of quality as to difference of aim. Difference of quality there is; the painting of the East, for example, has been described as an art of "line" in comparison with the painting of the West as an art of "mass".[1] But for my present purpose this difference of method between the two types is a matter of comparatively little moment. What is of importance is the difference of goal which is aimed at by art in general in India and in the Western world respectively. This difference in intention would be described by the Indian exponent somewhat as follows. The artist of the West, he would argue, seeks to reproduce accurately that which he sees around him. His aim as a sculptor or a painter is to produce a striking likeness of man or woman. He may idealise within limits; that is to say, he may minimise obvious imperfections in his model and he may emphasise good points, but his idealising is confined to producing perfection of the human form. He has no intention of attempting to suggest anything transcending the human form. His goal is realism rather than idealism.

I should perhaps pause here to explain that for the purpose of this argument I leave out of account those curious developments of modern European art known as post-impressionism, cubism and futurism. I am not myself competent to assess their value or to make any estimate of their vitality. But it is probably correct to say that they are widely regarded by contemporary opinion as being little more than ephemeral eccentricities. Some claim to imaginative novelty due to a subtle suggestion of unwholesomeness has been conceded to the first of these three schools by an artist of the day. But of cubism and futurism he has written that

[1] See Mr. Percy Brown's "Indian Painting".

they are "so meaningless that they are quite free from any unpleasant suggestion. Futurism pretends to have a most elaborate system of ideas behind it, but as its exponents have never succeeded in making these ideas in the least intelligible either in print or in paint, we can class it with cubism as merely a silly method which like other pictorial vagaries will lose its vogue as soon as its novelty is past."[1] Whether this estimate be correct or not, it is safe to assume that these types play no part in the traditional art of the average European. And the Indian critic, rightly regarding him as being imbued with the realism of the main currents of Western art, argues not unreasonably that his natural tendency is to condemn Hindu and Buddhist art unheard.

It is certainly the case that Indian paintings and frescoes often strike the European as grotesque; Indian images mere travesties of the human form. Much of the sculpture on the temples in certain parts of the country appears to him to be frankly obscene. And if the motif of Indian art were the same as that of Western art, he would be justified in his condemnation of it. But here the Indian exponent of his country's art would intervene, and would assert that its aim was altogether different. The Indian artist, he would explain, is not in the least concerned to reproduce a faithful likeness of his objective surroundings. His object is to catch the reality that lies behind the appearance of things. His art is in keeping with his philosophy. The world perceived by the senses is unreal; it is a veil behind which reality lies hidden. He has no desire to reproduce any part of the chequered pattern into which the veil is woven; rather does he strive to make manifest that which lies behind

[1] The Hon. John Collier in *The Nineteenth Century* for April 1919.

it. The same idealism that runs through his philosophy provides him with the inspiration of his art. He does not copy what he sees with his outward eye; he meditates upon his subject, and then gives form and colour to that which is created in his mind.

When it is realised that the object of the Indian artist is the suggestion of things unseen rather than a mere reproduction of things seen, the conventional and often unnatural forms of Indian religious figures become intelligible. Such things, writes Mr. O. C. Ganguli, "can hardly be represented in terms of a physically perfect and healthy human body. They can only be symbolised in ideal types and by forms not strictly in accordance with known physiological laws, but by forms which transcend the limits of the ordinary human body. The Indian artist was thus called upon to devise certain artistic conventions and a special system of anatomy suggestive of a higher and superior ethnical type for the purpose of intimating something beyond the form of things."[1]

Hence the many-headed and many-armed images which present a distinguishing feature of Indian religious imagery and which have been undiscriminatingly condemned by Western critics as being violations rather than expressions of legitimate art. Yet if "the vital characteristic of pure art is the expression of thought and not the exposition of form",[2] it is impossible to deny the artistic merit of, for example, the bronze images of Ṣrî Nataraja, the Lord of the Dance, commonly known as the Dancing Shiva, which are a famous product of the temple sculptors of Southern India. The image is invariably repre-

[1] Foreword by O. C. Ganguli to "Some Notes on Indian Anatomy," by A. N. Tagore.

[2] Mr. Samarendranath Gupta, "With the Five Fingers", contributed to the *Modern Review*.

sented as four-handed and with the left foot raised, the whole giving the impression of a figure in violent motion. Surrounding it is an aura of flame. Whatever may be the effect produced by these images upon the aesthetic sensibility of a foreigner, there is no doubt as to their meaning for an Indian. For the Indian the Nataraja is the plastic presentation of a whole philosophy. In the whirl of the dance he sees the primal energy which gives life to all existence and so sustains the universe. Other aspects of the figure speak to him of the destruction of desire and of the attaining of salvation. A detailed description of the image, together with extracts from a copious contemporary literature describing its significance, will be found in a volume of essays entitled "The Dance of Shiva", by Dr. Coomaraswamy. My object is merely to make it clear that from the Indian point of view the Western artist is not competent to compute the artistic value of a work the inner meaning of which is hidden from him.

And when a man of the attainments of Dr. Coomaraswamy sees in the Nataraja "a synthesis of science, religion and art", and feels impelled to declare that "no artist of to-day, however great, could more exactly or more wisely create an image of that Energy which science must postulate behind all phenomena", we may agree that it unquestionably does possess a value which we are not competent to assess.[1]

More familiar alike to the traveller and to the student of Eastern affairs, because of its wide diffusion throughout Eastern Asia, is the conventional figure of the seated Buddha. And equally with the Nataraja of Southern India, it

[1] I have touched upon the origin and present-day significance of these particular specimens of Indian iconography in the course of a brief examination of the religious quest of India in another volume. See pages 272 and 278 of "India: A Bird's-eye View".

illustrates the fundamental difference between the artistic conceptions of India and of Europe. Judged by Western standards it suffers from many imperfections. The face is expressionless. The figure is devoid of anatomical detail. There is nothing to indicate that the original possessed either veins, muscles or bones, and from this point of view it might be described as crude. Nevertheless it produces upon the mind the precise effect intended. I feel tempted to repeat a description of the impression made upon my mind by the great bronze Buddha of Kamakura, all the more so because the impression was made at a time when I was little conscious of the intention of Buddhist art:

"The great image stands in the open, in grounds of exquisite charm, a charm which it is impossible to ignore. . . . Yet amid all the charm of changing scene, the idea that rushes irresistibly uppermost in the mind is that of absolute immutability. In the infinite peace which seems to find materialisation in the expression of divine calm on the face of the Buddha is a mute and inexorable challenge to change and time. The setting varies with the season, but the great image remains the same, untouched by the passing of time, heedless of summer and winter, spring-time and autumn, unconscious of the men that come and the generations that have gone, wholly absorbed in sublime meditation and that perfect peace which only dawns with the final annihilation of passion and desire. All else falls into insignificance before that expression of unearthly calm — of complete and immense repose."[1]

If one attempts to analyse the factors which go to convey this impression, one is driven to the conclusion that it is this very absence of ex-

[1] From my "Wandering Student in the Far East".

pression and of detail that is chiefly responsible. The mind is not diverted by detail from dwelling upon the main idea suggested by the whole, namely, immobility. All is at rest. There is nothing to suggest movement of either body or mind. It is the embodiment of that ideal which throughout the ages India has sought with passionate tenacity—stillness, release from activity; that perfect peace which passeth all understanding to which she has applied the term Nirvana or Moksha—liberation from the evil of existence; in a word, salvation.

This difference of motif and of method is most noticeable in the plastic arts; but the same trait which characterises Indian imagery is observable in Indian painting also. Here let me anticipate criticism by admitting that this is a generalisation which requires very considerable qualification. What has been described as the classical period in the history of Indian painting stretches over approximately seven centuries from the birth of Christ. The best known extant examples of the work of this period are the Buddhist frescoes of Ajanta. Here the Buddhist painter-priest sought to present to the spectator the ideals of his creed. But while idealistic in aim the work of this school was essentially realistic in execution, so much so that it is recorded by the seventeenth-century historian Tara Nath that it deceived men by its likeness to the actual things depicted. In the same way realism is the keynote of the Moghul school of painting, "an outstanding feature of which is its devotion to the delineation of likeness".[1] But of this school it must be said that it was an importation from Persia and Central Asia and was therefore not a product of Indian soil. The Rajput school, on the other hand, which flourished alongside of the Moghul

[1] "Indian Painting", by Mr. P. Brown.

school and is the direct descendant of the older Indian schools, shows pronouncedly idealistic characteristics, notably in its treatment of animals, which were frequently given the forms of deities. Moreover, while the Rajput painter was an adept at depicting homely scenes from the daily life of the Indian peasant, he also sought frequent inspiration in the great religious epics, the Ramayana and the Mahabharata as well as in the legends of the Vaishnavaite and Shivaite creeds of his own day. His art was largely mystic. Nor is this all.

I have in my possession certain pictures of the Rajput school which possess a peculiar characteristic illustrating the paramount part played by suggestion in Indian art, and giving point to the claim made by Indians that appreciation of art is preponderatingly subjective, *i.e.* dependent upon qualities belonging entirely to the beholder, and transferred by him into the object before him. They represent figures of men and women grouped in various attitudes in landscape gardens presented in strange perspective, or in the verandas and on the platforms of highly ornamented pavilions standing in pleasure-grounds consisting of lawns and orchards broken here and there by stretches of ornamental water. The colouring is vivid, and the figures, though formal and, from a Western point of view, somewhat stiff and "unnatural", give an impression of animation. I certainly derive pleasure from contemplating them. But I do not understand them. They do not convey to my mind a suggestion of anything beyond what actually appears upon the paper. For the Indian artist, however, they possess something which is hidden from me. The Hindu connoisseur, on seeing any one of them will at once be reminded of a particular melody. For him the painting is visualised music, each picture being an interpretation in form and colour of a particular melody. Similarly, on hearing the melody he will call to mind the picture. This practice of weaving music and painting into a single composite whole provides us with a striking example of the intention claimed by the Indian for Indian art, namely, that of giving expression to the idea which lies behind the appearance of things—of making manifest the abstract; for it is, surely, ideas only and not objects, such as persons or things, that lend themselves to reproduction in two such different forms of artistic expression as music and painting. The case is comparable to that of the analogy drawn by Schopenhauer of architecture to music. To all outward appearances there is no connection between the two. The former exists in space without relation to time; the latter exists in time without relation to space. Yet the principles governing each, namely, symmetry and rhythm, are seen upon reflection to be closely akin, and to possess as their substratum a single idea. And it is this derivation from a common source that gives to F. von Schlegel's description of architecture as "frozen music" its pleasing appropriateness.

There is a well-known story of a famous musician at the court of Akbar, Tan Sen by name, which further illustrates this tendency of the Indian mind to look for reality in ideas rather than in objects, in the abstract rather than in the concrete. The singer was commanded by Akbar to sing at high noon a night raga, *i.e.* a melody based on a tonic series dedicated to the night season. Different ragas, it should be understood, are associated with different emotions, seasons of the year and periods of the day, and are intended to be, and usually are, employed at the proper time and in appropriate circumstances.

Obedient to the imperial command, Tan Sen sang the raga. And as he did so darkness descended upon the land for as great a space as was covered by the singer's voice. Here the idea of night conveyed by the melody converted day into night, or at least produced in the minds of his audience an impression amounting to conviction of the actual presence of night. It is but one of a number of anecdotes of the kind demonstrating the power of an idea to present itself in appropriate material form, even though this involves an interference with the orderly operation of natural law.

CHAPTER XIII

SEX SYMBOLISM

In the preceding chapter I have endeavoured to set forth the fundamental distinction which the Indian claims for his art, and to explain the reason for the unusual forms which, viewed from a Western standpoint, it so often assumes. For a time after the European invasion the Western point of view asserted itself in the sphere of art just as it had done in so many other directions. Indians adopted Western standards and accepted the criticisms which were levelled at their own. But here, as in other spheres, a reaction against this attitude is plainly apparent. A body of writers has arisen which repudiates criticism based on an alien theory and upholds the ancient tradition of its own country. And side by side with this new championship of Indian art has arisen a modern school of Indian painting which seeks its inspiration in the theory and practice of its own past. Outstanding representatives of these two movements are Dr. Ananda Coomaraswamy [1] in the world of letters and the group of artists associated with Dr. Abanindra Nath and Mr. Goganendra Nath Tagore in the world of art.

The writings of Dr. Coomaraswamy are directed to two ends: in the first place to combating European criticism of Indian art, and in the second to

[1] Although Dr. Coomaraswamy is not himself of Indian birth, he is one of the most effective exponents of the Indian point of view.

appealing to Indians to free themselves from the lure of the West and to return to the ideals of their own land. He asserts, for example, that the sex symbolism in Indian religious art, which has not unnaturally been the subject of much mordant criticism, is misconceived by the European critic. This feature of Indian art has, indeed, proved one of the greatest stumbling-blocks in the way of the Westerner who seeks to place himself *en rapport* with the Indian point of view. It provides the same difficulty which is raised by the tendency displayed in certain of the Indian scriptures to portray divine love in terms of human passion, as, for example, in the stories of Radha and Krishna, of which I have written elsewhere.[1] And the explanation given by Dr. Coomaraswamy and others, even if it fails to carry complete conviction, is therefore of considerable interest.

All love, he argues, is a divine mystery. In India the distinction between sacred and profane is meaningless, "and so it is that the relation of the soul to God may be conceived in terms of the passionate adoration of a woman for her lover". And he quotes with complete approval an observation by Sir Monier Williams that "in India the relationship between the sexes is regarded as a sacred mystery, and is never held to be suggestive of improper or indecent ideas". His contention seems to be that for the Indian, religion is not something apart from the experiences of his daily life, but on the contrary that all experience, however commonplace, has its religious aspect. Life and religion cannot be separated off into watertight compartments, the one to be opened only on every seventh day.

The student from Europe will probably find some difficulty in accepting this interpretation

[1] In "India: A Bird's-eye View", chapter xxi.

as a complete explanation of the sex symbolism which characterises certain examples of Indian religious art. He can scarcely be blamed if he sees in some of the sculpture which adorns the temples—the great temple of the Sun at Konarak in Orissa, for example—much that is kin to similar work characteristic of the later years of the Roman Empire. The fact is, I think, that the spiritual and intellectual life of India has ebbed and flowed much as has been the case with other peoples, though more noticeably, perhaps, on account of the longer span which it has covered. The decline of Buddhism ushered in a period of ebb-tide in the spiritual life of the people, during which the less reputable features of the mystic ritual of Tantrikism and other kindred cults took root and flourished, with results which, as Rai Bahadur Dinesh Chandra Sen has pointed out, were disastrous to the moral fabric of society. Indian writers naturally lay stress upon the symbolical meaning attaching to the doctrine and practice of such cults, and are inclined to overlook the inevitable results of placing too great a strain upon human nature. Thus Swami Vivekananda, speaking of the devotional exaltation of the Bhaktas in general, declares that it often happens that the devotees who sing in praise of divine love accept the language of human emotion in all its aspects as adequate to describe it. He admits that even the love of husband and wife is not intense enough for the inspired Bhakta. "So he takes up as his ideal the idea of illegitimate love, because the emotion in it is so strong." He explains that "the impropriety of it is not at all the thing which he has in view, but its power and intensity". And he is rather contemptuous of any one who expresses doubts as to the wisdom of the representation of love divine in terms of such violent human emotion. "Fools," he says, "do not understand this, and they never will, for they look at it only from the physical side." [1]

Unfortunately, human nature being what it is, the physical aspect is bound to obtrude itself. The Sahajiâ cult which was one of the products of the period which followed on the decline of Buddhism, is a case in point. The cult was based upon the idea that in sexual love there is a higher side pointing to love divine, and that through the former is to be found the path leading to the latter. In theory no doubt it was worship rather than love in its more worldly sense that it was sought to inculcate; but when the objects of such romantic attachment were young and beautiful women, and when further it was held that with a man's own wife the highest results could not be expected, the dangers of the creed become sufficiently obvious; and it is not surprising to learn that the early love poems inspired by the tenets of the cult and composed by a Buddhist scholar, Kanu Bhatta, late in the tenth century, were by no means free from obscenity.

A more spiritual emphasis was given to the teaching of the cult and of that of the kindred Parakîyâ Rasa cult of Vaishnava theology by Chandidas, a Brahman poet of the fifteenth century. "One who has crossed the region of darkness (passion) can alone have the light of Sahajiâ," he cries. The story of his own romantic love for Rami, a washerwoman, and one therefore whom he was debarred by caste from associating with, is well known; but while he addresses her in the fervent language of a lover he also declares "my love for your maidenly beauty has not any element of physical desire in it". Nevertheless he was as conscious as any one of the impossibility of the theory of the cult being lived up to in

[1] "Bhakti Yoga", by Swami Vivekananda.

practice so far as the majority was concerned, and he did not hesitate to assert the rarity of the self-restraint essential to its proper practice. " This love," he sang, " may be attained by one who can suspend the highest peak of Mount Sumeru by a thread, or bind an elephant with a cobweb." And again " to be a true lover, one must be able to make a frog dance in the mouth of a snake ", an aphorism which is described by Rai Bahadur Dinesh Chandra Sen as meaning that the lover while playing with dangerous passions—nay, while apparently running even to the mouth of destruction, must possess the self-control to return unhurt. Some indication of the popularity of the cult in Bengal may be gained from the extent of the literature dealing with it. Rai Bahadur Dinesh Chandra Sen mentions that he has come across as many as thirty authors in old Bengali literature who acclaim the principles of Sahajiâ, and he gives the names of nearly forty different books containing expositions of the doctrine, all written during a period of about two hundred years prior to the advent of British rule.[1] And researches in the royal library of Nepal in recent years have disclosed the existence of further works of a like character.

The love story of Radha and Krishna round which revolves the theology of the Vaishnavas is the perfect example of the cult of Parakîyâ Rasa. To outward appearance the story of Radha and Krishna is that of a love intrigue. Radha, the married daughter of a king, falls in love with a shepherd boy. The latter is portrayed in the guise of a passionate lover. But it is claimed that for the devout Vaishnava the love story possesses a purely symbolic meaning. Krishna is God incarnate, Radha is the human soul. The

[1] See his " History of Bengali Language and Literature ".

story which lends itself so easily to an earthly interpretation is to him an assurance that salvation is to be gained through love of God. This is the ideal attitude of the follower both of the Parakîyâ Rasa and the Sahajiâ cults, and there is no need to assume that the ideal has never been attained. "In cases where this feeling (of abstract love) has arisen, and the persons concerned possess noble moral qualities—social and moral barriers continuing to exercise their full power—it is easy to see that the highest romantic idealism is the inevitable result. We then find that the very restrictions imposed only accentuate the poetry of the passion. There is nothing which the lovers are not prepared to lay upon this the altar of their highest dream. Such love is the nearest approach in common life to the mystic longings of the devotee's soul for the realisation of God; and, in fact, in the purity of its sentiment and in its capacity for devotion and self-sacrifice, it approaches spirituality."[1] But in the case of persons less well equipped with moral armour such cults inevitably led to results the reverse of spiritual. "It goes without saying that in their earnest efforts to attain salvation by worshipping young and beautiful damsels, many a youth turned moral wrecks";[2] and it is, indeed, notorious that so great was the havoc which the doctrine created in certain strata of Vaishnava society that Chaitanya and other great fifteenth century leaders of the Vaishnava community vehemently condemned the cult, the former sternly forbidding his followers to associate with women. No branch of Indian scripture has come in for such severe condemnation on these grounds as that known compendiously as the Tantras. Sir John Woodroffe, who is probably

[1] "History of Bengali Language and Literature", by Rai Bahadur D. C. Sen.

[2] *Ibid.*

the greatest living European authority upon these works, protests indignantly against the sweeping charges of eroticism which have been laid against them; and his wrath against those who, armed with an admittedly defective knowledge of the subject, have judged the whole body of Tantrik doctrine by a small part only and who, failing to see in the works "the repository of a high philosophic doctrine, and of means whereby its truth may through bodily, psychic, and spiritual development be realised",[1] have incontinently dubbed them as "lust, mummery, and black magic",[2] is no doubt legitimate. Nevertheless, it is common knowledge that the elaborate system of worship laid down for Tantriks does include a ritual involving the practice of sexual intercourse. It is true that this particular ritual is in theory confined to a particular class of persons—those qualified for Vîrâchâra—who have reached a particular stage, that of Vâmâchâra (worship in which woman enters), on the ascending pathway which has to be trodden by all Tantrik worshippers; the first stage, that is to say, on the return journey of the soul to Brahman —the commencement of the process of involution after the evolutionary progress of the soul has reached its furthest point. It is also true that for the proper attainment of the objects of this stage—the destruction of the passions by the passions, just as poison is used as the antidote for poison, and their diversion in such a way that instead of binding the soul of man to earth they raise him to the universal life—it is laid down that the guidance of an experienced spiritual teacher is essential; and further that grave warnings are given as to the disastrous consequences of any false step taken by the worshipper

[1] See his preface to "Principles of Tantra", Part I.
[2] Brian Hodgson.

at this stage.[1] Yet it would be worse than useless to deny that such warnings have not always proved effective. And with all his admiration for the philosophy, and for much of the ritual of the Tantras, Sir John Woodroffe does not deny the abuses to which they have given rise. The Vîrâchâra ritual, originating possibly in a doctrine intended for the detached non-dualist initiate and kept closely secret, may, he suggests, have been perverted by the vulgar to whom some portions of it became later known. And he admits that the abuses of these commoner people as time went on, developed such proportions as ultimately to obscure all other matters in the Tantra, thus depriving them of the attention which is their due.[2]

If, then, Dr. Coomaraswamy's statement of the intended significance of the sex symbolism in Indian religious art may be accepted, it is less easy in the light of what has been written above, to accept the implication which he would, apparently, have us draw, that the influences which have been responsible for this particular phase of Indian art have been wholly spiritual.

[1] See Sir John Woodroffe's introduction to the "Mahanirvana Tantra".

[2] Introduction to "Principles of Tantra", Part I.

CHAPTER XIV

AN INDIAN RENAISSANCE

THE difficulty of ignoring a perplexing aspect of Indian culture has led me to digress somewhat from my main theme. Let me return to my examination of the attitude of the Indian nationalist in his rôle of champion of the art of his own country against the challenge of a rival culture. Dr. Coomaraswamy contrasts the idealism of Indian art with the realism of the art of modern Europe, which he attributes to the Western temperament "which more naturally than the Eastern seeks for the realisation of objective perfection". And commenting upon the adoption by certain Indian artists of an European style, he seizes the opportunity of emphasising the unsuitability of the latter as a means of giving expression to the *motif* underlying Indian art. By way of illustration he analyses a well-known picture of Saraswati by the late Raja Ravi Varma. In the picture in question the lotus-seat—essentially an abstract symbol of other-worldly origin—is represented in conformity with the realism demanded by the canons of Western art as a real flower growing in a lake with the result, as he points out, that "the spectator is led immediately away from the ideal to wonder how the stalk is strong enough to support a full grown woman".

But he is even more concerned to point to the

deplorable results following from the subordination of indigenous good taste to the influence of the art of Europe in its commoner forms. "There is no more depressing aspect of present day conditions than the universal decline of taste in India, from the Raja whose palace built by the London upholsterer or imitated from some European building is furnished with vulgar superfluity and uncomfortable grandeur, to the peasant clothed in Manchester cottons of appalling hue and meaningless design." And it is to Western domination that he attributes this unhappy state of things. British commercial policy directed to reversing the flow of textiles which at the beginning of the nineteenth century had been from India to Europe, was not only successful in achieving the end which it had in view, but resulted at the same time in debauching the taste of the people of India in dyed and printed goods. The beautiful Indian printed cottons of Madras disappeared before an avalanche of cheap machine-made goods from Manchester, ornamented with perfectly meaningless decoration such as rows of bicycles or pictures of bank notes. With equally disastrous results the British Government introduced into the country their own particular fancy in architectural style. By producing cheap and inferior carpets in their jails they inflicted irreparable injury upon the trade in good carpets; and they set up a series of art schools whose influence, whatever their intention, can only be described as pernicious. More serious than the actual direct influence of British domination upon the art of the country have been the changes in Indian taste and ideas, resulting from "a century of education, entirely false in aims and method". Native states no longer give employment to the hereditary builders[1]; for the individual Indian

[1] This is no longer altogether true.

an echo of the English suburban villa has become the architectural ideal; carpets from Brussels are purchased in preference to the products of Indian looms; Indian costume is discarded in favour of the clothes of Europe; the makers of Khincobs and kindred materials have discarded designs which are the outcome of centuries of evolution in favour of others culled from pattern books designed for English wall-papers.[1]

The cry is the same as that uttered by Mr. C. R. Das—India is losing her individuality through a vain and sycophantic mimicry of an alien race. "In the opinion of thinking men it must appear that it is not worth while being a nation at all, or making any attempts at political freedom, if India is to remain in the end thus enslaved at heart by purely material ideals. The national movement has no justification if it does not carry with it some hope of a new manifestation of the Indian genius in relation to the real things of life." Much more might be quoted; but the student interested in the subject will prefer to turn to the original works. Suffice it to say that a perusal of them can lead to no other conclusion than that arrived at and stated by Dr. Coomaraswamy himself, that the unrest which is permeating educated India "is a struggle for spiritual and mental freedom from the domination of an alien ideal", and that it is "not so much the material as the moral and spiritual subjection of Indian civilisation that in the end impoverishes humanity".[2]

The modern school of painting in Bengal has been brought into being by the same forces which have inspired the writings quoted above. It was founded by two cultured members of a famous

[1] In the above paragraph I have given a brief résumé of Dr. Coomaraswamy's indictment which is set forth at length in an essay entitled "The Influence of Modern Europe on Indian Art".

[2] Preface to a volume entitled "Essays in National Idealism".

Bengali family, the brothers Mr. Goganendra Nath and Dr. Abanindra Nath Tagore, C.I.E., nephews of the great Bengali writer of world-wide reputation. It is interesting to recall the fact that these two artists, now generally recognised as the founders of the modern Bengali school of painting, were at this time ignorant—so they have informed me—of the tradition and formulæ embodied in the Ṣilpa Ṣastras, the Indian classic on fine art. Yet impelled by a curious spiritual *malaise* they embarked upon the work which was so soon to bear fruit. It was as though deep down in the sub-conscious regions of their being the instinct of the old Indian masters was striving to find expression. The atmosphere amid which they worked may be gathered from a description of them given by an acute observer, as aiming at the development of an indigenous school of imaginative painting stimulated by their own example and by the study of the legends of Sanskrit literature.[1] In the family residence of the Tagores in Dwarka Nath Tagore Lane in Calcutta, they gathered round them a group of artists, many of whom—Nanda Lal Bose, O. C. Ganguli, Khsitindra Nath Mazumdar, Asit Kumar Haldar, Surendra Nath Kar, and Mukul Chandra Dey, to mention but a few—have since made names for themselves as exponents of the modern school of Indian painting. The studio where this interesting circle met was described by the same observer as being not so much a school for the encouragement of indigenous art as a place for the development of taste, for the cultivation of a sense of beauty, a love of beautiful things, especially such beautiful things as are expressive of the mind of India in its evolution.

The significance of these developments was at

[1] Mr. W. Hornell, C.I.E., at that time Director of Public Instruction in Bengal.

once fastened upon and made matter for comment by a political writer in Chandanagore, a town which, owing to its being beyond British jurisdiction, became a convenient and favourite resort of the Bengali revolutionaries. In illustration of his assertion that the reaction against the Europeanisation of India, which was inspiring all patriotic Indians, was already at work in literature and art, he quoted the formation of the Tagore school. "In Bengal the national spirit is seeking to satisfy itself in art, and for the first time since the decline of the Moghuls a new school of national art is developing itself—the school of which Abanindra Nath Tagore is the founder and master."[1]

No commentator indeed was necessary to interpret the meaning of these developments. To any one who took the trouble to trace back the sequence of events from causes, it was sufficiently apparent that the sources from which the revolutionary movement and the Tagore school of painting draw their inspiration were identical. It was equally obvious that while both were manifestations of the same spirit, the one called for the severest condemnation, while the other was worthy of all praise.

Quite apart from the interest which the new school possessed for me from the point of view from which the above has been written, it merited serious attention on the score of the actual work which it was turning out. There had been formed in Calcutta in 1907 an association of Indian and European gentlemen under the title of the "Indian Society of Oriental Art", the objects of which were the cultivation among its members and the promotion among the public of a knowledge of all branches of ancient and modern oriental art, and it was under the auspices of this

[1] From a pamphlet published by Manindra Nayak in 1917.

society that the work of the Tagore school had been exhibited annually to the public. As was the case with so many enterprises of a like nature, the activities of the society were checked somewhat by preoccupations arising out of the War; and the conclusion of hostilities seemed to provide a suitable opportunity for an appreciable step forward. I accordingly consulted leading members of the society, and as a result certain steps were taken with a view to giving it a more assured position and to widening somewhat the scope of its activities. With the assistance of a Government grant the society secured for the school suitable accommodation for a studio and a lecture hall; eminent exponents of the new school were engaged as teachers, and scholarships for indigent pupils were provided. A series of lectures was planned, and the publication of an art journal under the title of *Rupâm* (Form) arranged for. This reorganisation was explained at a gathering held at Government House on December 4th, 1919, at which recent works of a number of artists of the new school were on view, and an address, in part descriptive and in part critical of the new movement, was given by Mr. O. C. Ganguli, himself an accomplished artist and a discerning art critic.

Since the movement may be said to have reached a definite stage and to have firmly established itself, Mr. Ganguli's summing up of its aims and its achievements possesses a special interest. He began by calling attention to the greater tolerance and breadth of vision now characterising the standards of æsthetic criticism in Europe, due largely to the challenge flung at the claim of the artistic canons of Europe based on Greco-Roman traditions to finality, by the art-forms of Japan. And he went on to show how the discovery by the art critics of Europe and

America, that the Japanese school of painting was entitled to a recognised place in the art of the world, led them to revise preconceived ideas of the value of Indian art. From the Indian point of view the most important consequence of this change in the attitude of the art critics of the West, was the admission that artistic expression need not necessarily take effect through a scientifically complete representation of natural appearances, and that the most fantastic and unreal artistic forms may be the vehicle through which great and noble human feelings may adequately express themselves. A change, indeed, since the days when Mr. Ruskin declared of Indian art that it wilfully and resolutely opposed itself to all the facts and forms of nature ; that it either formed its compositions out of meaningless fragments of colour and flowings of line, or, if it represented any living creature, it did so under some distorted and monstrous form.[1]

And since in these days of rapid and unceasing intercommunication no body of men practising any particular profession in any particular part of the world can remain wholly unresponsive to external stimulus, this altered view-point of the art critics of the West has reacted favourably upon the new school. For the new school is consciously and intentionally idealistic. It is the avowed intention of its masters to escape from " the photographic vision, and to secure an introspective outlook on things which take one away from the material objectives of life to a rarefied atmosphere of beauty and romance. Instead of busying themselves with recording the superficial aspects of phenomena, they have worked with a deeper motive and a profounder suggestion,

[1] See "The Renaissance in India", by James H. Cousins, which contains an instructive essay entitled " Ruskin, the Indian Race and Indian Art ".

seeking to wean the human mind from the obvious and the external reality of the sense, disdaining to imitate nature for its own sake, and striving to find significative forms to suggest the formless Infinity which is hidden behind the physical world of forms." They have sought, that is to say, to maintain the distinctive and essential characteristic of ancient Indian art, and Mr. Ganguli thinks that they were right, therefore, when they adopted the traditional methods of Indian painting as a basis of their experiments. This necessity for studying and absorbing all the qualities of the traditional craft was responsible for a certain absence of originality in the early days of the movement. But its leaders realised that a period of gestation, characterised by imitation rather than creation, was inevitable before they could acquire the power of developing the old craft on new lines, if those new lines were to be in continuation of and in perfect consistency with its history and genius, and it was certainly not from any failure to realise the importance of evolving new forms of expression that they modelled themselves so closely upon works of the past. Mr. Ganguli's conclusion is that the school is still in a stage of transition. "It is undoubtedly inspired by national memories, but is hardly yet pulsating with the throb of modern aspirations." He seems to think that, generally speaking, the artists have held too much aloof from the more modern currents permeating Indian life. "They find no inspiration in modern Indian life, in its new attitudes and gestures, in its new environments and settings and its new occupations. The subjects which at first attracted them were almost entirely mythological scenes and legends from the national epics and popular folklores." In one respect he thinks they have been unsuccessful in upholding with any degree of courage the traditions of the older Indian schools; and by their failure to resort to the bright and pure colour schemes which were so pronounced a feature of the Moghul and Rajput schools, "have undoubtedly missed one of the chief characteristics of Indian pictorial art". But despite such criticisms, he concedes that a good deal has been achieved. The movement has already succeeded in bringing about a little revolution in public taste, while "the most critical views are agreed in admitting that the productions of the school have been inspired by a genuine respect for Indian sentiments and moods, and have succeeded in presenting Indian subjects in the true atmosphere of Indian thought and setting". He thinks that it has not only been successful in reviving the spirit of old Indian art, but has in many cases added its own contributions to the old stock. "And apart from its present achievements, its promises are more valuable, as its possibilities are many and diverse."

The future of the movement will undoubtedly be watched with ever-increasing sympathy and interest by all who believe in, and are well-wishers of, the Indian renaissance. Among them are many Englishmen. It gives me unbounded pleasure to bear testimony to the welcome which many Indian gentlemen, whose patriotism is beyond suspicion, are ready to extend to Englishmen who are sincerely desirous of co-operating with them. Yet I feel bound to add that the task of the Englishman anxious to work for a *rapprochement* between East and West is not always an easy or encouraging one. The extreme sensitiveness of a section of those Indians, whose pride in and affection for their country and all that it stands for in their eyes is strong, tends to make them suspicious of an Englishman's motives. An example of this was forthcoming in connection with the grant which I had secured for the school from Government. I had purposely arranged for the grant to be made free of conditions of any kind, lest it might be thought that Government was seeking to obtain a hold over the movement.

Nevertheless my action immediately became suspect in certain quarters, and these feelings found expression in the editorial columns of the *Modern Review*, an admirably conducted periodical of great merit with a wide circulation throughout Bengal and, indeed, beyond it. It was a mistake on the part of those interested to have accepted assistance from Government—so ran the argument. While admitting that I had laid stress upon the fact that the acceptance of the grant involved neither official inspection, interference nor control, the writer feared that it might, nevertheless, lead to a sense of obligation on the part of the school which in its turn might induce a conscious or unconscious deference to the official or European view of what Indian culture is or means, or ought to be or mean. To that extent, he thought, the recipients of the grant would prove subject to official or European influence. "We are subjected to European and official dominance, pressure and influence," he concluded, "in almost all spheres of life from so many directions that we could wish that the centre of Indian culture were located even in a hut, rather than that it should be subject to any kind of non-Indian obligation and influence."[1] The attitude here taken up is of interest as showing how deeply the antagonism arising out of the clash of ideals has permeated the minds of some at least of those who have been affected by it. Nothing but sustained effort and imperturbable patience will remove it.

[1] *Modern Review* for January 1920.

CHAPTER XV

INDIAN MONISM

THE idealism which permeates the art of India is but a reflection of her thought. Her sculptors and her painters have given expression in form and colour to that which her great thinkers have clothed with words. In her art and her philosophy alike one sees her favourite standpoint from which to approach the riddle of the universe. In common with idealists elsewhere, she has denied reality to the outward things brought to notice by the senses and in her search for ultimate reality has turned her gaze inwards. Starting from the premise that the world we see is, in fact, but a world of appearance, and consequently lacks reality, she has trodden a path which the average Westerner finds difficulty in following and which leads to a conclusion at once so daring and so bewildering, that he recoils from it as from something which is palpably absurd.

It is, indeed, startling to be told that individual man is God — not a personal God with attributes such as the God of theism, but the incomprehensible God of Absolutism ; that which is without qualities, attributes or limitations of any kind ; that which is both being and non-being ; that of which it can only be said that it is, " not so, not so " ; the One without a second ; the universal, eternal and only subject ; the knower that cannot be known, the seer that cannot be seen; the sum total of all reality and, therefore, the only reality. It is sufficiently difficult for the human mind to grasp any abstract idea such as that of time and eternity or of space and infinity, and there is no need to lay stress upon the impossibility of visualising Brahman, or the Absolute, of Indian monism. Yet an attempt to understand the conception must be made, for it is this overwhelming idea that is in the words of Mr. B. C. Pal, which I have quoted in the prologue of this volume, "the one everlasting and pre-historic fact in the life story" of the Hindu people, and it is this same idea that is to be "the corner stone of the new Indian nation".

The earliest indication of the great central idea of Indian speculative thought, namely, the singleness of all reality, involving the jettisoning of what may be described as the common sense or empirical point of view, that the things which we touch and see are in fact what they appear to us to be, is to be found in the Rig-Veda itself, the earliest of all the records of the Indo-Aryan people. It is therein stated that the poets give many names to that which is one only. At a later period, but still before the birth of Buddha, and therefore more than five hundred years before our era, the idea here tentatively put forward was developed in the Upanishads—that part of the whole body of Vedic literature which was devoted to metaphysics. The Upanishads themselves present no small difficulty on account of the variety and the contradictory nature of the ideas which they contain. It is not as if they were ordinary treatises propounding the theories of individuals or of particular schools of thought. Rather must they be regarded as the gradual accretions of a whole epoch of speculation, and in particular of the period between the wandering of the Aryan immigrants in the Ganges Valley and the rise of Buddhism, probably from 1000 to 500 B.C. Through all these speculations one sees the evolution of this great central idea—whence and however it arose—that all reality is one.

This rare product of the human mind did not flower without a struggle. It would, indeed, have been remarkable if an idea so contrary to experience had stood unchallenged. Subtle and penetrating though the minds of these early thinkers were, they nevertheless had constantly forced upon them the empirical point of view, derived from their daily contact with the world around them. Idealism and realism were in perpetual conflict, and out of the clash of these two conceptions which fought for the possession of men's minds came pantheism—the faith with which so large a portion of the India of to-day is credited. This is easy to understand. If, as the idealists maintained, the one and only reality was God (Brahman), and if, as man's daily experience assured him, the universe was ever present, tangible, refusing to be dismissed as a figment of his imagination, then God and the universe must be one; the latter must be a particular aspect of the former. In other words, the two were merely different names for the same thing.

Such were the main, though by no means the only conflicting, ideas which went to the making of the Upanishads. But the difficulty of steering a clear course through the Upanishads and the later works known as Sûtras is not due to the character of their matter only, but also to their form. Language was fashioned by man for the purpose of giving expression to his thoughts. A particular mode of thought gave birth to a particular form of language; and it would be unreasonable to expect, therefore, that the thought

—and particularly the speculative thought—of one race of men should not undergo some change in appearance when divested of its native costume and presented in a foreign garb. The thought produced in my mind by any particular passage of English will scarcely be identical with the thought produced in the mind of the ancient Aryan three thousand years ago by a corresponding passage of archaic Sanskrit, however technically accurate may have been the translation from the one language to the other. This difficulty is enhanced by reason of the fact that the literature of those early days—if we may use the word in this connection—was mnemonic. That is to say it was oral and not written. The necessity for having to commit to memory vast treatises in prose gave rise to a sort of oral shorthand, which developed into a recognised type of literature known as Sûtras—strings of terse aphorisms in which everything was sacrificed to brevity and condensation. The most remarkable example of achievement in this direction is probably the famous Sanskrit grammar of Panini, still studied in the tôls in many parts of India. This work, which deals exhaustively with the whole Sanskrit language, is so highly condensed that it can be printed in thirty-five small octavo pages.

It was in this style that the philosophic doctrine of the Upanishads first appeared in a systematised form, under the title of the Uttara Mîmâm̱sâ, or Vedanta Sûtras of Bâdarâyaṉa. Here the straining after conciseness has been so great that the work, though purporting to be one of exegesis, has proved to be more of the nature of a conundrum. The most essential words, according to their translator, Dr. Thibaut, are habitually dispensed with, nothing being more common than the omission of the subject or predicate of a sentence. Hence there arose a number of commentators; and it is in the commentary of the great theologian Sankara of the eighth century A.D. that the idealistic monism of India has found its most complete expression. The literal translation of the opening sûtras of the Uttara Mîmâṃsâ runs as follows:

1. Then therefore the inquiry into Brahman.
2. From which the origin, etc., of this.
3. From its being the source of Scripture.
4. But that because it is connected as their support.
5. On account of seeing is not it is not founded on Scripture.

The English translation of Sankara's commentary on these five cryptic utterances covers approximately forty-three large octavo pages of print. And it is not surprising to find that Sankara is but one of many commentators, or that the commentators themselves differ fundamentally as to the meaning of the texts which they claim to interpret. It is no part of my intention to discuss the question whether the interpretation of Sankara is the correct one. Whether it is or not, it undoubtedly meets with the acceptance of an important section of the Hindus themselves, and it is wholly congenial to the idealistic trend of Indian thought.

What then is the monistic (advaita) doctrine of the Vedanta as expounded by Sankara and his disciples? It is the elaboration of two famous aphorisms culled from the Upanishads, "Tat tvam asi" ("Thou art that"), and "Neti, neti" ("Not so, not so"). "Sa ya eshonima aitadatmyam idam sarvam tat satyam sa atma tat tvam asi Svetaketu" ("He that is the essence of Your Soul, He is the truth, He is the Self. Thou art that, O Svetaketu!").[1] "That" is equiva-

[1] From the Khândogya Upanishad, in which a young man, Svetaketu, is instructed by his father, Uddalaka.

lent to God. Thou art That; thou art God. And what of God? Can we form any conception of God? Christianity affirms the invisibility of God, for "no man hath seen God at any time".[1] The Vedantin is at pains to demonstrate not merely the invisibility, but the absolute unknowableness of God. We can form no conception of God, for if he is, indeed, the essence of our soul, the Self of ourself, the ultimate subject, it is clear that he cannot be objectified, for could he the ultimate subject be objectified, there would be no subject left to sustain an object. And if God cannot be objectified, and the Self within you is God, it follows that you cannot objectify your Self. Try to picture yourself dead. What do you see? Your body lying inanimate? Yes; but is the body the Self? And if so, who is it in your mental picture who perceives the dead body? Is it not your Self? You cannot picture your perceiving Self lying lifeless along with your body, for you cannot objectify yourself. "Thou canst not see the seer of seeing, thou canst not hear the hearer of hearing, thou canst not know the knower of knowledge, he is thy soul that is within all. In truth, Oh Gargi, the imperishable one sees but is not seen, hears but is not heard, knows but is not known. Beside him there is none that sees, beside him there is none that hears, beside him there is none that knows."[2]

Indeed the thoroughgoing advaitin is compelled by inexorable logic to go even further. If the ultimate reality is One without a second, there can be no object, *i.e.* no cognisable entity, since this involves duality—subject on the one hand and object on the other. And if there is no object it necessarily follows that there can be no

[1] The Gospel according to St. John, i. 18.
[2] Yâg̱ñavalkhya in the Bṛihadâraṇyaka Upanishad.

subject either, since to predicate a "knower" is to postulate something to be known.

If then there is in reality neither subject nor object, is not the Vedantin driven into acceptance of the doctrine of universal nihilism of the Sûnyavâda Buddhists who look for salvation in non-entity, and so postulate behind all phenomena a universal and eternal void? At first sight it may seem so. But Sankara, basing himself upon the 26th sûtra of pada II. of the second adhyaya of the sûtras of Bâdarâyaṉa—"Entity does not spring from non-entity, as it is not observed"—hotly contests this conclusion. And we find, therefore, that the ultimate reality of the Vedanta is, strictly speaking, neither non-entity nor a knowing subject, but knowingness, *i.e.* not a subject of which intelligence is an attribute, but pure intelligence itself. Brahman is also "being," since being connotes reality, and it is also said of him that he is pure bliss. The meaning of the word bliss in this connection is difficult to fathom. It is a state wholly unrelated to desire or the fulfilment of desire, and is likened to the state experienced by the spirit when a man is sunk in deep, dreamless sleep. What that state may be cannot be known, since the awakened man has no recollection of it, and if for this reason we put it down as mere insentience, we come perilously near to the void of the Ṣûnyavâdins. In so far, then, as Brahman can be described positively at all, he is said to be Sat-chit-ananda, pure being, pure intelligence, pure bliss. And since, for the reasons set forth above, this is to predicate something without attributes the Vedantin seizes hold of the aphorism from the Upanishads, and declares of Brahman, in respect of every conceivable description, "neti, neti" ("not so, not so").

Many consequences flow from these premises.

It is no doubt difficult, and possibly misleading, to picture that which is beyond time, space and causality by analogy with that which lies within these categories. But since the human mind itself is of the latter there is no choice. To obtain an idea, therefore, of the nature of the world according to the advaita Vedanta, one may regard it as that which is experienced in a dream. In a vivid dream people with all the appearance of reality, move and act in an apparently real world. Stage and actors alike appear to have an existence independent of the dreamer. And it is only when we wake up that we realise that they had no real existence apart from our own perceiving mind. Now conceive a single perceiving mind as the sole existing reality, and this manifold universe as nothing but the dream of such an one, and you have the nearest approximation in terms of time and space to the answer given by the advaita Vedanta to the riddle of the universe. If the analogy be pursued, it follows that when the dreamer wakes this manifold universe, and we with it, will fade away, for it has no independent existence apart from the one perceiving mind. The dream of our individual experience is but a dream within a dream. And that is precisely what the Vedanta holds. We are the perceiving mind—tat tvam asi—only our eyes are blinded by ignorance, and we do not realise the truth. So long as we remain in ignorance we shall grope our way wearily from life to life, caught up inextricably in the unending revolutions of the cycle of dream existence (saṃsara). And it is only when the scales fall from our eyes and the ignorance is dispelled, when we know—not merely say, which is quite a different thing—that there is but One reality without a second, and that we are indeed, therefore, that One, that heaven and earth shall pass away, and with them the whole vast fabric of this strange figment which presents itself to us as the universe.

It will be seen that the most stupendous consequences rest upon this blindness of ours (avidya), no less, indeed, than the heavens above and the earth beneath and the waters under the earth and all that therein is. And the question which naturally presents itself is, What is the nature of this ignorance and how did it arise? The word used by Sankara to denote both the state of ignorance and its cause, is maya, which is usually translated by the word illusion. This meaning is, however, a subject of controversy, and is said by some Vedantins to be misleading. Its use is challenged by the late Swami Vivekananda, one of the best known of modern exponents of advaita. Maya, according to him, is a statement of facts—of what we are and what we see around us. In other words it does not purport to provide an explanation of the phenomenal universe, but is merely a name for the world of experience, or nature, or to put it rather differently, for everything which is conditioned by time, space and causality. From the point of view of the Vedantin, however, this seems to come to much the same thing; and if by the word illusion is understood "a perception which is misinterpreted", there appears to be little reason to quarrel with its use, for to the Vedantin the world of experience is reality misinterpreted. Moreover, elsewhere the Swami himself with reference to the word maya, has declared that the whole universe is the apparent evolution of God, and in illustration of his meaning has quoted a simile well known in Vedanta literature, namely, that of a rope and a snake, where the former is mistaken for the latter. The person who mistakes the rope for a snake is convinced that what he sees is, indeed, a snake. Yet the rope, comments the Swami, "is changed into a snake only apparently; and *when the delusion ceases* the snake vanishes". The italics are mine. In another passage he explains that the Self appears as the manifold universe because we are "deluded by the mirage of personality. Having eyes we must see the apparent". But the apparent is like a screen that hides the Self which is unchanging. "When the screen is wholly removed we find that it really never existed." If it never existed, and we only thought that it did, it is surely no misuse of language to say that it was an illusion. And I think that it is correct to say that in the case of the generality of advaitist Vedantins, the word maya creates in the mind a picture of the universe as we see it with an explanatory footnote attached to the effect that while it possesses a relative reality, it is in fact an appearance without substance which on the fulfilment of certain conditions, namely, a realisation of the identity of the individual self with Brahman, will pass away and will be known never to have had any real existence at all. And after all a little reflection will show that ultimately this amounts to very much the same thing as the Christian doctrine voiced by St. Paul, that the things which are seen, *i.e.* the phenomenal universe, are temporal, *i.e.* relatively real only; but that the things which are not seen are eternal, *i.e.* absolutely real.[1]

To say so much, however, is merely to offer a conjecture as to the nature of the universe—to state that it is not the thing of substance which we ordinarily take it to be. And so far we need find little difficulty in accompanying the Vedantin, for though we may not be able to perceive that the world is unsubstantial, illusory, a misinterpretation by our understanding—being ourselves

[1] See 2 Corinthians, iv. 18.

part of the illusion, how could we ?—yet intellectually we can conceive that this may be so. It is otherwise when we come to grapple with the much more formidable problem how—the sole reality being Brahman—this misinterpretation can ever have arisen. If I am, indeed, Brahman the unconditioned Absolute, how came it about that I ever ceased to be conscious of my Brahmanhood ? Whence did this mist of ignorance descend upon my understanding ? How was it caused ? An answer to this question is obviously of supreme importance, and it is well worth while endeavouring to discover the answer which the thought of India has evolved.

CHAPTER XVI

A PROBLEM FOR THE PUNDITS

I ONCE laid the problem which is propounded at the close of the previous chapter before a convocation of the Sanskrit scholars of Eastern Bengal. " My difficulty ", I said, " arises when I ask how, if the sole reality is Brahman, did this ignorance occur ? I have read somewhere that it is stated in one of the Upanishads—the Maitrâyaṉa, I think—that Brahman entered the world of duality because he wished to taste both truth and illusion. But this, surely, involves a contradiction in terms since it imposes a limitation upon the Absolute. It amounts, surely, to nothing more than this—that you deny with one breath that which you have just affirmed with another. You associate the quality of desire with that which you predicate to be without attributes. This, then, is the question to which I seek an answer—how did the illusion of the phenomenal universe arise ? "

To this question I received a number of replies, which if they failed to satisfy, at least bore witness to the widespread interest taken in India in philosophic speculation, and brought into prominence the fascinating subtlety of the Indian mind. They also showed that different interpretations are given by Indians themselves to such terms as maya, avidya, and so on. Of this more presently.

The explanation quoted from the Maitrâyaṉa Upanishad along with other similar explanations such as, Brahman found himself alone without a second, and desiring to see himself in all his glory contrived maya as a mirror that should reflect him, was brushed aside as mere illustration to meet the requirements of minds of limited understanding.

So far the ground was common. Then there were those who admitted the main postulates in the problem as stated above—that Brahman is One without a second, that the world of experience is, therefore, unreal in the sense that Brahman is real; that the fact that it appears to be real is due to maya or avidya, that is, ignorance or false knowledge; and finally, that since ignorance can be destroyed by knowledge, the world of experience can be dissolved—seen to be unreal—which, looked at from the point of view of the individual, means that salvation or escape from the cycle of existence can be achieved. This last conclusion was reached by Sankara—though according to some as a result of false reasoning, as I shall presently show.

The discussion of the problem arising from these data provided a congenial field for the exercise of the peculiar genius of the Indian mind. The various replies which I received reached me for the most part in the form of essays. Many of them contained much common matter though often presented in different garbs. I can best present their substance to the reader by throwing it into the form of a dialogue between my correspondents whom I will designate pundit, and myself under the title of inquirer.

Pundit. You ask how did this maya, or ignorance, which is the cause of the phenomenal universe, arise? I reply that it did not arise, for it is without beginning.

Inquirer. You say that maya is without beginning? Then it is eternal, and must also be without end, so that it cannot be destroyed, and if this is so, how can salvation be achieved?

Pundit. I said that maya is beginningless, but I did not say that it is without end. On the contrary, it has an end.

Inquirer. What, is it possible that that which is without beginning may have an end? Can you refer me to any single thing that is without beginning but which has an end?

Pundit. That is not difficult. Consider for a moment any common object, such as an earthen jar or a piece of cloth.

Inquirer. I am doing so.

Pundit. Did not the previous non-existence of the earthen jar come to an end at the moment of its creation?

Inquirer. That is so.

Pundit. And was not its previous non-existence without beginning?

Inquirer. I must admit that it was.

Pundit. Is it not, then, true to say of any created thing that its previous non-existence is without beginning but has an end?

Inquirer. I can only remain silent in face of an ingenuity which baffles all comment. But I would ask for enlightenment on a further point. If Brahman is One without a second, how can it be said that there is such a thing as maya at all? If maya is real, must it not be second to Brahman?

Pundit. Maya is neither real nor is it unreal.

Inquirer. That sounds like a contradiction. Please explain it to me.

Pundit. Do you admit that before a thing can be destroyed it must exist?

Inquirer. Certainly.

Pundit. Do you admit that ignorance is destroyed by knowledge?

Inquirer. I do.

Pundit. Then it follows that maya exists, for it is destroyed by knowledge.

Inquirer. That surely is self-evident ; nor did I ever deny that such a thing as ignorance exists or may exist, for I cannot form any conception in my mind, surely, of anything which does not or may not exist or has not existed. Is not the mere fact that I can think of a thing proof in itself that it does or can exist ?

Pundit. By no means, for if that were so the conjuring up in your mind of such notions as a " hare's horn " or " the child of a barren woman " would prove the existence of such things.

Inquirer. We are agreed that ignorance or maya exists. It is also maintained that Brahman is one without a second, and it would seem, therefore, that maya must be identical with Brahman ?

Pundit. Such an idea cannot be entertained, because if that were so, the destruction of maya by knowledge would involve the destruction of Brahman also. And this is impossible, for it is knowledge of Brahman which destroys maya.

Inquirer. It seems that I have been driven to admitting that maya has an existence, that its existence is not apart from Brahman, and yet that it is not identical with Brahman, which seems to be contrary to sound logic. Can you throw any light upon this puzzle ?

Pundit. Have you by chance, when travelling across a desert, seen stretches of water, deep, cool and refreshing, shimmering in the sunlight ?

Inquirer. I have. And I have found that after all the water which seemed so real was but a mirage.

Pundit. And it was true to say that the mirage existed ?

Inquirer. I grant it.

Pundit. But the mirage ceased to exist when

you realised that the only reality was in fact the desert ? In other words, the mirage which had the desert for its *locus* was destroyed by your knowledge of the desert ?

Inquirer. I confess that it was so.

Pundit. And was the desert affected in the smallest degree by the existence of the mirage ?

Inquirer. It cannot be said that it was.

Pundit. Then is it not conceivable that maya exists, that it has Brahman for its *locus*, that it is destroyed by knowledge of Brahman, and that Brahman is indifferent to and wholly unaffected by it, or, to put it differently, that Brahman is One without a second ?

Inquirer. On the analogy of the mirage and the desert that would seem to be so. But just as the mirage has no real existence, does it not follow that maya has no real existence ?

Pundit. You have already admitted in the course of our discussion that it has existence. And now you are equally satisfied that it has no real existence. You have, therefore, accepted what I started by saying of maya, namely, that it is neither real nor is it unreal. You were right in saying that the mirage was an illusion, or reality misinterpreted, and, so, that it was not real. Yet you would be equally right in saying that the mirage *as such* was real. And from this you will perceive the wisdom of the Hindus, who characterise truth as absolute and relative. Relative truth is not the whole truth, but it possesses, nevertheless, the essence of truth.

In brief, the reply here given to the question asked is that the illusion of the phenomenal universe is without beginning, and therefore without cause. And to the obvious objection that this is equivalent to setting up maya as a principle co-equal and co-eternal with Brahman—

the One without a second—it is replied that this is not so, because the phenomenal universe is a misinterpretation of Brahman, just as the mirage is a misinterpretation of the desert. When further one asks by what is this misinterpretation caused, and one is told by ignorance (avidya), which, in its turn, is caused by, if it is not identical with, maya, one realises that one is wandering impotently in a maze of words, returning always to the point from which one started. And when I had sought a way out in vain, I was taken kindly by the hand and mildly chided, and told that it is only the great souls—Mahatmas—who, by austerity of life and profound and disinterested meditation succeed in transcending the bounds of time, space and desire, can understand these things. For the ordinary man to attempt to fathom the dark mystery of avidya by the light of his limited intellect is comparable to the case of a man who sets out to see darkness by means of a far-shining torch. And I was told that far from regretting it, I should rather rejoice that I had failed to discover an answer to the question, " How did the illusion of the phenomenal universe arise ? " or, to phrase it somewhat differently, " How has the Absolute become the relative ? " Since, had I done so, the Infinite and Unfathomable Being would have become measurable and fathomable by my limited human understanding. For, supposing we knew the answer, would the Absolute then remain ? Assuredly not. It would have become the relative. What is meant by knowledge in the vocabulary of common sense ? Anything that becomes limited by our own mind, we know ; but when a thing remains beyond our mind, we do not know it. Now if the Absolute becomes limited by the mind it is no longer the Absolute at all ; it has immediately become finite. Everything when limited by the mind becomes finite. Therefore to know the Absolute is again a contradiction in terms. That is why this question has never been answered, because if it were answered there would no longer be any Absolute.[1]

The logic of the above exposition is unanswerable and the conclusion final. And in face of it all further speculation might reasonably be put out of court as futile. To the Hindu, however, the Vedanta is much more than an exercise in ratiocination. In India there has never been any clearly marked boundary separating off philosophy from religion. Both draw their inspiration from the same source, and that source is revelation, and not reason. Whatever our opinion may be as to the extent to which the contents of the Upanishads can legitimately be described as inspired, there is no question as to the opinion of India herself on the point. To her the whole of the Vedas—hymns, brahmanas, aranyakas and Upanishads—are ṣruti, that which was heard by the seers, in other words, that which has been made known to man by divine revelation. Here, then, was a foundation not open to question, and the task of the philosopher was the interpretation of that which was set forth in the ṣruti to which he turned as the final authority in framing replies to all the questions which arose out of his speculations. First, then, there was the inexorable assurance of the Upanishads as to the sole reality and absolute nature of Brahman. Against this there was the empirical certainty of the phenomenal universe which, refusing to be brushed aside, obtruded itself upon the attention of man at every turn, and was for ever challenging the pure idealism to which certain outstanding texts

[1] "G̲n̄āna Yoga", by Swami Vivekananda, p. 111. I have quoted the words of Swami Vivekananda because they state the case rather more elaborately than was done by my actual correspondent.

of the Upanishads inevitably gave rise. There was also the weakness of human nature—man's hopes and fears, the parents of his worship and his prayer, and his natural repugnance at any explanation of the world of his experience as either an anonymous and soulless mechanism, or the unsubstantial figment of deluded fancy. There were, too, the inconsistencies and contradictions of the scriptures themselves. And out of all these things there arose, side by side with the philosophic idealism which is so marked a characteristic of Indian thought, the elements of a distinct theism which wove themselves, often incongruously enough, into the very warp of the idealism out of antagonism to which they themselves may be said to have arisen.

"Who is Īsvara, *i.e.* the Personal God?" asks Swami Vivekananda. And he replies, quoting from the Hindu scriptures, that he is "the Eternal, the Pure, the Almighty, the All-knowing, the All-merciful", and above all, "He the Lord is, of his own nature, inexpressible Love". And anticipating the question whether there are, then, two Gods—the Sat-chit-ananda of the philosopher, and the All-merciful God of Love of the bhakta (devotee), he adds that the Personal God worshipped by the bhakta is not separate or different from Brahman. "All is Brahman, the One without a second—only Brahman as unity, as the Absolute, is too much of an abstraction to be loved and worshipped, so the bhakta chooses the relative aspect of Brahman that is, Īsvara, the Supreme Ruler." And in further explanation he adds that "Īsvara is the highest manifestation of the Absolute reality or, in other words, the highest possible reading of the Absolute by the human mind".[1]

For the pure milk of the monistic doctrine one

[1] "Bhakti Yoga", pp. 17 and 18.

must turn to Sankara's famous commentary upon the sûtras of Bâdarâyaṉa. Then with a view to understanding how a philosophy which excludes prayer and worship can serve as a religion, one may turn to those who are adherents of the Vedanta system to-day.

CHAPTER XVII

THE LETTER OF THE VEDANTA

THE main outlines of the central theme propounded by Sankara in his famous commentary upon the Vedanta Sûtras, stand out in deep relief against a background of much wordy disputation. They have been set forth in the preceding chapter. There is but one ultimate reality—the absolute, undifferentiated, intelligent Brahman. All else possesses but a relative reality. The individual soul, if it but realised it, *is* Brahman. It only seems to be an individual soul on account of the limitations with which it is cumbered, and which, by cutting it off, as it were, from the universal, give it its individuality. But this individuality is apparent and not real because the limitations are due to ignorance—that is to say, to its failure to realise that it is Brahman. This idea is repeated over and over again, standing out clearly amid much that is tedious in the eight hundred and fifty-eight large octavo pages which are required to compass the English translation of the text and the commentary. And since there must be some cause for the empirical universe with its countless souls and its vast variety of animate and inanimate matter, and since Brahman is the sole reality, Brahman must be that cause. But Brahman is not affected thereby, for " as the magician is not at any time affected by the magical illusion produced by himself, because it is unreal, so the highest self (Brahman) is not affected by the world illusion ".[1]

This illusory world, however, which seems so real to us bound by the chains of ignorance, is a stubborn thing which insists on obtruding itself upon our thought and speculation however earnestly we may endeavour to brush it aside. And as one makes one's way through the long pages of argument and counter-argument by means of which Sankara seeks to establish his theory, one's grasp of the central conception is being perpetually shaken by the difficulties which keep cropping up in its way, and by the seeming contradictions and confusion of thought to which these difficulties give rise. At one time, for example, Sankara argues and proves to his own satisfaction that a S̲ûdra[2] is incapable of a knowledge of Brahman, on which knowledge a realisation of the unreality of the phenomenal universe depends. Certain consequences which seem to have escaped his attention follow necessarily from this conclusion, namely, that for the S̲ûdra *qua* S̲ûdra, it is the phenomenal universe that is the sole reality, since an ultimate reality of which *ex hypothesi* he can have no knowledge cannot, so far as he is concerned, be said to have any existence.

Another anomaly of a somewhat similar kind is provided by Sankara's dicta with regard to the beings occupying a higher place in the universe than man, *i.e.* the Gods. It is argued that the Lord of the Universe, a being corresponding to the God of theism, can have a knowledge of Brahman. It follows that he may, consequently, at any moment, realise his identity with Brahman, and

[1] Sankara's commentary adhyaya II., pada 1, sûtra 9.

[2] A man below the three great castes in the Hindu social scale which comprised the people of Aryan blood known as the " twice-born ". No one outside the charmed circle of the " twice-born " was permitted to attend the Vedic sacrifices or to hear the Vedas read. I have given a brief account of the caste system in " India: A Bird's-eye View ", p. 207 *et seq.*

so fade out of the phenomenal universe. But this, we deduce, does not, as a matter of fact, happen, because it is the Lord of the Universe who remains constant from one æon (kalpa) to another. And the succession of æons is infinite, the revolving cycles of the world of appearance being without beginning and without end. "Although ordinary animated beings do not, as we see, resume that form of existence which belonged to them in a former birth, still we cannot judge of the Lords as we do of ordinary beings." And one perpetually comes across passages in which the great central concept of the sole reality of Brahman seems to recede into the background, leaving one involved in the meshes of the manifold world as one finds it in ordinary experience. The word of the Veda, for example, is held by orthodox Hindus to be eternal, a contention, of course, which Sankara would never dream of disputing. It is heard by the prophets afresh at each succeeding creation—more properly according to Hindu ideas, re-manifestation—of the universe. But from this postulate certain consequences follow, namely, that each cyclic manifestation of the universe must be the same in kind as that which preceded it, and so on to infinity. Sankara accepts this. For him the universe evolves, reaches its farthest point of expansion, undergoes involution, is reabsorbed in Brahman and evolves again, the process being eternally repeated. And its nature is constant. "It is impossible to imagine", he says, "that in some new creation a sixth sense and a corresponding sixth sense-object should manifest themselves." If the whole thing is unreal, the figment of false knowledge, there does not seem to be any particular reason for the confidence with which this is asserted. But we here come across one of those passages which picture to us a universe in which all idea of its unreality is lost sight of. There is sketched out for us a marvellous scheme of things —the sun and moon and all the countless host of Heaven; men, animals and all forms of animate creation; the whole gamut of animate and inanimate existence as perceived by man, speeding eternally through time and space, evolving and involving rhythmically after the manner of the systole and diastole of the human heart. A universe, moreover, governed by Lords (Gods) who remain constant from one æon to another. A scheme of things in which a moral law is the determining factor, and in which "religious duty is enjoined and its opposite is forbidden in order that animate beings may obtain pleasure and escape pain", and in which "each new creation (at the beginning of each æon) is the result of the religious merit and demerit" of the previous cycle. A beginningless and endless procession of nights and days across the boundless background of Eternity. A scheme of things indisputably real to those engaged in the procession, and one, therefore, in which there is a God to whom to pray, deeds to be performed on which hangs that which is of supreme importance to the doer, namely, his future fate—a scheme of things wholly different in kind to the mazy shadow-show, the figment of false knowledge, which throughout the greater part of his famous work he sets himself to prove this world to be. Indeed at times he appears to reject idealism altogether, even the subjective idealism which many centuries later found so brilliant an exponent in the West in Bishop Berkeley. For he pours scorn upon the contention of those Buddhists who maintained that "no outward things exist apart from consciousness". The thing perceived and the idea of it are declared at the end of a long, argumentative dissertation to be distinct; and one finds it difficult to disabuse oneself of the belief that one is listening to the arguments of a thoroughgoing realist bent upon proving the existence of matter as a thing-in-itself. If the reader, in his attempt to maintain his grasp of the central conception, then turns to one of the many passages in which it is plainly set forth, he finds himself landed in a state of complete bewilderment. How, for example, is he to reconcile the attitude just described with Sankara's commentary upon the 22nd sûtra of the 1st pada of the 2nd adhyaya: "Moreover, as soon as, in consequence of the declaration of non-difference contained in such passages as 'that art thou', the consciousness of non-difference arises in us, the transmigratory state of the individual soul and the creative quality of Brahman vanish at once. . . . For that this entire apparent world, in which good and evil actions are done, etc., is a mere illusion . . . and does in reality not exist at all, we have explained more than once?" The only possible explanation seems to be that when Sankara asserts that the eternal world exists independently of our consciousness of it, he is thinking of it as Brahman—irrespective of our misinterpretation of Brahman, which results in it appearing to us as the manifold universe; and that when he is speaking of it as a mere illusion, it is exclusively our misinterpretation of Brahman that he has in mind.

But even this explanation does not enable us to escape from the difficulty which arises out of his constant assertion of the beginninglessness and endlessness of this misinterpretation—this shadow-show conjured up by Brahman by virtue of the magic wand of maya—an assertion which leaves us on the horns of an insoluble dilemma. For such an assertion amounts, surely, to an admission that there are two eternal verities, Brahman the magician and the empirical universe, which is the product of his magic. It is all very well to say that Brahman is not affected by the illusion which he disinterestedly produces, and that the realisation of Brahman and the consequent blotting out of the sensuous universe is within the grasp of the individual soul; but the fact remains that if the illusion itself is *eternal*, the assertion that it is unreal becomes meaningless.

A still greater difficulty confronts the student when he tries to reconcile the beginninglessness and endlessness of the empirical universe with the theory of the liberation of the individual. Liberation, or salvation, as defined by Sankara, is the intuitional realisation on the part of the individual that it is Brahman. It is when this intuitional realisation takes place that the phenomenal universe is seen to be unreal. But if this intuitional realisation can take place in one individual, it can occur in every individual, except, we must suppose, in a S̱ûdra. Supposing that this did, as a matter of fact, happen, what then would have become of the beginningless and endless illusion? For in course of time even the S̱ûdra would disappear, being got rid of by a process of elimination due to the fruit of works.[1]

Sankara is clearly conscious of some at least of these difficulties. And he seeks to get over them by declaring that knowledge is of two kinds, the higher knowledge which alone gives a realisation of Brahman, and the lower knowledge which is relative and not absolute, and as a result of which Brahman is not recognised as the Absolute, but appears as Ῑs̱vara, the Lord of the Universe. This theory, if it does not get over the difficulty last mentioned, at least opens the door to an almost unlimited field of speculation. The Vedantin who does not aspire beyond the lower

[1] For example, a meritorius life as a S̱ûdra would result in re-birth as a member of one of the twice-born castes.

knowledge finds a wide field for the play of his religious predilections. Brahman as seen through the veiled glass of the lower knowledge may appear as the Personal God of theism or the all-pervading spirit of Indian pantheism. The universally popular doctrine of Karma and transmigration can be accommodated. Sankara himself assigns to it an essential part in the scheme of things which prevails within the dominion of the lower knowledge. He does so, in particular, in dealing with the argument brought against him that Brahman cannot be the cause of the world, because if he were, the inequalities from which men suffer would prove him guilty of partiality, arbitrariness and injustice, whereas he is, *ex hypothesi*, without qualities. "Not so," he replies. "If the Lord on his own account produced this unequal creation he would expose himself to blame; but the fact is that in creating he is bound by certain regards; that is, he has to look to merit and demerit. Hence the circumstance of the creation being unequal is due to the merit and demerit of the living creatures created, and it is not a fault for which the Lord is to blame." This is, perhaps, one of the most difficult of all his assertions to follow. To begin with he is apparently speaking of the highest Brahman, *i.e.* the Absolute; and to predicate of the Absolute that he is bound by the relatively unreal merit or demerit of the relatively unreal creatures of the relatively unreal world seems to be the wildest of contradictions in terms. Moreover, the obvious objection at once presents itself that this is a postponement of, and not an answer to, the question. For if inequality is due to merit and demerit the question still remains to what are merit and demerit themselves due? This question is anticipated in the following **sûtra**: "If it be objected that it, viz. the Lord's having regard to merit and demerit, is impossible on account of the non-distinction of merit and demerit previous to the first creation, we refute the objection on the ground of the world being without a beginning".[1] And Sankara, in elaboration of the statement contained in the sûtra, adds that the objection would be valid if the world had a beginning; but that as it is without a beginning, merit and inequality are like seed and sprout, caused as well as causes, and there is no logical objection therefore to their operation. This, surely, is a disappointing answer to the question which of all questions has most insistently forced itself upon the mind of man.

It is possible, of course, to evade the difficulty by reminding the critic that since the phenomenal universe has no absolute reality, the highest Brahman is not really bound by any regards arising from it. This amounts to saying that in so far as Brahman appears to be bound by regards, it is Brahman as seen through the veil of nescience, *i.e.* Īsvara, Lord of the world; and its chief merit is, perhaps, that it admits the supremacy of the moral law in the realms of the lower knowledge.

It is all these problems of logic which bulk so large in Sankara's commentary, that make it difficult for the Western mind to appreciate the depth of the appeal which the Vedanta makes to the religiously minded Hindu. That the Vedanta is as much a religion as a philosophy in the eyes of its adherents I am convinced. And lest these pages in which I have tried to set forth the theory of the Vedanta as it strikes an average observer from the West should prove misleading in this respect, I feel bound to make an attempt to describe the nature of the religious appeal which it seems to me to make to the India of to-day.

[1] 35th sûtra of the 1st pada of the 2nd adhyaya.

CHAPTER XVIII

THE SPIRIT OF THE VEDANTA

If one wishes to understand the attitude of the Indian of to-day towards the Vedanta, one must take into account the existence of two deeply ingrained characteristics of the Hindu mind. The first is an implicit belief in Sruti, "that which is heard", *i.e.* the revealed word; and the second a certain curious inconsistency or something which is better described, perhaps, as an immense capacity for remaining unaffected by inconsistency of thought or action—a characteristic which, it may be observed incidentally, has proved a constant source of bewilderment and embarrassment to those engaged in the task of administration in India. Sankara has himself defined the attitude of the Hindu so far as the former characteristic is concerned in the following passage: "If it has been maintained that the scriptural passage enjoining thought on Brahman in addition to the mere hearing of the sacred texts treating of Brahman, shows that reasoning is also to be allowed its place, we reply that the passage must not deceitfully be taken as enjoining bare independent ratiocination, but must be understood to represent reasoning as a subordinate auxiliary of intuitional knowledge".[1] And he adds a little later that the Veda is the eternal source of knowledge, and that the perfection of

[1] Commentary on the 6th sûtra of the 1st pada of the 2nd adhyaya.

that knowledge which is founded on the Veda cannot be denied by any of the logicians of the past, present or future.

I had often come across examples of the second characteristic in everyday life, and I had discussed it with many people who, while admitting its existence, made no attempt to explain it. One Indian gentleman told me frankly that Hindus were not in the least troubled by contradictions where the teaching of the Vedanta was concerned. He quoted a sloka from the Īsopanishad—" That (the manifested one) is the whole. The whole takes its origin from the whole. If the whole is taken away from the whole, the whole remains as it has been "—and he commented as follows—" did you ever hear of such a thing that when ten is subtracted from ten, the result is ten? But this is what the Veda teaches us, and we believe it." And I do not think it is open to doubt that in the teaching of the Vedanta with all its difficulties and seeming contradictions, vast numbers of educated and cultured Hindus find that solace for which all thinking men yearn when they ponder upon the great mysteries of the here and the hereafter.

Not all Vedantins are monists. Far from it. There are many who read into the sûtras of Bâdarâyana a meaning differing widely from that given to them by Sankara. The name of Ramanuja stands second only to that of Sankara as a commentator. A Vaishnava of the twelfth century, he taught a less rigorous monism than Sankara, known technically as " qualified non-duality ", for which the authority of a long tradition prior to the actual production of the commentary is claimed. In Bengal a much more recent commentator, Srî Baladeva, has considerable vogue. A devout Vaishnava and follower of Srî Chaitanya, the famous prophet of Nadia, he is said to have written his commentary, to which he gave the title of "Govinda Bhashya", at the command of Lord Krishna at Brindaban. It gives a theistic interpretation of the sûtras. After what has been said as to the nature of sûtra literature, this wide diversity of interpretation will probably cause little surprise. Rai Bahadur Sris Chandra Basu, the translator of the "Govinda Bhashya", has expressed the opinion that the sûtras contain universal principles of religion and philosophy true for all times and ages, and that they were so constructed by Bâdarâyaṇa as to be of universal application and not confined to the exposition of any particular religion. And it is certainly the case that the term Vedanta, when used in its widest sense of the crown of the Vedas, *i.e.* the essence of the Vedic scriptures, covers a very wide field of religious and philosophic thought. And if one would catch anything of the spirit of the Vedanta at the present day, one must think of the term in its wider meaning rather than in its more restricted application to the interpretation of the sûtras associated with a particular school.

I have the vividest recollections of two visits paid to the "Garden of Meditation" of a great Indian nobleman. It might be said to correspond to the private chapel which is still a feature of some at least of the old landed estates of England. It was a large rectangular space cut off from the surrounding grounds and woods by high walls; and it was bathed in that atmosphere of mystic pantheism in which the Indian delights to bask, just as he does in the golden glory of his sunlit air. One felt here that God might be transcendent; but the idea more immediately present to one's mind was that of God Immanent. The spreading branches of a leafy tree, beneath which a small platform had been built, provided a bower for meditation; and often during those early hours of day, before the voice of nature is drowned by the din of man's activities, the noble owner repaired to it, to meditate amid these surroundings of harmony and repose upon the eternal mysteries which form the subject matter of the Vedanta. On all sides texts from the Upanishads selected by him have been graven upon the walls. At one end of the garden is a stretch of cool water, in the neighbourhood of which stand various shrines. In one stands a beautiful image of Buddha, beloved by the owner of the garden for the exalted code of conduct which he laid down for the guidance of man. In others repose the emblems of the mystery of the creation, the preservation and the destruction of the universe—the liṅga and the yoni of Shivaite symbology; and the mystic Aum (Om), the Sanskrit letters of white marble, themselves beautifully inlaid with symbolical figures in colour and gold, being let in to a panel of black stone. "Let a man meditate on the syllable Om"—thus the opening injunction of the Khândogya Upanishad, the purport of which is, as explained by Max Müller, to detail the various meanings which the syllable may assume in the mind of a devotee till at last the highest meaning is reached, namely, "that from whence", in the language of the Taittirîyaka Upanishad, "these things are born; that by which, when born, they live; that into which they enter at their death"; in other words, Brahman.

A short digression may be permitted here in explanation of the above definition of Brahman, because the particular episode in the Taittirîyaka Upanishad in which it occurs is quoted by modern Vedantins as a remarkable example of prescience, anticipating the main stages through which the higher thought of mankind has since passed.[1]

Brighu asks his father Varuna to teach him Brahman. Varuna tells him "that from whence these things are born, that by which when born they live, that into which they enter at their death, try to know that. This is Brahman." After meditating upon these words Brighu perceived that matter (or matter in the form of food) was Brahman, for from matter all things were produced, by matter (in the form of food) when born they lived, and into matter at death they entered. This theory is pointed to as clearly anticipating the materialism which was the outcome of the revolution in modern thought brought about by the writings of Charles Darwin. But Brighu was not satisfied by this first conclusion, and meditating further upon the matter he perceived that breath, or life, was Brahman; for from life all men are born, etc., thus anticipating the phase of thought known as vitalism. With further meditation this theory too was discarded, and Brighu perceived that mind was Brahman. The Sanskrit word here translated mind is *manas*, and means the highest sense organ which man possesses, *i.e.* the collecting station of all the sensations which reach him and the clearing-house of his ideas. It is neither man's self nor his power of reasoning. And this discovery made by Brighu amounts to this, that the universe consists of a variety of sensations—a form of idealism corresponding to the school of thought which goes under the name of sensationalism in the philosophic meaning of the word. But not even here did Brighu stop. From one thing he was led on to another, and in due course he per-

[1] Notably by the late Professor Benoyendra Nath Sen, and by Srî Arabinda Ghose. See four lectures published under the title of "The Intellectual Ideal" by the former, and a monograph entitled "Evolution" by the latter.

ceived that there was something higher than mind, and that was reason; and he then understood that this universe, governed as it is in all its aspects by rational law, is a manifestation of the sublime principle of Reason itself. Was there anything above and beyond reason? It seems that there was, and the final pinnacle to which Brighu attained is described in these words—"He performed penance. Having performed penance, he perceived that bliss is Brahman, for from bliss these things are born, by bliss when born they live; into bliss they enter at their death." What is meant by bliss? No explanation of the word Ananda (bliss) can be regarded as wholly satisfactory, for it has reference to that which transcends time, space and causality—the unfathomable mystery which lies beyond the range of human understanding. Let the Indian speak for himself. "We must remember that in the Upanishads we are in an atmosphere of pure intellect, so that we must guard ourselves against giving to the word bliss or joy the colouring and flavour it received when we pass into the world of love and passion, of action and its fruition. Ananda rather means perfection or fullness. . . . Here the ocean of life and thought is full, fathomless, shoreless, motionless, without the disturbance of a single ripple. No limitation of the slightest element of unreality or non-being corrupts that essence of pure and perfect Being. No limitation of the slightest shade of unreason or ignorance casts a shadow upon that pure and perfect light of Reason. No limitation of the feeblest flickering of desire or death can mingle with that pure and perfect Bliss. Perfect Being, Perfect Reason, Perfect Bliss—these constitute the essence of Brahman. . . . This much in explanation of the word; but it seems to me that the word really proceeds out of a silence which we shall in vain attempt to penetrate or analyse. Reason here is lost in the sense of the Infinite. The search after the ideal is no mere matter of metaphysical speculation to the Rishi of the Upanishads. By the hardest *tapasya* he has passed from one stage of thought to another, risen to a higher and still higher realisation of the mystery of Being—and now, when he has penetrated into the very heart of the mystery, the deep, eternal silences are around him and the darkness of Infinite Light dazzles his vision, and, lost in wonder and ecstasy, he can only exclaim—' From whence all speech with the mind, turns away unable to reach it '." [1]

Perhaps the best way of attempting to grasp the spirit of the Vedanta as contrasted with the dry bones of its letter, is to inquire into the meaning which it possesses for the Vedantin himself. Among those who have given to the world glimpses of their innermost thoughts in this respect are three men representative of very different types—the late Professor Benoyendra Nath Sen, the polished scholar and fine product of Indian culture combined with Western education, to whom reference has been made above; Ṣrî Ramkrishna Paramahaṃsa, the fervent devotee and type of India's ideal of renunciation; and Dr. Rabindra Nath Tagore, the inspired poet of Bengal, of whom one of his more recent biographers has said that his mind is the loftiest and most fastidious in India.

I

Professor Benoyendra Nath Sen

Professor Sen accepts the Hindu estimate of ṣruti which he defines as " the record of what is revealed to the soul of genius in the moment of

[1] The late Professor Benoyendra Nath Sen.

its highest exaltation" ; and while he agrees with Sankara that the testimony of reason is conclusive in favour of the view that the universe is of the substance of Brahman—*i.e.* that the sensuous world is an aspect of God Himself—he also holds with Sankara that the testimony of revelation to the same effect possesses a force overwhelmingly greater than that of mere reason. "Had the texture woven by the World-Spirit in the loom of time not been the visible garment of God Himself —had the universe not been the self-revelation of God", the idea of God could never have occurred to the mind of man. "Shut up in the hard opaque prison-house of matter, with pleasure and death for his masters, man had never thought of God at all."

Accepting the monistic view of Sankara that Brahman is the sole ultimate reality, he faces the two questions of fundamental importance to which this view gives rise—How can the Infinite and Absolute admit of anything different from itself? and How can a world of sin and suffering proceed from a perfect God? And he finds an adequate answer to them in Sankara's doctrine of maya, the latter being defined as the power by which the "Infinite Enchanter has contrived to put His own substance, which must be of the character of the infinite and absolute, into this texture which is woven in space and time". In his explanation of maya he dwells upon two characteristics attributed to it by Sankara, first, that of manifesting itself through name and form, and secondly, that of being not determinable either by Being or Non-being.

The first of these characteristics gives rise to little difficulty. There is nothing of which we take cognizance throughout the length and breadth of the universe that does not present itself to our senses through form or name. The precise meaning of the second characteristic is not, however, at first sight apparent. What exactly is meant when it is said of anything that it is not determinable either by Being or Non-being? Professor Sen explains that the characteristic of all knowledge of the universe is that it rests upon the superimposition of a concept upon the object, which attempts but is unable to express its true being. Hence it becomes necessary to change the concept the next moment as it seems that a truer realisation of the object has been attained; but this again has to be given up like the first, and thus the process of superimposition after superimposition goes on because the true being of the object is never reached. If we pause to consider the nature of manifested things, the meaning of the above passage becomes clear. Let us ask ourselves, for example, if the name or form under which a thing presents itself to us is rigid and constant?

The material objects which we see around us present themselves to us in the form of solid and inert mass, and under names appropriate to objects so constituted. And prior to certain recent discoveries in physical science we should have been justified in saying of these names and forms that they possessed the quality of "being", *i.e.* that the assumption that they corresponded to the objects with which they were associated was valid. Recent progress in physical science has shown, however, that the smallest particle of so-called solid and inert matter is a universe of infinitely minute entities in violent motion. This surprising discovery has provided a theme for many scientific writers in recent times. "There is now no matter," exclaims Dr. C. Nordmann in a fascinating exposition of the new physics associated with the name of Albert Einstein, "there is only electrical energy, which, by the reactions of the surrounding medium upon it, leads us to the fallacious belief in this substantial and massive something which hundreds of generations have been wont to call matter." And his comment upon this new knowledge is interesting—" A strange—*in a sense an almost spiritual*—turn for modern physics to take ".[1] Thus do we now perceive that in the very sphere in which our knowledge seemed to us to be absolute, the name and form which possessed for us the quality of " being " (validity) no longer do so, and in light of present knowledge would have to be characterised as " non-being " (invalid). And when we begin to think about it we perceive that what we are in the habit of regarding as absolutely true is in reality only relatively true; and that absolute truth lies beyond time and space. Standing in England and gazing up at the canopy of stars immediately overhead, I am convinced that I am looking upwards. But the man standing in New Zealand and gazing at the same moment in precisely the same direction is equally convinced that he is gazing downwards. Who is right? Am I or is the New Zealander? For me the name " upwards " is valid; for the New Zealander it is invalid. We label sensations with names such as heat and cold. Have these names any real validity? Is cold anything more than an absence of heat? And where precisely is the dividing line between the two? Can we mark any particular point on a thermometer at which heat exists (can be characterised as being), or ceases to exist (must be described as non-being)? And would the inhabitant of the Polar regions be in agreement with the denizen of the tropics on the point?

[1] " Einstein and the Universe ", by C. Nordmann, astronomer to the Paris Observatory. The italics are mine.

The shattering of our preconceived ideas as to the nature of matter is not the only shock which has been administered to us in those regions of knowledge in which, until quite recently, we were wont to think that we had laid hold of truths which were absolute. We are now learning that the foundations upon which we had built up vast and elaborate structures under the belief that they were of immovable rock are in reality nothing but shifting sand. Professor Einstein, " by separating far more completely than hitherto the share of the observer and the share of external nature in the things we see happen ",[1] has convinced a large and important section of the scientific world that laws hitherto regarded as absolute, such as Newton's law of gravitation and the laws of geometry formulated by Euclid, are in fact only relatively true. The conclusions as to the nature of things arrived at by Professor Einstein and his fellow-workers in the domain of physics bear indeed the most remarkable resemblance to those arrived at by the sages of India in the domain of metaphysics.

From the mechanical let us pass to the moral sphere and ask ourselves if it is possible to lay down any absolute line between good and evil. It may be urged that conscience does so with unerring judgement. Whose conscience ? it must be asked. The Christian conscience cries a halt at bigamy. Does the conscience of the most saintly follower of Muhammad do so too ? The disagreement must be admitted ; but it may be said that this is a matter of social custom rather than of moral rectitude. What, then, shall be taken as the test of right and wrong ? Shall it be the taking of another's life ? The taking of life is not in itself regarded as morally wrong by the generality of mankind, for the death penalty

[1] Professor A. S. Eddington in " Time, Space and Gravitation ".

finds a place in the penal code of the most civilised nations. And if the actual taking of life is not wrong in essence, the circumstances in which it may be taken become a mere matter of opinion. I have mentioned how I was struck with the apparent absence of any sense of moral guilt on the part of certain members of the revolutionary party in Bengal who tacitly admitted having taken the life of a police officer. And, indeed, that the dictum that political assassination is no sin is at present widely accepted by large sections of the human race, is only too painfully demonstrated by comparatively recent events in Ireland, Russia and elsewhere. It seems, then, that there is no standard of universal application by which we may lay down judgements as to conduct, placing this or that act or motive in a particular watertight compartment labelled right or wrong. And in this view it is evident that the doctrine of maya is a good deal more than a simple statement that the world of time and space is illusory. It predicates a state of affairs under which ignorance or false knowledge (avidya) prevails; but it also affirms the evolution of knowledge. We may try to picture it in this way. The true nature of reality is hidden from our eyes by a veil of many folds (avidya). The evolution of knowledge may then be likened to the gradual lifting of fold after fold, that which lies behind the veil changing in appearance as the removal of each fold admits of a clearer view. If this interpretation of the doctrine is accepted, the distinction which the Vedantin draws between Brahman the Absolute, and Isvara the personal God is seen to be a rational one. And it renders intelligible the changing conceptions of God, which have marked the different stages in the onward journey of mankind from savagery and superstition to the highest civilisation and the most lofty inspiration hitherto reached.

This seems to be the meaning which the maya of the Vedanta has for Professor Benoyendra Nath Sen. And thus interpreted it provides for him the answer to the second question to which I have referred, namely, How can a world of sin and suffering proceed from a perfect God? "If sorrow had been only the soul of bitterness, and joy only the overflowing of bliss, you might have charged God with partiality in distributing joy and sorrow unequally. But if sorrow has in its depths a hidden fountain of joy, and joy rests on a basis of deepest pain, nay, even if within the darkness of sin there is a hidden power that maketh for righteousness—there is no inequality to complain of; but every object, high or low, great or small, is equally a reflection of the infinite in the finite."

To what, then, does he look forward? He rejects Sankara's theory of individual liberation because it seems to him to be inconsistent with the true nature of maya, and reduces Sankara in the end to the necessity of regarding the universe as utterly unreal,—a position which is contrary to his teaching in respect of everything apart from this one idea of individual liberation. It is not easy to fathom the beliefs and hopes which he cherishes, but such indications as he gives of them suggest an expectation of a gradual approach towards ultimate truth, during which those things which wear the appearance of evil and suffering in the half-light of imperfect knowledge will, with an increasing realisation of God, gradually assume their true appearance until the totality of things is blended in the perfect harmony which is God—the bliss which has actually been experienced by the seers who have known communion with the Infinite.

However imperfectly one may have understood his beliefs and aspirations, one can at least have no doubt that for him the Vedanta is something a great deal more than a flight of the mind, however daring, in the vast realms of speculation; something beyond an excursion of the intellect, however bold, into a subtle world of metaphysic; something transcending an exercise of the faculty of ratiocination, however brilliant; a thing of the essence of religion, a thing capable of ministering to that craving of the soul which turns away unsatisfied from the highest that the intellect by itself has got to offer. For him, with all his reverence for reason, there stands something which is higher than reason, something which can only be vaguely indicated by the word Faith. "For I hold it truth," he declares, "—this that the Upanishads teach—that the ideal of the Intellect is Wonder and Reverence. Not wonder and reverence at the sacrifice of knowledge, or in opposition to it; but when knowledge has been brought to its utmost height, even that of realising that Reason is the Lord of the universe, there is still a mystery beyond, into which the intellect must look, and lose itself in that mystery. I also hold it truth that the intellect in its highest operation is intuitive and not discursive. The operations of reason we can analyse and know, but towards the Infinite the only attitude that is possible is Communion. To those ancient Rishis the privilege was given not simply to speculate and speak about metaphysical abstractions, but with purified hearts and devoted souls to hold communion with that which is beyond all speech or speculation, and realise in that communion the highest bliss of life."

CHAPTER XIX

THE SPIRIT OF THE VEDANTA (*continued*)

II

Ramkrishna Paramahaṃsa

A man travelling up the Hughli river from Calcutta is struck by the number of temples on its banks. They are built for the most part on a single model—a broad flight of steps leading down to the water to serve as a bathing ghât; a line of slate-grey shrines in whose architecture he will detect without difficulty, the curved roof of the Bengali cottage which is to be seen in many of the villages at the present day. These shrines dedicated to Shiva and containing the yoni and the liṅga emblematic of creation fashioned out of black stone, are identical in shape and size, and stand as many as a dozen in number in a straight line, along the river bank on either side of the porch or pavilion at the head of the bathing ghât. Behind these is a courtyard in the centre of which rises the main temple dedicated to Kâlî or some other incarnation of the deity. This is usually a building of imposing proportions, the main structure, which again follows the lines of the curved-roofed cottage, being surmounted by a cluster of pleasing cupolas.

The temple of Dakshineshwar, a few miles above Calcutta, is easily picked out by any one steaming up the river, by means of a group of tall casuerina trees, which can be seen from afar, standing in the temple grounds. It was built by a pious Bengali lady, Rani Rasmani, in the year A.D. 1855, and it was here that the famous saint of Dakshineshwar spent the greater part of his life. Few men have made a deeper impress upon the mind of Bengal in recent years than Gadadhar Chatterji, known to history as Srî Ramkrishna Paramahamsa, and his chief disciple Narendra Nath Dutt, better known under the title of Swami Vivekananda. At a time when the craze for the ideas and ways of the West was at its height these men stood for the ancient ideal of the East, for renunciation in an age of megalomania, for simplicity at a time when discoveries in mechanical science were making life elaborately complex.

The bright sun of a January day lit up the temple buildings and gave charm to the well-shaded grounds in which they stood, as I was shown the various objects which had acquired particular sanctity on account of their association with the departed saint. Here in the north-west angle of the courtyard was the room in which he had passed the greater number of his days. In the grounds on the north my attention was directed to a clump of five trees, the banyan, the pîpal, the nîm, the amlaki and the bael, planted at Ramkrishna's request. Here, it was said, he spent much time in meditation and the performance of religious exercises. Next it was explained that the two main shrines in the centre of the courtyard were dedicated to Radha and Krishna, representing God incarnate as love divine, and Kâlî, the Mother of the universe, standing for the personal aspect of the Infinite God which appealed most strongly to Ramkrishna.

Standing in the temple precincts surrounded by a group of Indian admirers of the saint, all eager to tell of his life and teaching, I found myself being carried away by their enthusiasm, and as I listened to their story I had little difficulty in conjuring up vivid pictures of the Master surrounded by his disciples, expounding his great doctrine of salvation along the path of self-surrender and devotion to God. The setting was there before my eyes. It required no great effort of the imagination to reconstruct events. One pictured the Master, a benign figure pacing to and fro along the terrace in the cool of the evening, halting now and then to engage in conversation with his disciples. As the shades of evening spread over the great courtyard one could see in imagination the lamps in the temple flaming into light, and the fragrant smoke ascending from the incense-burners as they were swung by the servants of the temple. And then one seemed to hear the sound of the evening service breaking in upon the stillness, the tintinnabulation of gongs, bells and cymbals echoing away over the murmuring waters of the holy river. Presently, as a silver moon rose in the sky, trees and buildings would emerge from the dusk of evening, thrown into sharp silhouette against the star-strewn background of the night. And appropriate to such a setting a venerable figure, bowing down before the Mother of the universe, rhythmically chanting the name of God, repeating the aphorisms in which were enshrined the guiding principles of his life; *Brahman Atman Bhagavân*, God the Absolute, God of the yogi, God of the devotee are one; *Saranagata, saranagata*, I am thine, I am thine; *Brahma-sakti Sakti-Brahman*, God the Absolute and the divine Mother are one. Thereafter the gradual assemblage of the disciples—keen, responsive young Bengalis in the white cotton chaddar and dhoti of the country, their dark eyes glowing with enthusiasm—followed by a discourse from the Master seated, cross-legged, in their midst.

* * * * * *

Born of Brahman parents on February 20, 1834, Gadadhar Chatterji found himself drawn to a religious life from his boyhood, and he became an assistant priest at the temple of Dakshineshwar from the date of its construction in 1855. He was no scholar, yet he possessed the power of attracting to himself men of light and leading of the day—Keshub Chandra Sen, Pundit Isvar Vidyasagar, Bankim Chatterji and Protap Chandra Mazumdar amongst others. The latter, one of the most devoted followers of Keshub Chandra Sen, seems to have been forcibly struck and a good deal puzzled by the influence which Ramkrishna exercised over educated men. "What is there in common between him and me?" he asked. "I a Europeanised, civilised, self-centred, semi-sceptical, so-called educated reasoner, and he, a poor, illiterate, unpolished, half-idolatrous, friendless Hindu devotee? Why should I sit long hours to attend to him, I who have listened to Disraeli and Fawcett, Stanley and Max Müller, and a whole host of European scholars and divines? . . . And it is not I only, but dozens like me who do the same." And after due deliberation he comes to the conclusion that it is his religion that is his only recommendation. But his religion itself is a puzzle. "He worships Shiva, he worships Kâlî, he worships Rama, he worships Krishna, and is a confirmed advocate of Vedantic doctrines. . . . He is an idolater, yet is a faithful and most devoted meditator of the perfections of the One formless, infinite Deity. . . . His religion means ecstasy, his worship means transcendental insight, his whole nature burns day and night with a permanent fire and fever of a strange faith and feeling."[1]

He studied the doctrine of the Vedanta at the feet of one Tota Puri, a holy man who took up his abode at the temple for the space of nearly a year. But it was along the path of worship (bhakta) rather than by the way of knowledge (gñâna) that he sought for the solution of the mystery of the universe. By temperament he was a mystic rather than a philosopher. The narrative of his life and teaching recalls inevitably the emotional figure of Chaitanya. Like the great Vaishnava saint of Nadia he gave vent to his pent-up feelings in song and dance. Hymns to the deity sung by his favourite disciples reduced him to tears, and frequently induced in him a state of trance. He was subject to such trances from his boyhood, his first experience taking place at the age of eleven, when, according to his own account, he suddenly saw a vision of glory, and lost all sense-consciousness while walking through the fields. His knowledge of God was intuitive, and he never felt the need of systematic study. A discussion on the subject of the study of the Scriptures was once in progress among his disciples when he exclaimed, "Do you know what I think of it? Books—sacred scriptures—all point the way to God. Once you know the way, what is the use of books?" A young man, typical of the educated middle classes of the day, obviously proud of his scholarship and knowledge of books and men, proceeded one day to the temple, attracted by the growing fame of the saint.[2] On

[1] From a monograph entitled "Paramahamsa Ramkrishna", republished from the *Theistic Quarterly Review*.

[2] Professor M. N. Gupta, a teacher in Calcutta who subsequently became a devoted disciple of Ramkrishna, and under the *nom-de-plume* of "M." wrote an account of his life and teaching entitled the "Gospel of Srî Ramkrishna". He still resides in Calcutta, and appreciating the difficulty which I experienced in understanding certain tenets of the Vedanta, drew my attention to passages in the gospel in which

learning that he was no scholar and had no use for books, he expressed extreme surprise, and at his first meeting embarked upon an argument with him on the subject of image worship. Ramkrishna swept aside his scholarly arguments. "Why must you worry yourself about things above you and beyond your reach?" he asked. "Does not the Lord of the universe abide in the temple of the human body and know the innermost thoughts of men? Seek then to know and revere God. Love God. That is the duty nearest you."

Apparent contradictions were nothing to him. God is the Absolute, the One, the All, the Brahman of the philosopher. But that does not prevent Him from manifesting Himself in different aspects in His relations with the phenomenal world—as Krishna in His aspect of divine love, as Kâlî in His aspect of creator of the universe and saviour of mankind. And when you realise God, such things cease to puzzle. "Sir, is it possible to see God?" asked the scholar. "Certainly," came the reply. "Cry unto the Lord with a yearning heart and you shall see Him." It is clear from the testimony of his disciples that he himself constantly attained that pitch of spiritual exaltation which is called by the Hindus samadhi, a state of trance induced by God-consciousness—that communion with the Infinite enjoyed by the Rishis of old and spoken of by Professor B. N. Sen as the bliss of Brahman, which is beyond all words and above all reason.

The pantheism so congenial to Indian thought was his by instinct. He was in the habit in his younger days of plucking flowers for the daily worship in the temple. On one occasion, we are

---

were set forth the teaching of Srî Ramkrishna on the points in question. The sketch of the saint and his teaching which I have drawn in this chapter is based upon Professor Gupta's narrative.

told, he was gathering the leaves of the bael tree when a portion of the bark was torn from the tree. It seemed to him that a severe wound had been inflicted upon the Divinity which was within him, and was equally manifested in all things. So deeply was the idea of God immanent rooted in his soul that he never again picked the leaves of the trees. Difficulties put forward by man's reason were brushed aside. If they could not be explained by reason they were discounted by faith. From the point of view of pure logic, consequently, his explanations were at times lacking in conviction. His reply to the question why, if everything is but a manifestation of God, should some things be harmful is a case in point. He quoted the story of a devout young man who refused, when warned to do so, to move out of the way of a charging elephant. The driver shouted, but the young man said to himself, " the elephant is a manifestation of the Divinity ", and instead of fleeing from him he began to chant his praises. When he was subsequently picked up and restored to consciousness, he explained why he had not moved away, but was chided by his guru in these words, " It is true that God manifests himself forth in everything. But if he is manifest in the elephant, is he not equally manifest in the driver ? Tell me then why you paid no heed to his warning voice ? "

With even scantier consideration he brushed aside the question of the apparent partiality of God. " Am I then, Sir," asked pundit Vidyasagar on one occasion, " to believe that we come into the world with unequal endowments ? Is the Lord partial to a select few ? " To which the Master replied, " Well, I am afraid you will have to take the facts of the universe as they stand. It is not given to man to see clearly into the ways of the Lord."

The value which he attached to ratiocination and inspiration respectively, is well illustrated by a scene which took place one afternoon in the presence of a number of his disciples in the grounds of the temple. "Is there any book in English on the art of reasoning?" he asked one of his Western-educated followers. He was informed that there were such treatises and, as an example, was told of that part of logic which dealt with reasoning from general propositions to particulars. He appeared to pay little attention to these explanations, which evidently fell flat upon his ear. And looking at him a little while after, his would-be instructor marvelled and became speechless. I give the description of the scene in his own words. "The Master stands motionless. His eyes are fixed. It is hard to say whether he is breathing or not. . . . The smile on his lips shows the ecstatic delight that he feels at the sight of the blessed vision. Yes, he must be enjoying a vision of unequalled beauty which puts into the shade the refulgence of a million moons! Is this God vision? If so what must be the intensity of Faith and Devotion of Discipline and Austerity which has brought such a vision within reach of mortal man?" The writer goes on to tell us that he wended his way home with this unique picture of samadhi and the ecstasy of divine love vividly reflected in his mind, and that there echoed within him as he went these words, "Be incessantly merged, O my mind, in the sweetness of his love and bliss! Yes, be thou drunken with the joy of the Lord!"

Ramkrishna did not dissent from the monistic explanation of the universe. It was only that he was driven by temperament to attach far greater importance to the Personal Aspect of God. The Absolute of Sankara could be realised; but only in perfect samadhi. On one occasion half returning to consciousness from a state of trance he was heard exclaiming, " Yes, my Holy Mother (kâlî) is none other than the Absolute. She it is to whom the six systems of philosophy with all their learned disquisitions furnish no clue." But when a man returned from samadhi he became a differentiated ego once more, and was thrown back upon the world of relativity so that he perceived the world-system (maya) as real. Why? Because with the return of his egoity he was convinced that he as an individual was real; and " so long as his ego is real to him (real relatively) the world is real too, and the Absolute is unreal (unreal relatively) ". He laid constant stress upon this.

The saint returning from samadhi could say nothing about the Absolute. " Once differentiated, he is mute as to the undifferentiated. Once in the relative world his mouth is shut as to the Absolute and Unconditioned." And since samadhi was not achieved by the average man, he must meditate upon and commune with the Personal God, for " so long as you are a person you cannot conceive of, think or perceive God otherwise than as a Person ".

In Ramkrishna's own case this latter difficulty was undoubtedly a predilection as much as a necessity, for by temperament he was emotional rather than critical. " As a rule ", he declared, " the devotee does not long for the realisation of the Impersonal. He is anxious that the whole of his ego should not be effaced in samadhi." And the reason which he gives is the one to be expected from a man of his temperament. " He would fain have sufficient individuality left to him to enjoy the Vision Divine as a person. He would fain taste the sugar in place of being one with the sugar itself."

His creed was summed up by him during a

visit to pundit Sasadhar in Calcutta one afternoon in 1884. Many paths lead to God, the path of knowledge, that of works and that of self-surrender and devotion. The way of knowledge is for the philosopher. His object is to realise Brahman the Absolute. He says "neti, neti" ("not this, not this"), and so eliminates one unreal thing after another until he arrives at a point at which all discrimination between the Real and the Unreal ceases. The way of works is that laid down in the Gîtâ, to live in the world, but not to be of the world; to practise at all times an exalted altruism. Neither of these paths is easy to travel in the present age. It is almost impossible in these materialistic days to get rid of the conviction that the self is identical with the body. How, then, can a man understand that he is one with the universal soul, the Being Absolute and Unconditioned? Similarly with the way of works. A man may form a resolution to work without expectation of any reward or fear of any punishment in this world or the next; but the chances are that consciously or unconsciously he will get attached to the fruit of his work. Let a man then choose the way of worship and seek communion with the Personal God, for the path of love, adoration and self-surrender to God is the easiest of all paths. It teaches the necessity of prayer without ceasing, it is in this age "the shortest cut leading to God".

Early in 1886 Ramkrishna was taken seriously ill. A graphic account of the suffering of his last hours in the garden of Cossipore surrounded by his disciples, is given by Professor Gupta in a passage of great pathos. He died not long after his fifty-second birthday.

Many of the young men who flocked to the temple at Dakshineshwar in the eighties of last century are preaching the gospel of the Master.

Those who, following his example, have adopted the path of renunciation have established a monastic order, the headquarters of which are at Belur Math on the opposite bank of the Hughli to Dakshineshwar, with branch monasteries in Bengal, the United Provinces and Madras. Associated with the monastic order which consists of sannyasins and bramacharins is a mission, these twin organisations standing for renunciation and service respectively, declared by the late Swami Vivekananda to be the two national ideals of India. The mission undertakes service of all kinds, social, charitable and educational. The monasteries are dedicated to the perpetuation through their spiritual culture of the great Ideal and Revelation which Srî Ramkrishna Paramahamsa embodied in his life.[1] One of these branch monasteries, the Ashram of Mayavati hidden away from the world in the vast labyrinth of the Himâlayas fifty miles north-east of Almora, is devoted exclusively to the study of advaita Vedanta, leading to knowledge of the Brahman proclaimed by Sankara, the absolute, impersonal and unconditioned God—the material and efficient cause of the universe.

Some of these men I have met at Belur Math. And having met them I know that it is for no colourless abstraction that they have renounced the world. Whether known as *saguna* Brahman (God Personal) or as *nirguna* Brahman (God Impersonal), it is to them the sole reality, the ultimate goal towards which sooner or later all mankind must direct its steps.

[1] First general report of the Ramkrishna Mission.

CHAPTER XX

THE SPIRIT OF THE VEDANTA (*concluded*)

III

Dr. Rabindra Nath Tagore

The flat alluvial tracts of deltaic Bengal are bounded on the West by undulating stretches of red laterite frequently covered, where cultivation has not extended, by large areas of sâl forest. They have a general elevation of from 600 feet to 800 feet, and on approaching them from the plains of the delta you become conscious of a change of climate. The air is dryer and possesses, consequently, a greater sparkle. In the winter the surface of the land is hard and dusty, though the suggestion of aridity for which the nature of the soil is responsible, is tempered by green clumps of palmyra palms and thickets of cotton and mango trees marking the sites of villages.

To these wide spaces there came sometime in the middle of the nineteenth century an austere figure, driven restlessly to and fro over the land by an absorbing quest—no less than that of God. A man who had searched the Scriptures of his race for a clue to the unravelling of the mystery of creation; who had found in much of them nothing but "vain imaginings"; who had rejected the pure monism of Sankara with the same impatience that he displayed in thrusting from him the idol-worship, which seemed to him to bulk so largely in the orthodoxy of the day. A man who, in the course of his quest had revivified the church founded by Raja Ram Mohan Roy under the name of the Brahmo Samaj, and had promulgated for its congregation a new book of faith compounded of texts from the Upanishads and of the out-pourings of his own soul, with the significant title of Brahma-dharma. And having come he pitched his solitary tent beneath the beckoning branches of three tall trees which the curious traveller may see to this day. And in due course he raised amid these surroundings, far removed from the distracting din of the world of men, a temple of worship to which he gave the name of Shanti Niketan—the "Abode of Peace". That man was Devendra Nath Tagore, known to the people as Maharshi or the great saint, a man of whom it can be said with confidence that he found that which he sought.

With Maharshi Devendra Nath Tagore, in 1872, came to Shanti Niketan for the first time his son Rabindra, then a boy of eleven years. One can enter into the feelings excited in the sensitive mind of the town-bred boy by the great free spaces of this new world into which he had stumbled. "The only ring which encircled me", he wrote, when describing his feelings in later years, "was the blue of the horizon which the presiding goddess of these solitudes had drawn round them."[1] Indeed, the impression made upon his mind was profound and lasting. It was the appeal of Nature knocking at the door of his heart, that opened a way into the innermost chambers of his being, by which there entered an unbounded admiration and reverence for the simple life lived by the early Aryan settlers amongst the forests of the Ganges Valley. It was amidst such surroundings that had dawned

[1] "My Reminiscences", by Rabindra Nath Tagore.

"the golden daybreak of the awakenment of India's soul";[1] and he has described how a time came when he dreamed of that towering age above all ages of subsequent history in the greatness of its simplicity and wisdom of pure life. The ideals originating from this golden age he has defined in glowing terms, "ideals of simplicity of life, clarity of spiritual vision, purity of heart, harmony with the universe and consciousness of the infinite personality in all creation".[2] These ideals, he believed, still flowed underground in the depth of India's soil, and it was with the determination of bringing them to the surface for daily use and purification that he returned to Shanti Niketan nearly thirty years later with a handful of pupils, to found the school which has since acquired world-wide fame.

* * * * * *

A two-mile walk from the station of Bholpur, up a gradual ascent through the bright sunshine of a February morning, was pure joy. Standing at the gateway of the *ashram* was a tall, commanding figure clothed in ample robes of white. With a charming courtesy he welcomed us to Shanti Niketan. I was conducted straightway to a stone seat in a shady grove. In front of me was a stretch of ground smoothed and polished until it resembled the surface of a threshing floor upon which had been chalked out a circular design. This served for a place of assembly which might be said to correspond to the speech room of an English public school. A little behind me, standing under the trees, were grouped the teachers, all clad in white. In front of me were the boys of the school drawn up in a semi-circle on the edge of the design. All were dressed in yellow—the colour of spring. On my right was

[1] An introduction by Dr. Rabindra Nath Tagore to Mr. W. W. Pearson's "Shanti Niketan". [2] *Ibid.*

a group of girls, pupils along with the boys at the school. Led by a pundit the gathering chanted Vedic hymns in Sanskrit with striking effect. The significance of the scene could not be lost upon any one acquainted with the outlines of ancient Indian history. Here was a reproduction in miniature of the conditions amid which the civilisation of India had been born, the life close to nature in the heart of the forests which provided the early Aryan settlers with all that they required. One recognised in all that one saw around one both a protest against the artificiality of modern life, and an offering of homage to the ideals and traditions of the past.

While the gathering was breaking up preparatory to the re-forming of the pupils in their classes, we wandered through the grounds and came to a rude seat beneath an ancient tree—a low stone block topped by two slabs of marble, marking the spot where Maharshi Devendra Nath Tagore was in the habit of sitting in meditation during his life of communion with God. We then returned to the classes, each one of which had its allotted place in the grove. Each class consisted of a group of pupils generally small in number, seated along with its teacher in a circle on the ground. The cultivation of man's instinctive sense of beauty, or in other words a development of his understanding of the harmony pervading all creation, appeared to me to run like a thread through the whole scheme of studies. Music and painting naturally found an honoured place in the curriculum.

A study of the motive which impelled Rabindra Nath Tagore to establish this school and of the ideas underlying the plan of the experiment, provides a key to his philosophy. His own school days were days of poignant memories. The dreary monotony of school routine had preyed upon his mind. A system devoted to the mere imparting of knowledge, as opposed to the development of the SELF, had entered like iron into his soul; and he had suddenly found his world—the world as God made it with its beauty, its music and its fragrance—vanishing from around him and giving place to wooden benches and straight walls which stared at him with the blank stare of the blind.[1] So wooden benches had given place to the lap of kindly mother earth, and straight walls to the varied lines of the Amlaki grove in the Abode of Peace; and the teacher sought not merely to impart information, but to bring the lives of those whom he taught into harmony with all existence. The mind of the author of this scheme was perpetually reaching back to the simple forest life of his remote ancestors, when the different elements in man, the spiritual, the intellectual and the physical were in complete harmony. The school of the present day, he declares, lays entire emphasis on the intellectual and physical, and thus unconsciously accentuates a break in the unity which is man's by nature. And when elaborating this view he gives us incidentally a simple statement of his creed—"I believe in a spiritual world—not as anything separate from this world—but as its innermost truth. With the breath we draw we must always feel this truth, that we are living in God. Born in this great world full of the mystery of the Infinite we cannot accept our existence as a momentary outburst of chance, drifting on the current of matter towards an eternal nowhere. We cannot look upon our lives as dreams of a dreamer who has no awakening in all time. We have a personality to which matter and force are unmeaning unless related

[1] "My School", a lecture delivered in America and republished in a volume entitled "Personality".

to something infinitely personal, whose nature we have discovered in some measure, in human love, in the greatness of the good, in the martyrdom of heroic souls, in the ineffable beauty of nature, which can never be a mere physical fact nor anything but an expression of personality." [1]

He was brought up, as he himself has told us, in a family where texts from the Upanishads were used in daily worship; [2] and it is not surprising, therefore, to find that the great central tenet of the Vedanta, the oneness of all, is the foundation on which his own creed is based. But his childhood was also spent in a circle where literature, music and art had become instinctive,[3] and it is not to be wondered at that this fundamental conception should have presented itself to his vision in the trailing draperies of poetry, rather than in the tight-fitting garment of philosophy.

The most connected presentment of his thoughts on religion is to be found in a volume entitled "Sâdhanâ," a word which may be interpreted as "the pathway of attainment". It is, however, very far from being a typical treatise on philosophy, and Professor Radhakrishnan is justified in his description of it as "a sigh of the soul rather than a reasoned account of metaphysics; an atmosphere rather than a system of philosophy".[4] As in the case of so many Indians, the religious idea most immediately present to his mind is that of God Immanent. It is the constant companionship of this thought that causes him to pour forth his soul in hymns in praise of the beautiful in nature. Natural beauty moves him to song much as the joy of summer does the nightingale, and he sings with the same

[1] "My School." [2] "Sâdhanâ."
[3] "Personality." See also "My Reminiscences".
[4] "The Philosophy of Rabindra Nath Tagore", by Professor S. Radhakrishnan.

spontaneity and abandon. The title of the best-known collection of his writings, "Gitanjali", "song offerings," is significant. He loves and trusts the world, unable to look on it either as a delusion of the Creator—a reference to ultra monism—or a snare of the devil.[1] He becomes intoxicated with joy at his discovery of God in everything, so that his perception of the unity of man and nature in God surges up from the deep places of his being in eruptions of poetry. His conviction that "the ineffable beauty of nature" must be "an expression of personality" determines the character of the imagery in which he indulges. He delights to speak of still Night "standing silently at the window like a pilgrim of eternity";[2] of "the stars gazing in, witnesses through untold ages of countless death scenes";[3] of the gentle south wind "kissing away the weariness of the world", and "the scent of jasmine and bela filling the garden with rejoicing";[4] of "the living power hidden in the beauty of a little flower more potent than a maxim-gun";[5] of "the crescent-shaped beach (at Karwar) throwing out its arms to the shoreless open sea like the very image of an eager striving to embrace the Infinite".[6] And he believes profoundly in "an ideal hovering over the earth—an ideal of that Paradise which is not the mere outcome of imagination, but the ultimate reality towards which all things are moving".[7] And he sees this vision of Paradise "in the sunlight and the green of the earth, in the flowing streams, in the beauty of spring-time and the repose of a winter morning".[8] Indeed he asserts with complete conviction that "everywhere in this earth the spirit of Paradise is awake and

[1] Letter dated October 1891. [2] "Mashi." [3] *Ibid.*
[4] "The Skeleton."
[5] "Paradise", an address delivered by Rabindra Nath Tagore in Tokio and republished in "Shanti Niketan" by W. W. Pearson.
[6] "My Reminiscences." [7] "Paradise." [8] *Ibid.*

sending forth its voice ".[1] True beauty is something real, " not ", to quote his creed once more, " a mere physical fact, but an expression of personality ". And this being so, beauty can find its way to the chambers of a man's soul by different channels. Writing to a friend in December 1892 he tries to describe the beauty which for him is the reality lying behind a sunset. He draws attention to the silence which broods over earth, sky and waters, and he falls to wondering. " If ever this silence should fail to contain itself," he questions, " if the expression for which this hour has been seeking from the beginning of time should break forth, would a profoundly solemn, poignantly moving music rise from earth to starland ? " And then, as if after reflection, " with a little steadfast concentration of effort we can, for ourselves, translate the grand harmony of light and colour which permeates the universe into music. We have only to close our eyes and receive with the ear of the mind the vibration of this ever-flowing panorama." For beauty is not a mere thing of the senses. Only those who cannot steep themselves in it to the full think of it as such. " But those who have tasted of its inexpressibility know how far it is beyond the highest powers of mere eye or ear—nay, even the heart is powerless to attain the end of its yearning." [2]

Over and over again we find stress laid upon the reality and meaning of beauty. The subject upon which all his writings have dwelt is, in his own words, the joy of attaining the infinite within the finite.[3] And it is beauty that is the link between the two, for " the beauty of nature is not a mirage of the imagination, but reflects the joy of the Infinite, and thus draws us to lose

[1] "Paradise." [2] Letter dated June 2, 1892.
[3] " My Reminiscences."

ourselves in it ".[1] The colour, form and fragrance of a flower all have their utilitarian purposes. They are the finger-posts directing the bee to the honey; and the attraction which the honey has for the bee possesses also a utilitarian purpose, that of the fertilisation of the plant by the bee so that it may carry on the work of reproduction and thus save the world from becoming a desert. From the point of view of science all these attributes of the flower have their appointed purposes in the economy of nature, the sum total of which is the survival of the species. Birth, growth, reproduction and decay follow one another inexorably in obedience to iron law; colour, form and fragrance are but links in the unbroken chain of causation, which is the essence of the law. From a materialistic point of view the explanation given by science is all-sufficient. Every attribute of the flower has been explained, the sufficient purpose of each pointed out. Yet the philosopher is not satisfied. There is something which science seems to have overlooked. The idea of beauty which the flower conveys to us is something over and above that which is required of its various attributes from the purely utilitarian point of view. The beauty which is made up of the sum of its attributes is something which is outside the economy of nature. Every function of the different attributes of the flower could be performed just as efficiently without their sum-total constituting a thing of beauty for the joy of man. These two things—the functions of the flower and its beauty—are different aspects of the same thing; one of thraldom, the other of freedom. "In the same form, sound, colour and taste, two contrary notes are heard, one of necessity, the other of joy."[2] The man who sees the flower only from this first point of view has reached an

[1] "My Reminiscences." [2] "Sādhanā."

elementary stage of knowledge only—the first stage reached by Brighu Varuni during his inquiry into Brahman; the stage at which he reached the conclusion that from matter all these things are born, by matter when born they live, into matter at death they enter. The stage at which the doctrine of materialism seems to supply an adequate answer to the problem of existence. The man who perceives the flower in its other aspect has travelled with Brighu Varuni to the final stage reached by him in his quest—the stage at which he perceived that from bliss, or joy, all these things are born, by joy when born they live, into joy at death they enter. It is in this final conclusion that Tagore revels; and it is his whole-hearted acceptance of it more than anything else that justifies the student of his philosophy in ranking him as a Vedantin.

It is in this final conclusion reached by Brighu that we find the nearest approach which the Vedanta provides to an answer to the question why there should be a universe at all. In the Brahma sûtras the world system has been likened to the illusion produced by a magician. But this illustration of the nature of the universe not unnaturally provokes the further question why the magician should produce an illusion at all? It can be neither of necessity nor of desire, because the magician being the Absolute is, *ex hypothesi*, without attributes. The answer given in the sûtras is that it is due to *lîla*, a word sometimes translated as playfulness. The conception seems to be rather that of spontaneity. The Infinite manifests itself in the finite because to do so is inherent in its nature. The universe in the words of the late Professor B. N. Sen, is "the divine exuberance blooming into a perpetual efflorescence". For Tagore it is equally out of the fulness of joy that God manifests Himself as creation. And if this be accepted, then the limitations to which God seems voluntarily to subject Himself need cause no surprise. For how could God exercise His power if He did not impose limitations upon Himself? Is it not by willingly imposing limits upon himself in the form of the rules of the game, and entering into definite relations with each particular piece that the chess-player realises the joy of his power? "It is not that he cannot move the chessmen just as he pleases, but if he does so, then there can be no play. If God assumes His rôle of omnipotence then His creation is at an end, and His power loses all its meaning. For power to be a power must act within limits."[1] And it is because joy cannot find expression in itself alone that it desires the law which imposes limitations upon it.[2] The joy of a singer expresses itself in the form of a song, and a song when analysed is found to be hedged around with limitations in the compass of each of its notes, and it is seen that if this were not so there could be no song. The Absolute is at all times greater than any assignable limit; but if limitation as such had never existed the Absolute would not have been complete. "On the one hand Brahman is evolving, on the other he is perfection; and in the one aspect he is essence, in the other manifestation—both together at the same time as is the song and the act of singing."[3] To refuse to recognise this is to ignore the consciousness of the singer, and to say that only the singing is in progress, and that there is no song. "Doubtless we are directly aware only of the singing and never at any one time of the song as a whole; but do we not all the time know that the complete song is in the soul of the singer?"[4]

It was, perhaps, inevitable in the case of a

[1] "Sādhanā." [2] *Ibid.* [3] *Ibid.* [4] *Ibid.*

writer who has written for the reading public of three continents that the source of his inspiration should be questioned. Is that which he professes essentially Indian ; or is it the offspring of Indian belief wedded to thought of an alien stock ? Professor E. J. Thompson, while admitting that the idea of many incarnations is found in his poetry asserts that he has no belief in the most characteristic of all Hindu doctrines, namely, that of karma and transmigration. It is with some diffidence that I venture to question any statement in this connection made by Professor Thompson. There is, however, much in Tagore's writings to show that this essentially Hindu idea presents itself to him instinctively. It is present to his mind when he is most deeply moved. Thus in describing the feelings which he experienced on the occasion on which he was taken for the first time to the country, he writes that the bank of the Ganges welcomed him into its lap " like a friend of a former birth ".[1] And in a letter dated May the 16th, 1893, he writes of his hopes and fears with regard to possible reincarnations. The thought that he may not be reborn in Bengal recurs to him daily ; and he is assailed with a fear that he may be reborn in Europe where the life of leisure which he loves might have to be exchanged for a life of hustle.

Other assertions have been made definitely charging him with drawing his inspiration from Christianity. Such charges have been challenged in their turn—notably by Professor S. Radhakrishnan. The professor quotes a writer in the *Spectator* of February the 14th, 1914, as saying that Tagore has employed his remarkable literary talents in teaching borrowed ethics to Europe as a thing characteristically Indian ; and a Christian missionary as claiming that his God whether he

[1] " My Reminiscences."

be explicitly Christ or not is at least a Christ-like God.[1] Whatever degree of truth there may be underlying such assertions, Professor Radhakrishnan is undoubtedly on sound ground when he points out that it is inconceivable that Tagore could accept any form of theism which identified its God with a part of the universe only—which set up two opposing forces, good and evil, allying God with one and altogether dissociating Him from the other. His view of good and evil is essentially that of the Vedanta, and there is little difficulty for all the difference of language, in identifying it with that of the late Professor B. N. Sen. Evil is due to limitations in the moral sphere; and once his explanation of the universe as the manifestation of the Infinite in the Finite is accepted, it is seen that such limitations, or in other words, Evil, must exist. And the question of real importance is not why imperfection exists, but whether imperfection is the final truth—whether evil is absolute? Neither Professor Sen nor Dr. Rabindra Nath Tagore has the smallest hesitation in replying to this question in the negative. A river has its limitations in its banks. But would any one suggest that the banks are the final facts about the river? Is it not rather these limitations that give to the river its onward motion? "The current of the world has its boundaries otherwise it could have no existence; but its purpose is not shown in the boundaries that restrain it, but in its movement which is towards perfection."[2] These limitations to which the Infinite subjects itself in order that it may experience the joy of self-realisation wear different appearances under different circumstances—evil in the moral sphere, suffering in the physical sphere, error in the sphere of intellect. If these

[1] The Rev. Mr. Saunders in the *International Review of Missions*, 1914.

[2] "Sâdhanâ."

limitations are looked at from this point of view there is little difficulty in perceiving that they have no permanence, or as Sankara would put it, that they possess only a relative reality. "To go through the history of the development of science is to go through the maze of mistakes it made current at different times."[1] Yet no one believes that the real purpose and achievement of science is the dissemination of mistakes. On the contrary, "the progressive ascertainment of truth is the important thing to remember in the history of science, not its innumerable mistakes. Error by its nature cannot be stationary; it cannot remain with truth".[2] It is shed like an outworn garment as soon as it has accomplished its purpose; for "it is the function of our intellect to realise the truth through untruths, and knowledge is nothing but the continually burning up of error to set free the light of truth".[3] In the same way "our will, our character has to attain perfection by continually overcoming evils".[4]

Belief in the infallibility of the Vedas had been jettisoned by Maharshi Devendra Nath Tagore in 1845. He and his associates in the Brahmo Samaj breaking away from the Sankara tradition, had then agreed that Reason and Conscience were to be the supreme authority, and the teachings of the Scriptures were to be accepted only in so far as they harmonised with the light within them.[5] To Rabindra Nath Tagore the light that is within him is a very real thing. "The vision of the Supreme One in our own soul is a direct and immediate intuition not based on any ratiocination or demonstration at all"[6]; and in the same way man has felt in the depths of his life that what appears as imperfect is the

[1] "Sâdhanâ." [2] *Ibid.* [3] *Ibid.* [4] *Ibid.*

[5] See an introductory chapter to the autobiography of Maharshi Devendra Nath Tagore by his son Satyendra Nath Tagore.

[6] Sâdhanâ."

manifestation of the perfect. And for an analogy to illustrate his meaning he returns to the singer and his song. "A man who has an ear for music realises the perfection of a song while in fact he is only listening to a succession of notes."[1] Joy is the cause of the song, the succession of notes is the means by which the song manifests itself; the song made up of each note which is in itself imperfect, is the perfect whole.

Is there any place in the scheme of things as thus interpreted for free will? Or does it follow from the belief that the universe is a manifestation of the Infinite in the Finite—a voluntary subjection by the Absolute of its absoluteness to limitations for the purpose of self-realisation—that man is subject to iron law? Are the limitations in their nature inexorable? Is man the mere sport of undeviating law? In his physical and mental organism where he is related to nature Tagore holds that he is. But in his soul a thousand times no. For what is the soul of man but *will* seeking manifestation in *will*—experiencing self-realisation as *will*? It is only in respect of man's SELF that anarchy is permitted. There could be no joy if *will* manifesting itself as the *will* of man were bound, for then there could be no freedom. The armed forces of God, the laws of nature, stand outside the chamber in which dwells the SELF of man "and only beauty the messenger of his love finds admission within its precincts".[2] If freedom is a reality—and without freedom there could be no joy—it follows that God's relation with the SELF of man is one of love and not of authority, "for this SELF of ours has to attain its ultimate meaning which is the soul, not through the compulsion of God's power, but through love and thus become united with God in freedom".[3] For

[1] "Sādhanā." [2] *Ibid.* [3] *Ibid.*

Tagore, let it be said once more, the teaching of the Taittirîyaka Upanishad is valid for it harmonises with the light that is within him—"From bliss all these things are born; by bliss when born they live; into bliss they enter at their death".

* * * * * *

However halting and imperfect the above sketch may be, however inadequately it brings before the mind of the reader the nature of the beliefs which it attempts to portray, it at least makes clear, I hope, that for the Indian the religious scriptures of the country are of living importance, and that they should be treated by Western inquirers as possessing something more than a "merely retrospective and archæological interest" fit only to be exhibited in labelled cases as "mummied specimens of human thought and aspiration preserved for all time in the wrappings of erudition".[1] It is the case, I fear, that the coldly critical and severely analytical mind of the West is prone to seize upon the skeleton of logic upon which the body of the Vedanta is built up, and to ignore the blood of faith and inspiration which courses through its veins, imparting vitality to the whole corpus of the doctrine. It is doubtless easy enough for the logician to dissect the central tenet of the Vedanta, namely, that Brahman is One without a second, and to prove therefrom that the God of the Vedantin is a colourless abstraction. He can point out that since the above definition rules out the existence of any object to be cognised, it follows that there can equally be no subject to cognise, for if there is nothing to cognise how can the act of cognition take place? Whence it follows that Brahman being neither subject nor object must be—if it is anything at

[1] Introduction to "Sâdhanâ."

all—pure cognition; not the knower or the known, but the knowing, or in other words not an entity possessing intelligence as an attribute but pure abstract intelligence itself. With equal plausibility he can point out that the bliss by which term Brahman is also described can be nothing but insensibility, for active enjoyment predicates a subject to enjoy and an object to be enjoyed. Basing himself upon the premises which he finds in the sûtras he can—as Jacob has done—legitimately depict the Supreme Being of their teaching as "a cold impersonality, out of relation with the world, unconscious of its own existence and of ours and devoid of all attributes and qualities". And he can continue his criticism in the words of the same writer and point out that "the so-called personal God, the first manifestation of the Impersonal, turns out on examination to be a myth; there is no God apart from ourselves, no Creator, no Holy Being, no Father, no Judge—no one, in a word, to adore, to love or to fear. And as for ourselves we are only unreal actors on the semblance of a stage."[1]

It has already been stated in Chapters XV. and XVII. that the Vedantin, if he is an adherent of the advaita school, accepts these conclusions, and it has now to be added that he is wholly unmoved by them. Dreamless sleep is accepted as the earthly analogy of a realisation by the individual soul of its identity with Brahman. Only for the Vedantin and the Western critic the words possess different values. The nature of deep sleep is discussed by Sankara in his comments on the 18th sûtra of the 3rd pada of the 2nd adhyaya, in the following words: "The objection that sleeping persons are not conscious of anything is refuted by Scripture where we

[1] See chapter iii. of Dr. Sydney Cave's "Redemption, Hindu and Christian".

read concerning a man lying in deep sleep, 'and when there he does not see, yet he is seeing though he does not see. For there is no intermission of the seeing of the seer because it cannot perish. But there is then no second, nothing else different from him that he could see (Bṛi. iv. 3. 23). That means: the absence of actual intelligising is due to the absence of objects, not to the absence of intelligence; just as the light pervading space is not apparent owing to the absence of things to be illuminated, not to the absence of its own nature." The conclusion that Brahman is pure intelligence is also accepted. "Intelligence alone constitutes the nature of the self. . . . Hence the soul manifests itself in the nature of pure intelligence, free from all manifoldness, calm, not capable of being expressed by any terms."[1]

These things cannot, in fact, be defined by human language. They are such that from them in the words of the Rishis of old, "all speech with the mind, turns away, unable to reach them". And it seems to me that if they are to be measured in accordance with the limited and imperfect standards of such logic as the human mind is capable of, the Vedantin can employ such standards as effectively as his critics. Could he not ask, for example, if perfection is not the ultimate goal towards which humanity irrespective of race or creed, is necessarily striving? And if he were to receive the obvious assurance that this was so, could he not, employing the weapon of logic relied upon by his critic, point out that perfection is necessarily One without a second, since logic insists that where there is duality there must be difference, and where there

[1] Sankara's commentary on sûtras 6 and 7 of the 4th pada of the 4th adhyaya.

is difference there must be superiority and inferiority, and where there is inferiority there cannot be perfection ?

For a true appreciation of the spirit of the Vedanta a man must bring to bear upon its study faith, reverence and insight, or he will inevitably lose himself in a jungle of mere words.

EPILOGUE

In the body of this volume I have endeavoured to describe the birth of modern India and to analyse the influences which are now shaping her growth. The conclusion to be drawn from what has been written is that a struggle is in progress between two main influences for the acquisition of the upper hand in determining her future—inherited tendencies and acquired characteristics. The period of growth, so far as it has gone, has produced individual cases in which one or other of these two influences has been in the ascendant, to the almost complete exclusion of the other. Examples of the triumph of acquired characteristics over hereditary tendencies are to be found in the case of a number of the Anglicised Indians, particularly of the second generation of Western educated Bengalis, of the nineteenth century. Cases of the reverse process where inherited tendencies have vanquished acquired characteristics have been seen of late. Mr. M. K. Gandhi may be taken as an outstanding example. If between these two extremes there exists a golden mean, it must be the offspring of a reconciliation between these two forces.

Such a golden mean should not be beyond the genius of India, for it was one of the greatest of Indian sages who preached and popularised the essential wisdom of the Middle Way. "What do you think," asked the Lord Buddha of one who played upon a lute, "if the strings of your lute are too tightly strung, will the lute give out the proper tone and be fit to play? Or if the strings of your lute be strung too slack, will the lute then give out the proper tone and be fit to play?" And on receiving the answer: "But how if the strings of your lute be not strung too tight nor too slack, if they have the proper degree of tension will the lute then give out the proper sound and be fit to play"? The lute-player assented and received this exhortation: "In the same way energy too much strained tends to excessive zeal, and energy too much relaxed tends to apathy. Therefore cultivate in yourself the mean."

But if we are to urge the Indian to cultivate the mean—to avoid giving too loose a rein to his inherited tendencies on the one hand, and on the other to adopt with a wise discrimination the garb of a civilisation and culture that are not his own—we must also ourselves remember that the Indian is not as inanimate clay to be moulded at the potter's whim, but a complex living organism with a strong distinctive individuality of his own. An educationalist who has had long personal experience of Indian boys of the upper classes does not hesitate to say that the Indian boy's mind is nearly the antithesis of that of the English boy. He finds his mind, in fact, precisely of the type that one's study of ancient Indian culture would lead one to expect—"highly imaginative and delighting in subtleties . . . at home in mental speculations which are nearly inaccessible to his Western schoolmates". More definitely still he describes the average Indian boy of his acquaintance as having "a great reverence for abstract truth, the field of concrete fact only appealing to him as a stepping-stone to the field of abstract thought". And realising the significance of differences so profound, he argues that a system of education must be evolved in India to suit the Indian boy. "Take what is best and most effective in the Western systems, and in as much as they are adaptable adapt them to the East; but these can only be accessories; the essential and more substantial parts of the Indian system must be Indian and suited by their nature to the nature of the Indian mind." The India of thirty years hence, he observes, will in the main be what the Indian boys of to-day will make it, and the closer the understanding between the governing and the governed the better. "The highest degree of this understanding will be obtained in India, not by merely grafting upon the Indian mind foreign methods of thought necessarily uncongenial and artificial, but by giving the fullest development to the indigenous plant of the soil. This must be borne in mind and adhered to in the planning of the Indian school system, mapping out the curriculum of studies and defining the lines along which these are to be pursued."[1]

The course thus indicated by the Rev. T. Vander Schueren is already being pursued by Dr. Rabindra Nath Tagore at Bholpur. I have referred to this interesting educational experiment in Chapter XX. When I was at Shanti Niketan early in 1920 the founder was already dreaming dreams of a large expansion of the original scheme. The school was to become a university, not an educational store stocked with foreign imports, at whose counter India stood as a beggar bent upon borrowing that which she had ceased to desire to produce herself, but a living organism, drawing its vitality from the soil on which it stood. India must shake herself free

[1] The Rev. T. Vander Schueren, S.J., in a monograph entitled "The Education of Indian Boys belonging to the Better or Upper Class Families", November 1919.

of the lethargy which had sapped her vitality and left her content to become a passive mimic of others. She had her own contribution to make to the progress of the world. But before she could do so she must search in her own household for that which she had mislaid. The first step must be to secure a true understanding of all the real wealth that had been produced and cherished by every section of those who composed the varied life of India. "With the realisation of the ancestral wealth of our own culture comes our responsibility to offer to share it with the rest of the world."[1] The university which was growing in the mind of its architect was to be at one and the same time a centre of research into the past, and a great hostelry at which all who desired to accept the gifts which Indian culture had to offer would be freely welcome. A resuscitation of Indian civilisation was to be the main work to be carried out, but with no narrow end in view, for the new university was to be an example of education established "on a basis, not of nationalism, but of a wider relationship of humanity".

Research was already in progress. In the library I found a Sanskrit pundit at work, intent on proving that the idealistic monism of Sankara drew its inspiration from Buddhist sources, and later on I came across a Buddhist Thera thumbing the dusty pages of ancient pali manuscripts. I saw the paintings of pupils at the school, and I listened to the performance of an expert Indian musician. There was one skeleton in the cupboard and that was the matriculation examination of the Calcutta University, for which the parents of some at least of the boys insisted on their sons being prepared. And when once a boy entered the matriculation classes his interest in

[1] The *Visva-Bharati Quarterly* for May 1923.

painting and music evaporated, for these things possessed no mark-earning value.

Great strides have been made since my visit early in 1920. The matriculation classes have gone, the university planned by Rabindra Nath Tagore has come into existence under the title of Visva Bharati, with Pundit Vidhusekhara Bhattacharya Sastri as its first Principal; great oriental scholars from the West have received and have responded to the invitation of its founder to accept its hospitality, among those who have already done so being Professor Sylvain Levi, M. Benoit and Dr. Stella Kramrisch, Mlle. A. Karpellez and Dr. Winternitz.

It is not in the sphere of education only that we have woven upon a Western warp where we might well have produced a more harmonious blending in the pattern upon the loom had we worked upon an Indian frame, introducing such alterations as seemed desirable by the use of Western thread amid the woof. Indeed, it is in our work in India more than elsewhere, perhaps, that we are likely to be held by the historian of the future to have suffered from the defects of our own qualities. Emerson was a great admirer of the vigour, the determination and the self-assurance of the English people; but with unerring insight he pointed to certain failings which were the outcome of these qualities, when he asserted that the Englishman's confidence in the power and performance of his own nation made him provokingly incurious about others. I have shown elsewhere[1] that in our confidence in the superiority of the system of local self-government which we have evolved for ourselves, it did not occur to us that there could be any other which India might prefer; whereas a people more diffident might well have sought, and had they

[1] In chapter xi. of "India: A Bird's-eye View".

done so would certainly have discovered, the foundations of an indigenous system laid firm in the soil of India by Indian genius long centuries before, upon which to build a structure more in consonance with Indian aptitudes and tradition. Has not experience in this case proved that in our attempts to bring East and West, India and Great Britain together, to weave into the tapestry of Indo-Anglian history, so to speak, the threads of Indian and British theory and practice in the science of government and the art of life, we have tended to make too large a use of the material of the West?

At the present time we are making herculean efforts to establish in India in the higher sphere of government, a constitution modelled as faithfully as possible upon our own. Is it certain that a constitution which has been evolved gradually with our own growth from childhood to nationhood is the one best suited to the genius and the circumstances of the Indian peoples? There are, at any rate, Indians of widely differing schools of thought who entertain serious doubts upon the point, and who are clearly far from thinking that the possibilities of political science have been exhausted with the evolution of the democratic constitutions of the West. Nearly a quarter of a century ago Mr. B. C. Pal sounded a note of warning. With impressive emphasis and unwavering insistence he asserted that to ignore the peculiar genius of a people in schemes of reform, whether of their political or their social institutions, was "to foredoom those schemes to failure, to court disappointment and to risk disaster". And he added that reform on national lines involved "the recognition of and due obedience to the supreme genius of the nation in devising means for its advancement".[1] More

[1] In a paper entitled "Reform on National Lines," published in December 1901.

recently Mr. C. R. Das has expressed the opinion that " a highly centralised form of parliamentary government is contrary to the economic, social and religious nature of India ". But beyond asserting that " the organisation of village life and the practical autonomy of small local centres are more important than either provincial autonomy or central responsibility ", and that " the ideal should be accepted once for all that the proper function of the central authority, whether in the provincial or in the Indian Government, is to advise, having a residuary power of control only, in case of need, and to be exercised under proper safeguards ", he has hitherto said little in public from which any idea can be formed of the sort of constitution which he has in mind.

A constructive contribution towards the solution of the problem of Indian Government comes from an entirely different quarter. In the autumn of 1922 an announcement was made by order of His Highness the Maharaja of Mysore of certain developments in the constitution of the State upon which he had decided, and of the appointment of a Committee to work out the details of the plan. The Committee under the chairmanship of an eminent scholar of Bengal, Dr. Brajendra Nath Seal, Vice-Chancellor of the Mysore University, issued its report in March 1923. The goal at which the Committee aimed was a constitution which, while taking cognisance of present-day tendencies throughout the world, should yet be based upon Indian rather than upon Western theory, and give expression to Indian rather than to European ideals. The report is of particular interest, therefore, at a time when we ourselves are engaged in setting up machinery by which the government of the vast continent which we have shouldered for so long, is to be transferred gradually to its many peoples ; and for the benefit of those who may be sufficiently interested I have drawn up an appreciation of it which I have added as an Appendix to this volume.

I do not suggest that a constitution suited to a self-contained Indian Native State such as Mysore in which the position and prestige of an hereditary ruler are factors of paramount importance, would be equally suited in all its details to British India. But the scheme is based on principles which are capable of general application. The actual process of law-making; the organs by which that process is to be carried out, and the constitution of these organs, could be adopted where conditions varied widely from those prevailing in Mysore; and an outline of the recommendations of the Committee on these points is, therefore, relevant here.

The process of law-making is regarded as a threefold one. The first part of the process consists of the presentation of matters in respect of which legislation seems to be required. Such presentation should be made by the people themselves, and the organ designed to give effect to this part of the process is a Representative Assembly so constituted as to be an epitome of the people. Its members are expected "to articulate the intuitive and unsophisticated views and wishes of the people".[1] The second part of the process is a technical one, namely, the scientific examination of legislative proposals before they are submitted to the legislature; and the machinery by which this task is to be discharged consists of Standing Boards of experts so constituted as to be qualified to advise both the executive government and the legislature. The final part of the process—the actual discussion and amendment of draft bills—is to be performed

[1] This and other quotations are from the report of the Committee.

by a body much smaller than the Representative Assembly made up of persons of knowledge and experience, a body which would be not so much an epitome of the people as "an assembly embodying the collective wisdom and virtue".

The means by which it is sought to make of the Representative Assembly an epitome of the people, deserve attention. Territorial constituencies provide a general basis on which to build up a system of popular representation; but there are other considerations in addition to the mere accident of an individual's residence in a particular locality which must be taken into account. "Neighbourhood", argues the Committee, "is no doubt a vital bond . . . and territorial electorates are a necessary basis of representation . . . but the ties of common interests and common functions that bind men into groups and associations independently of the tie of neighbourhood, acquire greater and greater importance with the more complex evolution of life and society. . . . A citizen of a state is a citizen not merely because he resides in a particular locality, but really by virtue of the functions which he exercises and the interests he has at stake in the body politic." The constituencies should, therefore, be not territorial only, but vocational as well. Those who are familiar with the social organisation of the Aryan settlements in the Ganges Valley two thousand years and more ago,[1] will see in this idea a reaching back to the guilds and other corporations which were one of its outstanding features. The Committee itself claims the support of the ancient Sanskrit works on political science for its contention that representation of this kind is in strict accordance with the political genius of the Indian peoples.

[1] Described in chapters iii. and xi. of "India: A Bird's-eye View".

The ministers who form the Executive are the agents of the Ruler of the State, chosen by him as his advisers, and they are, therefore, neither responsible to nor removable by the legislature. And in this respect the new constitution of Mysore is essentially monarchical. It is a monarchy, however, which lays no claim to absolutism, for the ruler, according to the theory upon which the scheme is based, rules by virtue of his representative character; and a referendum to the people—as represented in the case of Mysore by the Representative Assembly—is the means whereby the unity between the ruler and his people is made real and effective. The referendum, consequently, is regarded as fundamental in the constitution, and it is by its operation that the primacy of the people is assured. Under such circumstances there is no *a priori* reason why the head of the State should be an hereditary monarch. The position could equally well be filled by an elected head in a non-monarchical State or by the representative of the King Emperor in a province of British India. Indeed the adoption of some at least of the principles embodied in the constitution of Mysore had been urged for British India before ever the Committee had been appointed, by so gifted an Indian statesman as His Highness the Aga Khan. Both in his writings and in his evidence before the Parliamentary Committee which was concerned with the framing of the Reforms Act of 1919, he made it abundantly clear that in his considered opinion an Executive irremovable by the legislature, but brought into close organic union with the people by means of the initiative and the referendum, was far better suited to India than the British model. "The Indian peoples," he asserted, "with an instinctive sense of their need, have asked for self-government within the Empire, not for Parliamentary institutions on the British model." And he went further and pointed out that none of the draft schemes prepared by Indians, from that of Gokhale to the joint representation of the National Congress and the Moslem League, hypothecated full and immediate responsibility of the Executive to the legislature.[1] The employment of the word "responsible" in its technical constitutional sense in the famous Reforms Declaration of Parliament was in his view unfortunate, because it carried the technical meaning of a government responsible for its existence to an assembly elected by the people, whereas the ministers should be responsible through the Governor to the Crown and, so far as tenure of office was concerned, free from the control of the legislature. "It would be a disaster," he declared, "for India to be forced into the narrow form of constitutionalism that developed with its essential condition of two great rival parties in England through historical and natural causes."[2] These representations left unshaken the conviction deeply rooted in the British mind that the British model must be the best; and once again the British Parliament provided justification for the criticism passed by Emerson upon the British people.

* * * * * *

There is, then, ample evidence derived from many spheres of modern Indian life—from that of political science of which the constitution of Mysore is an example, from that of education of which the Visva Bharati provides an illustration, from that of literature as witness the works of Bankim Chandra Chatterji, of Rabindra Nath Tagore, of Miss Sita Devi and other well-known Bengali writers of the present day, and from that

[1] See "India in Transition", by His Highness the Aga Khan, published in 1918. [2] *Ibid.*

of art [1]—of the existence of something which has all the appearance of an Indian civilisation, the direct descendent of and heir to that born and nurtured on Indian soil, but vivified and to some extent modified by contact with the thought of the West. Do these things represent living growths or are they artificial products—the result of clever but mechanical dovetailing together of pieces organically unrelated to one another, held together by no more intimate a tie than that which binds the stones of a mosaic? There are some who maintain that no more intimate union than this is possible between the genius—or, as Mr. Pal would say, the thought-structure—of one nation and another. "Growth is a question of organism", declares Mr. C. R. Das, "and you cannot grow into a different thing from what you are unless the seed and germ of this different thing is already present in your organism", and in further illustration of his contention, "just as no permanent union can be effected by gluing together two separate physical things, so no permanent union can be effected by importing special features from the life of a foreign nationality and seeking to graft them upon the genius and character of our own nation".

I have no desire to embark upon a discussion of vexed questions of heredity to which the science of biology itself has not yet given its final answers. Nor is there any need of doing so, for few will deny that the intellectual outlook of the educated Indian of the twentieth century has been modified by a hundred years of contact

[1] "Mr. Mukul Dey is a young Indian artist belonging to that Calcutta school which seeks to revive the traditional styles and motives of Indian art. With a view to strengthening his draughtsmanship and science he came to England and studied at the Royal College of Art, where he has gained a diploma. He has not, however, Westernised his art, and has a devout admiration for those great classics of Indian painting, the now famous frescoes in the rock temples of Ajanta." The *Morning Post* of February 5, 1924.

with the thought-structure of the West. Dr. Rabindra Nath Tagore is an outstanding product of Indian genius; yet Mr. Das would hardly suggest, I imagine, that the thought-structure of this great figure in the world of literature would have been precisely what it is had no contact ever taken place between India and Europe. A far truer appreciation of the realities of the problem, surely, was displayed by the late Sir Asutosh Mukherji when he established the post-graduate department of the Calcutta University. Speaking of his hopes and beliefs concerning this enterprise, he characterised the doctrine held in some quarters that what is foreign should be excluded from the field of Indian education as "hateful", and the claim that what is Indian must necessarily be the best, as "ignorant and presumptious". And he summed up his argument in the following words: "The root of the matter is that though the things which have universal human value are the things of most importance in education, the universal can be fully apprehended only where it lives in concrete embodiments. Consequently, while we recognise and appropriate all that is wholesome in the culture of the West, we are equally concerned with the preservation and development of the organs of our national culture and civilisation." [1]

The India of to-day is giving birth to men great in science—that branch of the tree of knowledge which has been in special degree a gift to India from the West. Sir J. C. Bose is one, Sir P. C. Roy is another. No one would ever dream of describing these men as in any respect un-Indian. The latter in particular has been closely identified in recent years with movements

[1] Address at the convocation of the Lucknow University on January 7, 1924. This was one of the last pronouncements made by him before his sudden and tragic death early in the summer of the same year.

which are essentially nationalist. Among the younger men is Dr. J. C. Ghose, less known as yet to the general public, but known already in scientific circles in the West for valuable original work which places him in the front rank of the physico-chemists of the day.[1] The thought-structure of the race as represented by such men has unquestionably been modified by the changed mental environment which has arisen out of the contact effected between India and Great Britain. Have they for this reason been uprooted from their own cultural and intellectual soil? Surely not. It is true that there is an extreme school of thought in India which would dissociate the life of her people altogether from the science of the West; but this school derives its teaching in the main from Mr. M. K. Gandhi, who in his turn has been profoundly influenced by the teaching of Tolstoy. In his condemnation of railways, for example, Mr. Gandhi asserts that God set a limit to a man's locomotive ambition in the construction of his body, and after observing with pained disapproval that man immediately proceeded to discover means of overriding the limit, added that God had gifted man with intellect that he might know his Maker, whereas man had abused it so that he might forget his Maker.[2] To any one less curiously dogmatic on such matters, it would surely have occurred that God had also equipped man with the brain that discovered and then applied the locomotive power locked up in steam.

If this attitude towards progress were typical of the genius of India, then her future would be dark indeed. Happily it is exceptional rather than typical. Nothing impressed me more when visiting the high schools and colleges of Bengal

[1] In particular for his theory of electrolytic dissociation.
[2] "Indian Home Rule", by M. K. Gandhi, second edition, p. 47.

than the demand which has arisen in recent years for instruction in chemistry and other physical sciences. Nor shall I easily forget the enthusiasm which was aroused when Sir Jagadis Bose dedicated the Institute in Calcutta which bears his name to the Indian nation. In the course of his dedicatory address he said : " It is forgotten that He who surrounded us with this ever-evolving mystery of Creation, the ineffable wonder that lies hidden in the microcosm of the dust particle, enclosing within the intricacies of its atomic form all the mystery of the cosmos, has also implanted in us the desire to question and understand ". Therein is to be seen the difference between the Indian lost in the mazes of an extravagant extremism and the Indian who has chosen the middle way. But more than that. Sir J. C. Bose stands to-day a living witness of the success with which, in spite of Mr. C. R. Das's denial, " the special features from the life of a foreign nationality "—in this case the analytical methods of experimental science—can be " grafted upon the genius and character " of the Indian nation. For with all his wonderful grasp of the scientific methods of the West he remains essentially a product of Indian genius. He draws his inspiration from what Mr. Pal has described as " the particular World idea " of the Indian race, the idea that is to be " the corner-stone of the new Indian nation as it was of the old Hindu race " [1] —the idea of an all-pervading unity underlying the apparent diversity of the universe. Over and over again in speech and writing he has given expression to this thought. " The excessive specialisation of the West has led to the danger of our losing sight of the fundamental truth that there are not sciences, but a single science that includes all." In his investigations into the

[1] See the Prologue.

action of forces upon matter he tells us that he was amazed to find boundary lines vanishing, and to discover points of contact emerging between the living and non-living. He can conceive of no greater contribution to knowledge in the realm of science than the establishment of a great generalisation " not merely speculative, but based on actual demonstration of an underlying unity amidst bewildering diversity ". And straight from his heart comes the cry: " Shall this great glory be for India to win ? " [1] And speaking at the Institute in Calcutta at which research on the lines marked out by his own life's work is being vigorously prosecuted, he has said: " Here will assemble those who would seek oneness amidst the manifold. Here it is that the genius of India should find its true blossoming."

The last time I saw him before I left India was once again within the precincts of that building which some years before, I had heard him dedicate " not merely a laboratory but a temple ". A laboratory, for within its walls would be carried on investigation with those marvellously delicate instruments which have excited the admiration of scientists throughout the world—instruments of such amazing sensitiveness, that variations in the rate of the growth of plants so minute as one-fifteen millionth of an inch per second have been detected—along the lines which he has made peculiarly his own; a temple, for there are other truths which must remain beyond even the supersensitive methods known to science, truths which can only be revealed by faith—" faith tested not in a few years, but by an entire life ". He was standing beneath a picture which I have heard described as an " allegoric masterpiece ", the picture of two figures, those of Intellect feeling

[1] See an address delivered by Sir J. C. Bose at the foundation of the Hindu University at Benares in February 1916.

the sharp edge of the sword with which he has to cleave his way through the dense darkness of ignorance, and his bride Imagination inspiring him to effort with the music of her magic flute. It is the work of Nanda Lal Bose, one of the masters of that school of Indian painting whose birth I have described. He was the scientist speaking of what had been accomplished in the Institute. He passed on to say something of his hopes for the future. His face was lit up by the fire of enthusiasm, and expression and voice alike became those of the seer—of the man with a message for mankind. There could be no shadow of doubt that in treading the pathway of the golden mean he had not merely retained, but had enhanced the value of his Indian parentage, or that in the empirical knowledge of the West he had found the complement of the intuitive knowledge of the East. But let him speak for himself. Telling the world long since of his discovery of the thinness of the partition between organic and inorganic matter, he said: "It was when I perceived in them (the results of his experiments) one phase of a pervading unity that bears within it all things—the mote that quivers within ripples of light, the teeming life upon our earth, and the radiant sun that shines above us—it was then that I understood for the first time a little of that message proclaimed by my ancestors on the banks of the Ganges thirty centuries ago:

"'They who see but one in all the changing manifoldness of this universe, unto them belongs eternal truth—unto none else; unto none else!'"

APPENDIX

CONSTITUTIONAL DEVELOPMENTS IN MYSORE

Memorandum summarising the Recommendations of the Committee

The Report of the Committee sets forth proposals for framing a Constitution which, while taking cognisance of present-day tendencies throughout the world, yet seeks to base itself upon Indian rather than Western theory, and to give expression to Indian rather than to European ideals. The basic fact of such a Constitution is the existence of the Head of the State as the supreme executive head as well as the source and sanction of law; and in the view of the Committee this provides the key to the fundamental difference between a typically Indian form of Government and a modern democratic Constitution, such as that of Great Britain. The one is unitary in origin and in fact: the other dualistic in origin, if not at the present time, altogether so in practice. For if the British Constitution has "reached a basis of unity under an arrangement by which the Cabinet controls Parliament *de facto*, while Parliament controls the Cabinet *de jure*", this does not alter the fact that it is the product of a system under which sovereignty was divided between two originally separate elements, namely, the Head of the State and the people composing the State.[1] In the case of a unitary State the Head

[1] Strictly speaking the Indian constitution had a pluralistic origin, as a reference to chapter xi. of the first volume of this series ("India: A Bird's-eye View", pp. 132-138) will show. But the Committee when speaking of the Mysore Constitution as being unitary *in origin* is referring to the period when the State proper had come into existence and not to those earlier days of guilds and other corporations before the rise of kingship. When once the idea of "the state" had arisen, "the monism of the Hindu mind", to quote the words of Dr Seal in a letter to me on the subject, "stamped its impress on the polity by emphasising the need of the monarch as the wielder of *Danda* (sanction, punishment) for the preservation of *Dharma* (the Law of Laws); and in the end the latter-day Indian states in practice became monistic and absolute".

thereof, as the symbol of *Dharma* or the law, is regarded as representing the people " directly and primarily in his person . . . and as standing in a more direct and vital relationship to them " than the members of any representative body. He may seek the advice of individuals or of corporations; he may delegate his functions to individuals or to chambers; but he remains the head of the body politic, such other limbs as may evolve or be created being but subordinate members— " organs of one Will centred in the Head " wherein resides " the permanent reservoir of law-making power ".

This being the recognised position of the Head of the State, the object of the introduction into the Constitution of other bodies is in the main to provide machinery for perfecting the process by which effect is given in the domain of legislation and of administration, to the one undivided Will of the State. Those bodies of the ancient Indian polity to which reference is made in the Report—the village assemblies, the guilds and other similar associations—having disappeared, new bodies must be created for this purpose. And to this end, in the view of the Mysore Committee, the process of law-making may most conveniently be treated as a threefold one, each part of the process being assigned to a separate organ. The first part of the process is the enumeration of matters in respect of which legislation is desirable. Legislation having been decided on, the next part of the process consists of a technical and expert examination of the matter, and, finally, there is the actual work of discussion and amendment in the course of which the measure assumes its final form for presentation to the Head of the State for ratification or, if he thinks fit, rejection.

The Committee found the rudiments of these three organs already in existence in Mysore, having grown up " under the silent forces of natural evolution ", and proceeded to make recommendations for their formal incorporation in the Constitution. The first of these organs, to be known as the Representative Assembly, should be so constituted as to be an " epitome of the people ", and as such its functions should be to voice the popular will in all the acts of Government affecting the life of the people. It should serve two important ends—the initiative and the referendum. Its members would " articulate the intuitive and unsophisticated views and wishes of the people". It would not perform the actual work of legislation, but would express its opinion on legislative measures both before and after they had been dealt with by the organ—namely, the Legislative Council—to which this function is assigned. It should be in fact a "conference of the delegates of the whole people". The number of members suggested for this body is 250.

The actual work of legislation should be performed by a smaller body of fifty members, consisting of persons of knowledge and experience, a body which would not be so much an epitome of the people as "an assembly embodying the collective wisdom and virtue"; while work of a more technical character—the scientific examination of legislative proposals before they are submitted to the legislature, and of proposed administrative action, etc.—should be discharged by Standing Boards of experts constituted for advising the Government and the legislature.

One of the most interesting features of this machinery is its suggested composition. In the case alike of the Representative Assembly and the Legislative Council, the Committee urges that representation should not be merely general, but should include minorities and a variety of interests as well. The Constituencies, that is to say, should be not merely territorial, but vocational. This is an essentially Indian tradition going back to the days of the guilds and caste corporations, and great stress is laid upon it in the Report. "Neighbourhood is no doubt a vital bond . . . and territorial electorates are a necessary basis of representation . . .; but the ties of common interests and common functions that bind men into groups and associations independently of the tie of neighbourhood, acquire greater and greater importance with the more complex evolution of life and society. . . . A citizen of a state is a citizen, not merely because he resides in a particular locality, but really by virtue of the functions he exercises and the interests he has at stake in the body politic."

The ancient Sanskrit treatises on political science—the Arthashastras—are quoted in support of the claim that representation of this kind is in accordance with "the political temper and political genius of the Indian peoples". But continuity is not the only advantage urged for such a system. The greatest advantage claimed for it is that it is bound to work for the softening of differences in general, and of communal differences in particular. The dividing lines of the professions—so runs the argument—cut across those of the communities. " So far as rigid communal barriers in the matter of vocations and functions are breaking down, and a free inter-change and inter-flow are being established in society at large, the representation of interests and functions on a non-communal and non-ethnic basis will be an influence for unification and concord ".

For the present it is suggested that provision should be made for the representation of seven or eight different interests, to be spread over fifteen seats in the Representative Assembly; but a large development of this element in the composition of the Assembly is aimed at in the future, and the number of different interests which the Committee would like to see specially represented, includes agriculture, manufacture and trade, land and capital, law, medicine, engineering and teaching, labour, social service, women and children, the depressed classes, and even dumb animals.

Prima facie one would have expected that the particular category of interests which bulks so largely in India and which has proved a source of so much difficulty where it has had to be fitted into the framework of the parliamentary system which is being established in British India, namely, the communal, would have been regarded as the most important of the special interests to be provided for in an Indianised form of a modern Constitution. But this is not so.

The Committee draws a sharp distinction between the " function groups " described above which " form no *imperium in imperio*, no independent centres of the citizen's loyalty or allegiance conflicting with the growth of the national sentiment or with a sense of the common weal ", and the different communities with " creeds and customs that sunder ", which constitute " so many independent and original centres ". Nevertheless—though the Committee was far from unanimous as to the means by which it was to be achieved—it was recognised that some scheme must be devised to afford protection to communal minorities which were proved in practice to be unable to secure representation through the ordinary electorates. The device of communal electorates, adopted in British India in the case of the Mohammedans and the Sikhs, after being condemned in vigorous terms by the chairman, was rejected by the Committee, though the scheme eventually adopted by the majority, necessarily possessed certain features in common with the system which was condemned. Briefly it was laid down that any minority community of not less than 20,000 souls, failing to obtain representation through the general electorate, should be entitled to representation through special electorates consisting of such *bona fide* associations, numbering not less than 100 members, as had been established for the advancement of the communities. The chief advantages claimed for this scheme are, first, that it displays no discrimination in favour of, or against, any particular community. The measure of protection which it affords is offered to any community which is proved by experience to require it. Secondly that it will act as a stimulus to the communities affected by it, since representation will only be accorded if suitable associations conforming to certain prescribed conditions are established. And finally, that sooner or later the scheme will automatically work itself out as the progress made by the various minority communities enables them to obtain representation in the ordinary way. This result will be hastened when the general standard of education and political experience permits of the introduction of some form of proportional representation. It is thought that some ten or twelve out of about thirty minority communities will secure representation through the general electorates from the start.

These different bodies, as has been pointed out, have been designed to facilitate the translation into concrete form of the one undivided Will of the State. They have no power to tap " the permanent reservoir of law-making power " vested in the Head of the State. For the " constitutional unity between the Head and his people is the central fact in an Indian state like Mysore, built on the unitary plan ". It follows from this that the executive or ministry is not responsible to, or removable by, the legislature, for the ministers are the agents of the Head of the State chosen by him as his advisers, and responsible to him. And the wisdom of this conception of the unitary state—of this close organic relation between the sovereign and his people—is extolled on various grounds, but particularly on this, that it works for the perpetuation of *dharma*, that is to say of righteousness or the moral justice which is the lawful due of every individual of whom the State is composed. For " no Court of Areopagus, no Justiza of Aragon, no Federal Supreme Court, no Hague arbitrations, nor any other machinery that ever has been invented by man has served as a material check on that most perfect of all tyrannies, the irresponsible will of the majority in any democracy ". The only safeguard against such tyranny is the willing homage of all wills in the State to the Law of Laws, King Dharma, the inscrutable and inexorable Ruler of the Universe, of whom the Head of the State is the Representative on earth. And if it be objected that such a constitution is in effect nothing but an autocracy hiding behind an ingenious camouflage, its authors reply that this is not so, for the crucial feature of the constitution—the means by which the primacy of the people is secured and the unity between them and the Head of the State made living and effective—is the referendum. It is this right of initiative and referendum vested in the General Assembly of the delegates of the whole people that constitutes the pivot upon which the machine of government is poised, for without it "the one undivided Will of the State" could neither be ascertained nor *a fortiori* given effect to.

The Committee was precluded by its terms of reference from dealing in any detail with the reorganisation of local self-government. But in touching briefly upon this question, which it regards as one of the highest importance, it urges the re-construction of the machinery of local self-government on lines according with ancient Indian sentiment and tradition. Until the edifice of local self-government is rebuilt on a foundation of bodies characteristic of the ancient Indo-Aryan polity, such as village panchayats and guilds, local self-government will remain " an exotic, unacclimatised and unrooted on Indian soil ". With the re-creation of such a foundation on which such bodies as District Boards may rest, there will come into existence the " true Jacob's ladder " giving access to " the democrats' Heaven ". This is the plan of Indian rural organisation, " which is still visible in outline, however dilapidated may be the walls; and ", in the opinion of the Committee, " it may even now be restored with some facings and buttresses from modern county council developments in the agricultural countries of the West ".

INDEX

Adam, Mr., 28
Adhikari, Dwarkanath, 31
Aga Khan, His Highness the, 242, 243
Agamvâgîşa, Krishnânanda, 36
Agartolla, 41
Ajanta, frescoes of, 139, 244 *f.n.*
Akbar, the Emperor, 141
Aligarh, university of, 63, 64
Almora, 213
Amherst, Lord, 19, 20, 29
Amrita Bazar Patrika, the, 58
Ananda, 167, 194, 208
"Ananda Math," 86, 104, 130; the story of, 106-115
Anderson, J. D., 29
Arabic, 28
Arjuna, 119, 122, 124, 126, 127
Art, Indian, contrasted with the art of Europe, 134-142, 151; idealism of, 135, 136, 140, 141, 151, 157, 161; sex symbolism in, 144-150
Arya Samaj, the, 65, 69-72, 74, 75
Âryâvarta, 96
Asceticism, 5, 6, 49
Atman (the Self), 91
Avidya, 169, 172, 173, 177, 200
Ayurveda, 56

Bâdarâyaṇa, compiler of the Vedanta sûtras, 14, 164, 167, 180, 190, 191
Baladeva, Şrî, 190
Balasore, 114
Bande Mâtaram, 103, 104, 114, 115
Banerji, Hemchandra, 105
Banerji, Jitendralal, 58, 59
Banerji, K. M., 30
Banerji, Dr. Pramathanath, 10
Banga Darsan, the, 31, 32, 105
Barrow, J. R., 12 *f.n.*
Basu, Rai Bahadur S. C., 191
Belur Math, 213
Benares, university of, 59, 64
Bengal, assassinations in, 80, 81, 115; high schools of, 11, 246; modern school of painting of, 153-160, 249; partition of, 88; revolutionary movement in, 79-87, 89, 103, 112, 114, 115, 126, 127, 130, 200; students of, 4, 14, 15, 18, 45-47; tôls in, 55
Bengal Gazette, the, 31
Bengal Spectator, the, 20
Bengali language, the, 18, 28-32, 46, 62, 104-106
Benoit, M., 237
Bentinck, Lord William, 20
Berkeley, Bishop, 184
Besant, Mrs. A., 120 *f.n.*
Bhagavad Gîtâ, the, 46, 116, 126, 127, 212; the philosophy and theology of, 117-125
Bhagirathi river, the, 35
Bhairab river, the, 65, 68
Bhakti, 39, 129, 145, 179, 207
Bhattacharji, Gangadhar, 31
Bhattacharya, Krishna Kamal, 105
Bhawani, 101, 107, 128, 129
Bholpur, 65, 216, 235
Birt, F. B. Bradley, 28 *f.n.*
Bishwambhar, *see* Chaitanya
Biss, E. E., 11 *f.n.*
Bombay, 70
Bose, Sir Jagadis, 245, 247-249
Bose, Nanda Lal, 154, 249
Bose, P. N., 31 *f.n.*
Bose, Raj Narain, 47
Bose Institute, the, 247-249
Brahma, the god, 6
Brahmacharya, 72, 84
Brahma-dharma, 215
Brahman, the Absolute, 103, 117, 125, 149, 161, 162, 167, 170-179, 181-183, 185-188, 192-194, 196, 200, 205, 208, 210-213, 223, 224, 228-231
Brahmanhood, 6

Brahmo Samaj, the, 49, 51, 215, 227
Brighu, 193, 194, 223
Bṛihadāraṇyaka Upanishad, the, 166 *f.n.*, 231
Brindaban, 41, 191
Brown, Percy, 134 *f.n.*, 139
Buddha, 49, 69, 91, 92, 162, 233; image of, 138, 192
Buddhism, 120, 123, 145, 146, 163, 236
Buddhists, the, 2, 184

Calcutta, 4, 16-18, 54, 58, 80, 81, 154, 155, 203, 212, 247; Madrassa, 16; Medical College, 20; University, 60, 67, 76, 77, 97, 236, 245; University Commission, 8, 11, 13-15, 22, 23, 33
Carey, the Rev. W., 17, 29
Caste-dharma, 117, 122, 127
Cave, Dr. Sydney, 230 *f.n.*
Chaitanya, Ṣrî, 36-41, 110, 148, 190, 207; chatuspathi, 37
"Chaitanya-charit-amrita," the, 39, 40
Chandanagore, 155
Chandi, 97
Chandidas, 146
Chandravati, the poetess, 95
Chatterji, Bankim Chandra, 31, 32, 54, 85, 99, 104-107, 114, 206, 243
Chatterji, B. C., 87 *f.n.*
Chatterji, Basanta Kumar, 127
Chatterji, Gadadhar, *see* Ramkrishna.
Christianity, 51, 166, 170, 225
Christians, 2
Collier, the Hon. J., 135 *f.n.*
Committee of Public Instruction, the, 20, 28
Connaught, H.R.H. the Duke of, 4
Coomaraswamy, Dr. A. K., 137, 143, 144, 150, 151, 153
Cossipore, the garden of, 212
Council of Indian Education, the, 62
Cousins, J. H., 157 *f.n.*
"Cow of Plenty", the, 5-7
Cunningham, J. R., 55 *f.n.*

Dacca Anushilan Samiti, the, 115, 125
Dakshineshwar, the saint of, *see* Ramkrishna; the temple of, 203, 206, 212, 218
Dancing Shiva, the, *see* Nataraja
Darwin, Charles, 193
Das, C. R., 93, 95, 96, 100-102, 153, 239, 244, 245, 247
Datta, Akshay Kumar, 30, 31
Datta, Bibhutibhuson, 8, 33 *f.n.*
Datta, Govinchandra, 17
Datta, Michael Madhusudan, 62
Dayanand, Swami, 69, 70
Dayanand Anglo-Vedic College, the, 71
Denationalisation, of India, 26, 33, 45-47, 61, 77, 86, 90, 93, 94, 97-100, 143, 151-153, 236-239
Derozio, H. L., 18
"Desher Kotha," 85
Dey, M. C., 154, 244 *f.n.*
Dhritarashtra, 118, 119
Duff, the Rev. Alexander, 19
Durga, 107, 128
Dutt, Narendra Nath, *see* Vivekananda

East India Company, educational policy of, 16
Eastern Bengal ballads, 94-96
Economic pressure, on Indian middle classes, 48, 57, 86
Eddington, Professor A. S., 199 *f.n.*
Education Commission, of 1882, 22, 23; of 1902, 23
Educational system, the, in India, 8-15, 25, 57, 60, 74, 77, 96; origin and growth of, 16-23; indigenous, 34-38, 55-57, 67, 96, 97
Einstein, Professor A., 197, 199
Emerson, R. W., 237, 243
English, as the medium of instruction in India, 8, 10-12, 20, 24, 26, 29, 33, 61, 78, 97
Englishman newspaper, the, 4, 34 *f.n.*, 60 *f.n.*

Famine, in India, 95
Fort William College, 29, 31
Frazer, R. W., 105
Friend of India, the, 17

Gandhi, M. K., 3, 4, 6, 7, 58, 233, 246
Ganges, river, 73, 225, 249; Valley, 162, 215, 241
Ganguli, O. C., 136, 154, 156, 157
Gargi, 166
Gauranga, Lord, *see* Chaitanya
Ghose, Arabinda, 89, 91, 128, 193 *f.n.*
Ghose, Barindra Kumar, 91, 92
Ghose, Dr. J. C., 246
Ghose, Sir Rashbehary, 59

Ghose, Sarat Chandra, 93
" Gitanjali ", 220
Gñâna, 207
Gokhale, G. K., 243
" Govinda Bhashya ", the, 191
Guṇas, the three, 110, 120-122, 124
Gupta, Isvar Chandra, 31
Gupta, Professor M. N., 207 *f.n.*, 212
Gupta, Madusudan, 20
Gupta, Samarendranath, 136 *f.n.*
Gurukul, the, 71-75
Gyanuneshun, the, 20

Hakim, 56
Haldar, A. K., 154
Hardinge, Lord, 21
Hardwar, 71, 73, 75
Hare, David, 17, 18, 30, 60
Hare's school, 20
Hastings, Warren, 16, 106
Himâlayas, the, 5, 73, 100, 111, 113, 128, 213
Hindi, 74
Hindu Academy, at Daulatpur, 65-68, 75
Hindu College, the, 18, 45, 48
Hindus, the, 2, 3, 7, 10, 22, 74, 75, 112, 113, 162, 165, 176, 190
Hodgson, Brian, 149
Hooloo, 36
Hornell, W., C.I.E., 154 *f.n.*
Household, H. W., 79 *f.n.*
Hughli river, the, 17, 203, 213
Hyderabad, state of, 63

Idealism, a characteristic of the Hindu mind, 84, 91, 128, 135, 136, 140, 151, 161, 165, 179
India Act, of 1813, 16 ; of 1833, 19, 20
Indian National Congress, the, 88, 243
Indian Society of Oriental Art, the, 155
Indo-Anglia, 38, 44
Infanticide, 101, 102 *f.n.*
Ireland, 200
Isopanishad, the, 190
Isvara, 179, 186, 188, 200
Iyengar, S. S., C.I.E., 59

Jagaddhatri, 107, 108
Jaganâth, temple of, 39, 41
Japan, 89
Juguntur, newspaper, 126

Kâlî, 107, 108, 115, 128, 203, 204, 206, 208, 211
Kamakura, Buddha of, 188
Kanu Bhatta, 146
Kar, S. N., 154
Karma, 117, 129, 187, 225
Karpellez, Mlle. A., 237
Kaviraj, 56
Kenaram, the ballad of, 94, 95
Khândogya Upanishad, the, 108, 165 *f.n.*, 192
Khulna, 65
Konarak, temple of, 145
Koran, the, 51
Kramrisch, Dr. Stella, 237
Krishna, 39-41, 70, 92, 119-124, 144, 147, 191, 204, 208
Krishnadas, author of the Chaitanya-charit-amrita, 39
Kurukshetra, 119
Kurus, the, 118
Kusumâñjalî, the, 35

Lahiri, Ramtanu, 20
Lahore, 70
Lakshmi, 108, 128
Lala Lajpat Rai, 72 *f.n.*
Levi, Dr. Sylvain, 237
Lîla, 223
Linga, 192, 203
Literacy, in India, 10, 14
Logic, *see* Nyâya
Lucknow University, 245 *f.n.*

Macaulay, Lord, 19, 20, 25, 28, 32, 45, 76
Madras, 57, 59, 60, 62, 152, 213
Mahabharata, the, 5, 46, 118, 140
Mahadeva, the god, 5
Maitrâyaṇa Upanishad, the, 172, 173
Manu, the code of, 84
Manusaṃhitâ, the, 68
Marshman, the Rev. W., 17
Materialism, 92, 96, 193
Mathura, 70
Max Müller, 192, 206
Maya, 169, 170, 172-177, 185, 196, 200, 201, 211
Mayavati, the ashram of, 213
Mazumdar, K. N., 154
Mazumdar, P. C., 46 *f.n.*, 47 *f.n.*, 206
Metropolitan school, the, 48
Misra, Paksadhara, 36
Missionaries, educational work of, 19
Mithilâ, 35, 36
Mitra, Dinabandhu, 31, 54, 105
Mitra, Kisori Chandra, 30
Mitra, Peary Chand, 30 *f.n.*
Mitra, Dr. Rajendralal, 30

Modern Review, the, 61 *f.n.*, 160
Moghul Empire, disruption of, 44, 106
Moghul school of painting, 139, 159
Moksha, 139
Moreno, H. W. N., 31 *f.n.*
Moslem League, the, 243
Moslems, the, 2, 9, 10, 16, 22, 75, 86, 110, 112, 113
Mukherji, the late Sir Asutosh, C.S.I., 76, 77, 245
Mukherji, Jotindra Nath, 114
Mulshankar, 69
Munshi Ram, Mr., 72, 73, 75
Mymensingh, 95
Mysore, the constitution of, 239-243, and Appendix

Nalanda, 72
Nâm-kirtan, 39
Nataraja (the Dancing Shiva), 136, 187
Nationality, defined, 1-3
Navadvîpa, 35-38, 41, 55, 99
Nawab Hyder Nawaz Jung Bahadur, 63
Nawab Masood Jung Bahadur, 63
Nayak, Manindra, 155 *f.n.*
Nepal, Royal Library of, 147
New Dispensation, the church of the, 49
New Zealand, 198
Nirvana, 139
Nityananda, 39, 41
Nizam of Hyderabad, the, 63, 64
Nobel prize, awarded to Dr. Rabindra Nath Tagore, 32
Nordmann, Dr. C., 197, 198 *f.n.*
Nyâya philosophy, 35

Odantapuri, 72
Om !, 103, 104, 115, 192
Oriental Conference, the, 75
Orissa, 145
Osmania University, the, 63, 64

Paine's "Age of Reason", 46
Pal, Bepin Chandra, 2, 89, 91, 104, 107, 132, 162, 238, 247
Pala dynasty, the, 78
Pandavas, the, 118, 119
Panini, 164
Pantheism, 163, 187, 191, 208
Parakîyâ Rasa Cult, the, 146, 148
Parsis, the, 2
"Pathrabali", 85
Paul, Saint, 170
Pearson, W. W., 216 *f.n.*
Persian, 28 ; supersession of, as language of the courts, 21
Phelps, Myron, 73, 74
Philosophy, high place accorded to, in India, 14 ; the six systems, 14, 70, 211 ; *see also* Nyâya, Sânkhya, and Vedanta
Pindharis, the, 102
Prakriti, 120-122
Probhakar, the, 31
Public Instruction, Department of, 21
Punjab, the, 65, 71, 74
Purânas, the, 5, 51, 70
Purandar, Jaganâth Misra, father of Chaitanya, 39
Puri, 39-41
Puri, Ishvar, 39
Purusha, 120, 121

Radha, 128, 144, 147, 204
Radhakrishnan, Professor, 188, 219, 225, 226
Raghunandana, 36
Rajput school of painting, 139, 140, 159
Rama, 206
Ramanuja, 14, 190
Ramayana, the, 5, 46, 97, 140
Rami, the washerwoman, 146
Ramkrishna Mission, the, 213
Ramkrishna Paramahamsa, 51, 90, 129, 195 ; religion of, 203-213
Rani Rasmani, 204
Rayaningar, Rama, 63
Reforms Declaration of Parliament, 243
Renunciation, an Indian ideal, 3-7, 69, 111, 115, 117, 213
Rigveda Samhitâ, the, 68, 162
Rowlatt Act, the, 6, 7
Rowlatt Commission, Report of the, 80
Roy, Amrita Lall, murder of, 181
Roy, Raja Ram Mohan, 18-20, 28, 45, 48, 60, 215
Roy, Sir P. C., 245
Rupâm, 156
Ruskin, on Indian art, 157
Russia, 89, 200

Sabdakalpadrûma, the, 68
"Sadhabar Ekadashi", 54
"Sâdhanâ", 219
Sahajiâ cult, the, 146-148
Sama Prakas, the, 31
Samadhi, 208, 210, 211
Sanâtana Dharma, 9
Sanjaya, 118, 119

Sankara, 14, 125, 165, 169, 173, 180-183, 185-190, 196, 201, 210, 213, 214, 227, 230, 236
Sâṅkhya system of philosophy, 120-123
Saṅkîrtan, 41, 97
Sannyasi Rebellion, the, 106
Sanskrit, 28, 37, 38, 71, 74, 76, 78, 104, 164, 172, 217
Saraswati, 108, 151
Sarkar, Akshoy Chandra, 105
Sarkar, Jadunath, 40 *f.n.*
Sarvabhauma, Vasudeva, 35
Sasadhar, Pundit, 212
Sastri, Pundit Siva Nath, 52
Sat-chit-ananda, 167, 179
Satyagraha, 4
Saunders, the Rev., 226 *f.n.*
Schlegel, F. von, 141
Schopenhauer, 141
Scott, Sir Walter, 105
Sen, Benoyendra Nath, 193 *f.n.*, 195-202, 208, 223, 226
Sen, Dinesh Chandra, 29, 30 *f.n.*, 94, 145, 147, 148
Sen, Keshub Chandra, 48-53, 118 *f.n.*, 206
Sen, Ramdas, 82
Sen, Ramkamal, 30, 45, 48
Sen-Gupta, Nares Chandra, 105-107
Sensationalism, 193
Serampore College, 17, 19
Shachi, mother of Chaitanya, 39, 40
Shanti Niketan, 215, 216-218, 235
Shiva, 203, 206
Shraddananda, Swami, 75
Shuddhi movement, the, 75
Ṣilpa Ṣastras, the, 154
Ṣiromaṇi, Raghunâtha, 36
Sita Devi, Miss, 243
"Society for the Acquisition of General Knowledge", the, 20
Soul-force, 4-6
Sridhanya Katak University, 72
Ṣruti, 189, 195
Stephen, Dorothea Jane, 125 *f.n.*
Ṣûdra, 182, 186
Sûnyavâda Buddhists, the, 167
Sûtras, the, 163-165, 191
Suttee, 101, 102
Svetaketu, 165
Swadeshi movement, the, 99

Tagore, Abanindra Nath, C.I.E., 76, 136 *f.n.*, 148, 154, 155
Tagore, Devendra Nath, 49, 51, 215, 217, 227
Tagore, Goganendra Nath, 143, 154
Tagore, Rabindra Nath, 32, 60-62, 65, 132, 133, 195, 215, 235, 237, 243, 245; religion and philosophy of, 216, 218-229
Tagore, Satyendra Nath, 227 *f.n.*
Taittirîyaka Upanishad, the, 192, 229
Tan Sen, 141, 142
Tantras, the, 36, 148, 150
Tantrikism, 145, 149
Tara Nath, 139
Tattva-cintâmaṇi, the, 35
Taxila, 72
Theism, in the Bhagavad Gîtâ, 123, 124; in the Vedanta, 179, 187
Thibaut, Dr., 164
Thompson, Professor E. J., 225
Thought-structure, Hindu, 2, 3, 5, 7, 162, 244, 246
Thugs, the, 101, 102
Tilak, Bal Gangadhar, 126
Tôls, 34, 36, 37, 55, 164
Tolstoy, 246
Tota Puri, 207
Tripura, 41

Uddalaka, 165 *f.n.*
Ujaiyanta Palace, the, 41
United Provinces, the, 65, 71, 213
Upanishads, the, 46, 73, 90, 103, 162-165, 167, 172, 178, 179, 192, 194, 195, 202, 215, 219
Urdu, 63

Vaishnava dance, 41, 42
Vaishnavism, 36, 39-41, 110, 146, 148
Vâlmîki, 92
Vâmâchâra, 149
Vander Schueren, the Rev. T., 235
Varendra, 78
Varma, Raja Ravi, 151
Varuna, 193
Vasishta, the Brahman, 5, 6
Vedanta, system of philosophy, 3, 14, 51, 67, 92, 103, 120, 123, 125, 129, 165-171, 178, 180; as interpreted by Sankara, 181-188; the religion of the, 189-232
Vedas, the, 5, 46, 51, 70, 73, 90, 92, 178, 183, 189-191, 227
Vernacular Press, the, 31
Vernaculars, capacity of the, 25, 28, 29; as the medium of instruction in schools and colleges, 13, 33, 34, 68, 72, 74, 76, 77, 97

Vidhusekhara Bhattacharya Sastri, Pundit, 237
Vidyakalpadrûma, the, 30
Vidyasagar, Isvar Chandra, 31, 206, 209
Vikramasila, 72
Vîrâchâra, 149, 150
Virjananda, Swami, 70
Vishnu, 110, 119
Visva Bharati, 65, 237, 243
Visvamitra, King, 5-7
Vitalism, 193
Vivekananda, Swami, 85, 129, 145, 169, 178 *f.n.*, 179, 204, 213
Vyasa, 92

Ward, the Rev., 17
Wellesley, Lord, 29
Williams, Sir Monier, 144
Winternitz, Dr., 237
Wood, Sir Charles, 21
Woodroffe, Sir John, 148, 150

Yâgñavalkhya, 166
Yogis, the, 122

THE END